wedding planning & management

WEDDING

PLANNING & MANAGEMENT

CONSULTANCY FOR DIVERSE CLIENTS

Maggie Daniels and Carrie Loveless

LONDON AND NEW YORK

First published by Butterworth-Heinemann
This edition published 2012 by Routledge
2 Park Square, Milton Park, Abingdon, Oxon OX14 4RN
711 Third Avenue, New York, NY 10017, USA

Routledge is an imprint of the Taylor & Francis Group, an informa business

Library of Congress Cataloging-in-Publication Data
Daniels, Maggie, 1969–
   Wedding planning and management : consultancy for diverse clients /
authors, Maggie Daniels, Carrie Loveless.
      p.   cm.
   Includes index.
   ISBN-13: 978-0-7506-8233-6
   ISBN-10: 0-7506-8233-7
   1. Wedding supplies and services industry. 2. Wedding supplies and
services industry—Management. 3. Weddings—Planning. 4. Consultants.
I. Loveless, Carrie, II. Title.
   HD9999.W372D36 2007
   392.5068—dc22

                                                                        2006038016

British Library Cataloguing-in-Publication Data
A catalogue record for this book is available from the British Library.

ISBN 13: 978-0-7506-8233-6
ISBN 10: 0-7506-8233-7

Printed and bound in India by Replika Press Pvt. Ltd.

we dedicate this book to brides
and grooms around the world.

contents

section one

foundations

section two

❧ practice

section three

building your business

xi

list of case studies

consultant in action

culture corner

research roundtable

vendor spotlight

list of figures

list of tables

preface

his book was written to fill a void in wedding planning literature. When Maggie found that her events management students at George Mason University were increasingly asking for a class that specifically dealt with the planning and management of weddings, she designed the course and walked it through a rigorous approval process. The next step was finding the right instructor. Maggie met Carrie and knew she was the perfect fit. As the owner of Carried Away Events, Carrie was excited to share her extensive wedding planning and implementation knowledge with an eager audience.

The third step was finding the right book. While we located numerous excellent texts that pertain to weddings, we did not find a single book that had everything we needed. Specifically, we were looking for a book that would cover four vital areas. First, the reader would need a strong foundation in the cultural, historical, social, and political influences on weddings and marriage; second, the book had to include all of the elements essential to the practice of planning weddings; third, the text should provide a clear overview of what it takes to start a wedding consulting business; and finally, the book had to be visual so that the ideas it presented would be brought to life and spark the imagination of every reader. This comprehensive book did not exist, and we were faced with having our students purchase multiple texts or writing a book that brought all of these areas together. We chose the latter alternative, and the result is *Wedding Planning and Management: Consultancy for Diverse Clients*.

Although originally conceived with a student audience in mind, the project evolved and broadened so that anyone with an interest in the business of weddings would benefit from the content. Thus, this book is not just for current and potential wedding consultants. Instead, it is designed so that brides, grooms, vendors, scholars, and those simply fascinated by weddings can also appreciate and apply the material.

The emphasis on understanding diverse clients is one that you will find consistently throughout this text. This book originated in the greater metropolitan area of Washington, DC, one of the most culturally diverse regions in the world. Our surroundings encouraged us to be responsive to diversity, and we amassed widespread research so that individuals around the globe could relate to the information in this text.

We sincerely hope that *Wedding Planning and Management: Consultancy for Diverse Clients* enlightens, challenges, and inspires you. Whether you are a student taking a wedding planning class, planning your own wedding, acting as a vendor for weddings, or preparing to start your own consulting business, the ideas, cases, and images within this text are designed to stimulate both your curiosity and creativity.

Maggie Daniels and Carrie Loveless

JANUARY 2007

acknowledgments

hillary rodham clinton popularized the african proverb, "it takes a village," in light of raising children. this same idea applies when authoring a book.

Our village consists of many people whom we would like to acknowledge. We relied on the generous support and expertise of many wedding professionals. Foremost is Rodney Bailey whose stunning images bring this book to life. Wendy Joblon, who sets a gold standard for wedding consultants, supported our efforts from day one. The many vendors, consultants, experts, and couples who graciously agreed to share their stories and keys to success include Patricia Borosky, Kristina Bouweiri, Cassie, Doug, and Russ Brayley, Randy Christian, Ed Chung, Aubrey Cote, Susanne Dubrouillet, Fred Elting, David Fletcher, Suzuki Fusako, Giselle, Rachel Gittins, Leslie Goldman-Poyourow, Wayne Hager, Brigid Horne-Nestor, Diane Haworth, Jennifer Johnston, Page Karami-Adgani, Susan Lacz, Tom Lally, Marc McIntosh, Iwamura Michiyo, Duarte Morais, Carola Myers, Jerry O'Connell, Marianne Raub, Barbie Richardson, Davis Richardson, Ellen and Pierre Rodgers, Kubo Sanae, Lynne Sandler, Bernadette Thompson, Asai Toshiko, Takeuchi Yayoi, and Soga Yoshiko. Special thanks to Yao and David Wosicki for their detailed insights regarding Chinese wedding traditions. The students taking Wedding Planning and Management at George Mason University (GMU) were a tremendous source of feedback and inspiration regarding the information that should be included in this text. Thank you for your enthusiasm and patience while the materials were test-marketed in class. Dave Wiggins of GMU was a constant sounding board, while Sandy Smith, Lisa Reeves, and Davi Mohammad helped make things happen. Diane Loomis tracked down the hundreds of research sources used in this text, while Karin Emmons transcribed our lectures and interviews. Janet Daniels tirelessly read and reread the manuscript in search of errors and inconsistencies. Jane Macdonald of Elsevier saw the potential for this book and was the liaison that supported the expansion of the material as well as the number of images and color printing of the text. Thanks also to Dennis McGonagle, Melinda Ritchie, Betty Pessagno, Alisa Andreola and the production staff at Elsevier, as well as Anjel Van Slyke and Connal Hughes at Cabbage Design Company. We would like to thank our friends and family members who kept us laughing and motivated. The Sudley tennis players, especially Dianne Webber, Rose Mary Davis, Joyce Johnston, Ceil Boyle, Lindsey Bailey, and Christy Mohl, were constantly supportive of Maggie's efforts on and off the court. Carrie's cheerleaders included the Boylans, Donna Fancher, Nancy Smith, and especially Toni Mahmud. Thanks to the Daniels, Michel, Wosicki, and Loveless clans who kept us grounded. Finally, we want to joyfully acknowledge 100 years of marriage. As of January 2007, if you total the years of marriage between our parents, Peggy and John Daniels and Judy and Walt Wosicki, and then add in the number of years Maggie has been married to Matt Michel and Carrie to Bruce Loveless, you arrive at an exact total of 100 years. In this day of fly-by weddings and quickie divorces, this is truly a cause for celebration.

about the authors

maggie daniels

Maggie Daniels is an Assistant Professor of tourism and events management in the School of Recreation, Health, and Tourism at George Mason University (rht.gmu.edu). She enjoys teaching classes in wedding planning, event management, meeting planning, and tourism policy. She simultaneously partners with events managers and tourism agencies in the Washington, DC metropolitan area to assist them with event and tourism implementation and evaluation. Maggie is a prolific researcher and has a combination of over 50 published papers, book chapters, professional presentations, and technical reports to her credit. She received her B.A. from Miami University of Ohio, her M.A. from the University of Georgia, and her Ph.D. from Clemson University. When not working, Maggie is a tennis enthusiast and also runs and practices yoga. She enjoys traveling with her husband, Matt Michel, and simply relaxing by their pond while watching the antics of their fish.

carrie loveless

Carrie Loveless is the owner of Carried Away Events (www.carriedawayevents.com), a wedding planning and event management company based in Washington, DC. She has more than 20 years' experience managing corporate and social events ranging from large trade shows to intimate weddings. She has been a guest lecturer at the Rhode Island School of Design and an adjunct professor teaching wedding planning at George Mason University. She received her B.A. in English from Chestnut Hill College in Philadelphia and her M.B.A. from George Mason University. She studied interior decorating and design at the Corcoran School of Art in Washington and the Rhode Island School of Design in Providence, and floral arranging at the Judith Blacklock Flower School in London and U. Goto Florist in Tokyo. Carrie enjoys traveling and living around the world with her husband, Bruce Loveless, a Captain in the United States Navy. They currently reside in Yokohama, Japan, with their Wheaten Terrier, Dunkin.

rodney bailey

Rodney Bailey of Wedding Photojournalism by Rodney Bailey (www.RodneyBailey.com) is a photojournalist in the purest sense. He does not manipulate his surroundings, orchestrate his subjects, or distract from the moments he is capturing. He has documented weddings for 16 years using this unobtrusive (and now, trendy) approach and is one of the most sought-after wedding photographers in Washington, DC. He has also worked in destinations such as Bermuda, Paris, and Rome. Rodney's work has been featured in many of today's top bridal magazines including *Modern Bride*, *The Knot*, *"I Do" for Brides*, *Grace Ormonde Wedding Style*, *Engaged*, *Elegant Bride*, and *Wedding Dresses*. Rodney is also commissioned for corporate, fashion, and commercial photography projects, though weddings still remain his passion.

He has captured images for the Library of Congress, *Vogue*, and Disney, as well as Oprah Winfrey and *O Magazine*. Rodney has been voted the top photojournalist in the *Washingtonian Magazine* for eight consecutive years and is featured in *Grace Ormonde Wedding Style Magazine* as one of the top five photographers in Washington, DC. During his down time, Rodney can still be found behind the camera; however, his subjects are sharks and sea life as he is an avid scuba diver and underwater photographer.

about the photographer

section one

FOUNDATIO

the beautiful traditions that we see each
time we witness or plan a wedding are
influenced by culture, religion, history, the
media, family, and politics. thus, it is
essential that you explore these dynamics to
become an informed consultant with an
appreciation of and sensitivity to the diverse
needs of your clients.

CHAPTER 1   begins with an overview of the role and scope of wedding consultancy by presenting statistical information that explains why careers dealing with the business of weddings have grown substantially over the past 50 years. This chapter also introduces the multitude of roles held by wedding planners and offers an overview of the main features found throughout the text.

CHAPTER 2   details how culture and religion influence marriage socialization, mate selection, pre-wedding rituals, wedding customs, and changes in identity due to marriage.

CHAPTER 3   follows with a discussion of the historical power relations associated with weddings and marriage, and how power imbalances have been continually challenged.

CHAPTER 4   explores the influence of the media on wedding planning by considering the persuasive nature of film, television, and the Internet.

CHAPTER 5   reviews significant trends that are resulting in a changing family dynamic. Specifically, this chapter tracks the evolving definition of family by considering workforce changes, cohabitation, divorce, same-sex relationships, and blended wedding traditions.

CHAPTER 6   reflects on consumerism and how the quest for perfection can hamper the wedding experience. This chapter also considers ways in which consultants can help couples plan anticonsumptive and conservationist weddings.

CHAPTER 7   looks at how weddings contribute to community economic development through tourism, with attention given to guest travel, honeymoon travel, and destination weddings.

The information provided in this section is designed to establish a context for the rest of the book. The material will allow you to approach the practice and business of weddings with an understanding of where and how many traditions and beliefs about matrimony originated. The perspective gained through this section will give you added sensitivity and confidence as you step into the practice of wedding planning.

PHOTO 1-1 *Consultants help wedding parties work as a team.*

role and scope of wedding consultancy 1

Countries across the globe commemorate the institution of marriage with a ceremony commonly referred to as a wedding. Few events are as tradition-laden and culturally bound as weddings, with heritage, history, symbolism, and superstition playing important roles in the options that are debated and the selections that are ultimately made by the couple and those in supporting roles. Over the past 100 years, some of these decisions have become easier to make while others have grown increasingly complicated. Influences such as globalization, technology, the media, economic development, law, changing sex-role dynamics, and altered definitions of family facilitate the decision-making process while simultaneously posing unique challenges to the couple.

enter the wedding consultant. This cutting-edge field of study represents a growth occupation. A spinoff of the larger discipline of event management, the business of wedding planning is not an industry unto itself but instead encompasses a broad array of support industries such as hotels, retail, and catering services. United States government and market estimates support associated conclusions about the increasing demand for wedding planners:

ESTIMATE   The average wedding in 2006 will cost approximately $26,000 versus $15,000 in 1990, representing a 73 percent growth. With close to 2.2 million weddings anticipated, the total market value of weddings is projected to be over $57 billion (Fairchild Bridal Group, 2005; McMurray, 2005).

CONCLUSION   Weddings entail significant financial output on typically first-time purchase decisions. A wedding consultant brings experience to the process.

ESTIMATE   45 percent of couples report spending more on their wedding than they had planned (Fairchild Bridal Group, 2005).

CONCLUSION   Weddings involve emotionally laden decisions and external pressures. A wedding consultant brings logic to the process.

ESTIMATE   Women have better educational preparation and career opportunities than ever (Ashford, 2005) and are thus marrying later. The proportion of women ages 30 to 34 who have never married more than tripled, from 6 to 22 percent, between 1970 and 2001 (U.S. Census Bureau, 1995; 2005). Similarly, the proportion of men ages 30 to 34 who have never married increased from 9 to 30 percent in that same time period (U.S. Census Bureau, 1995; 2005).

CONCLUSION   Couples are marrying later, have less time and more disposable income, and thus can afford to hire a wedding consultant to handle their wedding details.

ESTIMATE   15 percent of first marriages will end in separation or divorce within five years, while over 25 percent will end within 10 years. Of those who divorce, over half will remarry, typically within 3.5 years (U.S. Census Bureau, 2005).

CONCLUSION   Second marriages are a common occurrence. Wedding consultants can assist in making arrangements that support blended families.

ESTIMATE   Interracial marriage has increased fivefold since 1970, with younger and better educated couples more likely to intermarry than older, less educated individuals (Lee and Edmonston, 2005).

CONCLUSION   Wedding consultants can help successfully blend different ethnic traditions and rituals into the ceremony and reception (González, 2005).

These estimates and associated conclusions clarify why an estimated 19 percent of couples hired a wedding consultant in 2006, with an increase projected for the future (McMurray, 2005).

While these estimates are based on U.S. statistics, these same trends are being evidenced across the globe, as are the associated opportunities and dilemmas that these movements pose. For example, the average cost of a wedding in the United Kingdom is estimated to be between £16,000 and £17,000 (approximately $25,000 to $27,000 U.S. equivalent), with prices continuing to rise (Gold, 2005; Papworth, 2005). Furthermore, women's educational attainment and participation in the global workforce continue to rise. Specifically, of all wage earners, women accounted for 38 percent in the early 2000s, up from 35 percent in 1990 (Ashford, 2005). When just considering more developed countries, women make up 47 percent of the workforce (Ashford and Clifton, 2005). Thus, women across the globe are advancing their educations and putting those skills to use. For instance, women in Japan are increasingly choosing careers over marriage, either putting off marrying or foregoing it altogether (Buckley, 2004). Education in India has been found to be an important precursor to marriage, where students who plan to attend college "expect significant improvement in income, career opportunities, social prestige and marriage prospects regardless of post-school choice" (Dhesi, 2001, p. 14).

Global trends indicate that wedding consultants are bound to be increasingly in demand. Accordingly, the specific roles of the wedding consultant bear examination.

⤷ titles, packages, and roles

An individual entering the wedding business from a planning perspective has many titles from which to choose. Some of the more common include wedding consultant, wedding planner, bridal consultant, wedding coordinator, wedding director, and wedding designer. Although all of these titles may be equally marketable, the terms *wedding consultant* and *wedding planner* will be primarily used in this text for the sake of consistency. Simultaneously, the word "you" will also be used throughout the text to get the reader in the mind frame of thinking like a wedding consultant. Regardless of the title, a wedding consultant fulfills a number of identifiable tasks, which vary based on the package the couple picks.

CONSULTANT PACKAGES

Consultant packages (which will be discussed in more detail in Chapter 24) generally come in three types: comprehensive packages, partial packages, and day-of packages. Consultants often also provide indi-

vidualized à la carte or ad hoc services. While services will vary from planner to planner, Goulet and Riddell (2005) offer an overview to differentiate the primary package types. For a comprehensive package, also known as a full package, the consultant is generally involved from the onset of the planning process. This is the most expensive type of package, where the consultant offers initial and ongoing assistance with any or all of the following services: (1) budget preparation; (2) vision and theme determination; (3) creation of timelines and check-lists; (4) selection, negotiation with, and booking of vendors; (5) design of invitations and other stationery elements; (6) compiling of guest lists, mailing out invitations, and tracking; (7) ceremony and reception preparation; (8) direction in the completion of necessary contracts, forms (e.g., marriage license), and tests (e.g., blood tests); (9) on-site direction of rehearsal, ceremony, and reception; and (10) final payment and wrap-up with vendors. Specifics in each of these service areas will be offered throughout this text. Some planners will only accept comprehensive packages, because they want to be involved with every step of the planning process. When starting your business, however, you will most likely want to diversify your services.

Partial wedding packages are generally vendor-based and occur when the couple primarily requires assistance in pinpointing and selecting the service providers appropriate to their vision and budget. A wedding consultant can offer invaluable advice to the couple that does not have the time to comparison or quality shop. The partial package allows the consultant to assist with vendor selection, contract negotiation, scheduling of appointments, day-of coordination, final payment, and follow-up (Goulet and Riddell, 2005).

Day-of packages have become increasingly common and are designed for clients who have completed the planning process, yet desire assistance and coordination during the wedding day and often during the rehearsal as well. The consultant is involved prior to this period on a limited basis, primarily to obtain the necessary information to make the day flow. Specifically, the consultant will need a list of all vendors and will help in the preparation of the wedding day timeline. These materials will ensure that the consultant can be the primary point of contact during the rehearsal and wedding so that the couple can enjoy themselves without constant interruptions. The drawback of this type of package is that if the couple has made less-than-ideal vendor decisions, then the consultant will end up troubleshooting more than is the case when consultant-informed decisions are made. Generally, wedding consultants can recommend a variety of trusted and established

PHOTO 1-2 *(opposite) Wedding consultants must pay careful attention to details.*

vendors. These relationships greatly facilitate the day-of process. Therefore, in cases where the consultant has not been involved in the vendor selection process, it is imperative to obtain the vendor list as soon as possible. By touching base with each of the selected vendors in advance and confirming all arrangements, the consultant can more readily mitigate problems that may arise on the wedding day. See Consultant in Action, Case 1.1, for an example of a day-of consultant challenge.

In addition to packages, many consultants offer à la carte or ad hoc services on a for-fee basis. While this may entail just about anything that pertains to the wedding process, some of the more common added services include the writing and placement of announcements; the coordination of engagement parties, showers, post-wedding events (e.g., day-after luncheons), and honeymoons; gift selection and purchases; preparation of seating lists; and the sending of thank-you cards.

PHOTO 1-3   *Partial wedding packages occur when couples primarily want assistance choosing vendors.*

the groom's cake

You have been hired as the day-of consultant for a 140-person wedding, and the bride and groom gave you a list of their selected vendors. As you made contact with each of the vendors two weeks before the wedding, you saw next to "Groom's Cake" the name "Aunt Jenny" and a telephone number. From Aunt Jenny you learned that the mother of the groom wanted a groom's cake and that Aunt Jenny agreed to make a French Croquembouche, which is a traditional French wedding cake made up of individual cream puffs that are filled with pastry cream, caramelized, stacked in a tower and decorated. She saw a recipe in a magazine and, because the groom is of French descent, thought it would be a great idea. You expressed your concerns to the bride and groom, based on the fact that Aunt Jenny was not a licensed pastry chef, but they were insistent. Resigned, you verified with Aunt Jenny that she would be bringing the filled pastry puffs to the reception site at 2:00 P.M. on the day of the wedding, between the ceremony and the reception, and then would caramelize and stack them on-site so the cake would be fresh. She assured you that she felt confident to do these tasks.

On the wedding day, you arrive at the reception site at 1:30 P.M. to meet with the vendors and get everything set for the 5:00 P.M. start time of the reception. At 3:45 P.M., Aunt Jenny arrives looking harassed and flustered. She said that with all of the excitement she got a little behind, but that she caramelized the puffs at home before the ceremony to save time. She hands you a box containing 5 dozen puffs that are stuck together in a gluey mess, as well as a bag containing powdered sugar and accent decorations. Aunt Jenny says, "Here is a picture of what it should look like. Please take care of the arrangement because I have to go get ready for the reception."

What do you do?

As a consultant, it is important that you carefully delineate the services that go with each package type as well as which services are considered add-ons. As will be discussed in the third section of this text, you need business savvy to stay in business.

ROLES

The wedding consultant will fulfill a variety of roles throughout the planning and implementation of any wedding. The nature of the package will influence those roles, as the comprehensive package will allow the consultant to become more fully involved in the lives of the couple and their families, whether desirable or not! For any given couple, the consultant may take on seven common roles: service provider, decision maker, organizer, artistic designer, psychologist, mediator, and friend.

First and foremost, it is critical to remember that the consultant is in a business relationship with the couple. As a service provider, you have specific obligations to fulfill and must maintain the highest standards of professionalism. (The third section of this text is devoted to establishing and building a sustainable business.)

Although the business relationship is paramount, other roles will emerge, some related to the nature of the business and others to human nature. The consultant will often become the decision maker by default. In particular, couples who select a comprehensive wedding package may do so because they simply do not have the time or desire to make all of the decisions that pertain to their wedding. In such cases, it is still important to give the couple the sense that they were involved in the final decisions. Even limited participation provides a feeling of ownership and accountability. As will be explained more fully later in the text, as the consultant you should never sign any contract on behalf of the couple, nor should you sign your own name to any vendor contract.

A third role you will take on as a wedding consultant is that of organizer. As the couple's consultant, the assumption is that any person involved in a given wedding can turn to you for direction. Timelines, checklists, and itineraries are crucial to maintain a sense of order and clarity amidst all the confusion that can arise. A key facet of organization is time management. The wedding consultant must be able to prioritize the tasks that need to be completed and to decide when each must occur. Having a comprehensive calendar for each wedding and written agendas for each meeting will help keep both you and the couple on task.

Your fourth role will be that of artistic designer. Many individuals get into the business of wedding planning because they have inherent good taste and a sense of flair that friends and family members have commented on throughout their lives. These traits lend themselves to helping couples make their visions reality. Consultants must be careful, though, to not overimpose their views on the couple. Generally, however, a wedding consultant is hired in part because the couple wants artistic design advice regarding cake selection, stationery essentials, floral décor, and other decorative elements.

Few weddings are stress free, and so the fifth role that a consultant often acquires is that of psychologist. The bride is typically the primary point of contact and spends on average 17 months in the wedding planning process (Fairchild Bridal Group, 2005). If you are involved from the onset, the bride will likely turn to you in moments of anxiety, pressure, and strain. The line between business communication and interpersonal communication blurs as trust develops (Knapp and Vangelisti, 1996; Littlejohn, 1989), and the bride may seek reassurance from you in times of emotional stress.

Should the stress of wedding planning move beyond the individual level, the consultant often acts as mediator, a sixth role. Mediators are not problem solvers per se; instead they respond to conflict-laden situations by encouraging empowerment, constructive listening, recognition, and negotiation (Bush and Foger, 1994). As a mediator, the wedding consultant can help disputing parties by creating a forum where each gets to speak and listen, then allowing the parties to work together to clearly define the problem, seek alternative and creative solutions, and ultimately implement an agreed-upon strategy (McKinney, Kimsey, and Fuller, 1995). Many wedding planners form vendor relationships with marriage counselors, whom they can recommend to clients who are facing significant relational crises.

Finally, the relationship between the couple and the wedding consultant may evolve to the point of friendship. In many cases, consultants start their businesses by working with friends and family members. Because consultants depend on referrals, often friends will suggest your services to other friends, and your business grows from there. It is important to recognize that you do not have to befriend your clients to have a successful business. In fact, you may have clients whom you do not like at all, which does not mean that you cannot have a successful working relationship with them. Friendship should be viewed as a natural outcome of some client-provider interactions rather than a forced business necessity.

the organization of this book

This book is presented in three main sections: Foundations, Practice, and Building Your Business. Section I comprises the first seven chapters and delves into the foundations of weddings, including the cultural, historical, mediated, political, and social factors that influence

II

PHOTO 1-4 *(top) Consultants help wedding parties work as a team.*

PHOTO 1-5 *(bottom) Consultants rely on positive word-of-mouth advertising from satisfied clients.*

our widely held beliefs, values, and preferences pertaining to weddings. Section II, which includes the middle 14 chapters, is devoted to practice, and concentrates on the services and associated vendors with whom the couple and consultant will interact. Consultant checklists will be found at the end of each of these chapters. Section III contains the final seven chapters and concentrates on the steps needed to establish your wedding planning business.

Throughout the text, you will find four different types of specialized information, presented as case studies, to complement the chapter material, entitled Consultant in Action, Culture Corner, Research Roundtable, and Vendor Spotlight. First, Consultant in Action cases will pose management situations based on scenarios that actual wedding planners or vendors have faced. You will be asked to specify how you would contend with the issues raised in these cases. Second, Culture Corner cases will highlight unique and blended traditions, customs, and practices. Third, each Research Roundtable will summarize academic and applied research that pertains to weddings and wedding planning. Finally, Vendor Spotlight segments will present tips of the trade as offered by top wedding vendors.

Whether you are a student interested in becoming a wedding consultant, an already practicing wedding or events specialist, a vendor who provides wedding services, or whether you are in the process of planning your own wedding, this book offers you the information and tools necessary to successfully engage in the business of weddings. Our focus on diversity broadens the meaning and applicability of the principles, while the case studies and photojournalism bring the concepts to life.

REFERENCES

Ashford, L. (2005). Taking stock of women's progress. Population Reference Bureau, available at http://www.prb.org

Ashford, L., and Clifton, D. (2005). Women of our world. Population Reference Bureau, available at http://www.prb.org

Buckley, S. (2004, September 28). Japan's women wary to wed. BBC News, World Edition, available from http://news.bbc.co.uk

Bush, R. A. B., and Foger, J. P. (1994). *The Promise of Mediation*. San Francisco: Jossey-Bass.

Dhesi, A. S. (2001). Expectations and post-school choice: Some data from India. *Education + Training* 43: 14–24.

Fairchild Bridal Group. (2005). The American wedding 2005. Microsoft PowerPoint research presentation.

Gold, T. (2005, August 23). Oh happy day. Guardian Unlimited, available from http://money.guardian.co.uk

González, I. C. (2005, June 23). Down the aisle, into the melting pot. *Washington Post*, H1; H5.

Goulet, C., and Riddell, J. (2005). *FabJob Guide to Become a Wedding Planner*. Alberta, Canada: FabJob.

Knapp, M. L., and Vangelisti, A. L. (1996). *Interpersonal Communication and Human Relationships*. Boston: Allyn and Bacon.

Lee, S. M., and Edmonston, B. (2005). New marriages, new families: U.S. racial and Hispanic intermarriage. *Population Bulletin* 60: 1–38.

Littlejohn, S. W. (1989). *Theories of Human Communication*. Belmont, CA: Wadsworth.

McKinney, B. C., Kimsey, W. D., and Fuller, R. M. (1995). *Mediator Communication Competencies: Interpersonal Communication and Alternative Dispute Resolution*. Edina, MN: Burgess International Group.

McMurray, S. (2005). The Wedding report: 2006 statistics and market estimates, available from http://www.theweddingreport.com

Papworth, J. (2005, June 18). For richer or poorer. Guardian Unlimited, available from http://money.guardian.co.uk

U.S. Census Bureau. (1995). Marital status and living arrangements: March 1994. Current Population Reports, Population Characteristics. Report Number P20–484.

U. S. Census Bureau. (2005). Number, timing, and duration of marriages and divorces: 2001. *Current Population Reports*, Household Economic Studies. Report Number P70–97.

review questions

1. Explain three reasons why the percentage of couples who rely on the services of a wedding consultant is increasing.

2. Name and differentiate three common types of wedding packages.

3. Name and briefly describe four of the seven roles that are commonly held by wedding consultants.

terminology

- À la carte / ad hoc wedding services
- Comprehensive wedding package
- Croquembouche
- Day-of wedding package
- Mediation
- Partial wedding package

weddings, culture, and religion

Weddings, as an area of study, have attracted "surprisingly little attention from researchers" (Leeds-Hurwitz, 2002, p. ix). When considering the multitude of topics available to students, practitioners, and scholars interested in the meaning and development of weddings, the cultural traditions, under-pinned by religion, have received more focused consider-ation than other areas. Cultural subject matter is particularly compelling, as norms pertaining to (1) socialization for mar-riage; (2) mate selection; (3) pre-wedding rituals; (4) wedding customs; and (5) changes in identity due to marriage are bound by both geography and heritage. These five points will form the framework of this chapter, and Culture Corners throughout the text will supplement this material.

PHOTO 2-1 *(opposite) Religious traditions play a major role in many weddings.*

althhough this chapter cannot begin to cover the wedding-related intricacies of every unique human culture and subculture, the norms presented offer an overview of areas where significant variation, yet common threads, can be found. As a consultant you are urged to carefully interview each couple with whom you work to help them pinpoint the unique elements that will highlight their cultural identities. The blending of traditions that occurs in intercultural and interfaith marriages is discussed throughout the text, with specific attention given to the many unique cultural customs that accompany wedding ceremonies highlighted in Chapter 13.

socialization for marriage

In most cultures marriage is assumed to be a viable option for the group's members; however, the expectation of and preparation for marriage vary quite significantly among different peoples. For example, in a primarily Muslim, Hausa-speaking Mawri society in Niger (Africa), "To become adults, both boys and girls must marry: non-marriage is simply not an acceptable option, a situation that is attested by the absence of Hausa terms that define physically mature women and men who have never married" (Masquelier, 2005, p. 59). This norm may appear extreme in most Western societies, yet individuals who were raised under certain rule structures may still be held accountable for those rules, even if they no longer reside in the geographical locale where the beliefs are held. For instance, Bekker et al. (1996, p. 330) detail the prescription for virginity, using the case of Islamic women residing in Western countries:

> In Islamic countries, staying a virgin until the wedding night is very important. Many young women are raised with the impera-tive to save their hymen for their husband. This norm implies no sexual intercourse, the avoidance of certain sports and a cau-tious approach to physical exertion. Before the wedding and around the wedding night, rituals take place that have to prove the bride's virginity. Some women are taken to medical doctors to get a certificate of their virginity. In other cases, a cloth with the woman's blood has to be demonstrated to the relatives, friends and neighbors after the defloration.

Bekker et al. explain that Islamic young women who reside in Western countries are torn between two forms of socialization, including their tra-ditional culture that enforces virginity and their more permissive country of residence that allows for sexual experimentation prior to marriage.

Many socialization rituals have abated over time. For example, tradi-tionally, young women around the world were instructed in Home Economics, learning skills related to menu preparation, cooking, sewing, crafts, housekeeping, etiquette, childcare, and language arts to prepare them for a domestic role and to be a gracious hostess. Classes and books regarding Home Economics were widely available between 1840 and 1950 but largely disappeared after the beginning of the women's movement, as this discipline was seen to restrict females to domestic roles (Heggestad, 2005). The modern film, *Mona Lisa Smile*, depicts some of the formal coursework and informal socialization that took place to prepare women to become housewives.

mate selection

Human mate selection may or may not include the input of those who are getting married. Mate selection by capture and by arrangement are two approaches in which at least one party has little say in the matter. The idea of a woman being abducted into marriage seems archaic, and the idea is generally relegated to discussions of ancient customs (see Ingoldsby, 1995). However, this form of mate selection still exists in some areas, as summarized in the Culture Corner, Case 2.1.

A second form of mate selection, marriage by arrangement, was historically enacted for economic reasons, to preserve bloodlines or to advance political agendas (Ingoldsby, 1995). This approach to mate selection is still commonly practiced in many societies. For instance, in Japan couples often meet through an arranged introduction called *miai marriages* (Dunn, 2004). Similarly, in India, "marriage is largely an arranged affair. Parents, relatives and family friends play an important role in the choice of partners. The matrimonial columns of newspapers are also used to seek wider response. However, in the majority of cases, it is the parents/relatives who carry out negotiations" (Dhesi, 2001, p. 15).

In societies that commonly practice arranged marriages, selection by choice or out of one's social class may have repercussions. For example, when Princess Sayako of Japan wed a commoner in November of 2005, she lost her title and royal status (Argetsinger and Roberts, 2005). As she is no longer considered a member of the Imperial Family, she can never again stay at her family's residence, the Imperial Palace. Furthermore, her visits to her parents are strictly controlled, with only one or two meetings allowed per year.

Even if a marriage is not fully arranged, culture may place boundaries on acceptable mate selection. The Amish, whose numbers are largely situated in the American states of Pennsylvania, Indiana, and Ohio, "socialize with and marry their own and are not involved in ecumenical activities with other denominations" (O'Neil, 1997, p. 1133).

If a marriage is not arranged or restricted, individuals are left to their own devices to select a suitable partner. Even in these cases, social cues will influence selection. Primary determinants of selection are social mobility and, increasingly, educational or occupational similar-

bride kidnapping in kyrgyzstan

In the country of Kyrgyzstan, located in Central Asia, the practice of nonconsensual bridal abduction or kidnapping is the beginning of approximately one-third of all marriages (Sadiq, 2004). This illegal and often violent custom is known as *ala kachuu*, or "grab and run," and is often chosen so that men will not have to pay a bridal price or because they wish to prove their manliness (Smith, 2005, A1).

Once girls have reached their teen years, they often suffer anxiety and the fear of being kidnapped because the abductions generally involve hysterical women screaming for freedom and being denied food, drink, and sleep while they are cajoled by the groom's female relatives to accept him (Lom, 2004). While most women eventually submit and often are ultimately content, cases of rape and suicide exist (Sadiq, 2004).

This common occurrence, though a largely taboo topic in Kyrgyzstan, gained worldwide attention when academic Petr Lom filmed a graphic documentary on the subject that was broadcast on PBS (Lom, 2004).

Case submitted by Aubrey Cote

ity. Prandy (2001) looked at six countries, including Australia, Britain, Germany, Hungary, Ireland, and the United States to determine the occupational status similarity of cohabiting and married couples. Even excluding cases where the couple had the exact same occupation (e.g., both were lawyers or both were farmers), a strong relationship occurred suggesting that social similarity in terms of career paths was an indicator of mate selection. Interestingly, the occupational status relationship was weakest in Australia and the United States. Prandy explains this finding by noting that these two countries are generally regarded as being more socially egalitarian than countries such as Hungary and Ireland, which had the strongest likelihood of occupational status similarity.

Indirect cues can also be used to select a mate. In the animal kingdom, females of a given species have been shown to prefer males that another female has already chosen (Uller and Johansson, 2003). This phenomenon is known as mate-choice copying or imitation, and suggests that a female may seek an already chosen male because the fact that he has already been selected indicates his suitability as a mate (Uller and Johansson, 2003). The phenomenon was evidenced in the popular National Geographic film, *March of the Penguins*. The mate-choice copying behaviors evidenced in animal species might also play a role in human mate selection. A study that investigated the wedding ring effect by determining if imitation influences human mate selection is summarized in the Research Roundtable, Case 2.2.

Once a mate has been selected and prior to formal engagement, the courtship period occurs as a time of exploration and negotiation. In analyzing the courtship stories of 344 young, newly married couples, Holmberg, Orbuch, and Veroff (2004) found that nearly one-third of the stories focused on negative occurrences and tensions that impacted this period in their lives. These tensions most frequently originated from within the relationship (e.g., physical separation, resistance to deepening the relationship), whereas other obstacles pertained to external issues such as family or finances. Another one-third of the couples' courtship plots were neutral, focusing on a pragmatic intertwining of lives, and the final one-third were focused on a general positive progression, where the relationship descriptions centered on "a continuous increase in positive commitment to each other with no major hitches or setbacks along the way" (p. 58).

pre-wedding rituals

Once a couple decides to marry, rituals pertaining to the engagement or prematrimonial period are carried out. In some societies, these customs can be as elaborate as the wedding itself. In certain African regions, a gift exchange is used to signal preparedness to marry (Masquelier, 2005, p. 59):

mate-choice copying

Purpose: To determine if men wearing wedding rings are perceived as more desirable than those not wearing a wedding ring.

Methods: A sample of 97 female undergraduate students met two men and were given five questions to ask them. The men did not state their marital status but were either wearing or not wearing a wedding ring. After the interactions, the women answered questions regarding their impressions of the marital status, attractiveness, and socioeconomic status of the men, as well as items pertaining to their willingness to have dinner, engage in sex, and start a serious relationship with each.

Results: The presence or absence of a ring did not influence how the women perceived the men. The wedding ring effect was not supported. In fact, though not statistically significant, the pattern of results suggested that when the men were not wearing the rings, they were generally perceived as more attractive and the women indicated a higher willingness to have dinner, engage in sex, and start a serious relationship with each.

Conclusion: Females found single men to be equally desirable as men who were perceived as being in a committed relationship. Mate-choice copying does not appear to impact the human species as much as it does animal species.

Source: Uller and Johansson (2003).

Before a boy and girl can tie the knot, however, bridewealth (sadaki) must be exchanged. While the bride's mother spends the sadaki payment on the bowls, cooking implements and furnishings that will adorn her daughter's new home, the groom, assisted by his friends and kin, must make an additional series of gifts to his future in-laws to demonstrate his ability to secure land, labour, and capital.

Dowry practices can be distinguished from bridalwealth or bride price: "Bride price refers to goods or money given by the groom's family to the family of the prospective bride in return for the realization of the intended marriage. Dowry, on the other hand, involves the gifts given to the bride, the groom and the groom's family by the bride's parents" (Sandıkcı and İlhan, 2004, p. 150). Although the meanings and experiences differ, dowry practices and other financial settlements continue in parts of South Asian countries such as China, India, and Turkey (Sandıkcı and İlhan, 2004). For example, three forms of dowry still practiced in Turkey are (1) the chest dowry, comprised of hand-produced, decorative textile items such as embroidery, needlework, and lace; (2) appliance dowry, including kitchen items and household durables; and (3) gift dowry, which includes hand-produced items such as headscarves and linens that are given to the groom's immediate and extended family (Sandıkcı and İlhan, 2004).

The Westernized wedding shower, also commonly referred to as the bridal shower, is an anticipated pre-wedding ritual that was historically conceived as an offshoot of dowry practices to prepare brides for marriage. Legend has it that bridal showers originated in Holland. According to Clark (2000), a young woman wanted to marry a poor Dutch miller whose generous nature had led him to give all of his possessions away to those in need, "so that when the time came to marry, he had nothing left to offer his prospective bride" (p. 7). The girl's father, fearing that the miller would not be able to adequately provide for his daughter, forbade the marriage and refused to provide a dowry. Out of appreciation for the miller's longstanding kindness, the community came together and showered the girl with household items so that she could marry the miller (Clark, 2000). An adaptation of this same idea has spread, and most women in the United States have bridal showers, regardless of their financial status. Bridal showers offer women an opportunity to "embrace their femininity and celebrate an upcoming wedding" as they "gather, eat, socialize and watch the bride open presents" (Montemurro, 2005, p. 13).

More recently, men have been intentionally included in wedding showers. Montemurro (2005) identifies and describes three situations where men take part in shower rituals: fiancé-only shower, groomal shower, and coed wedding shower. The fiancé-only shower follows a similar format to that of the traditional bridal shower, but the groom-to-be is present throughout the entire event and is the only male present. In cases such as these, the male may be there in support of the bride, in particular if there are many women present (i.e., relatives of the groom) with whom she is not familiar. A similar, more common, situation occurs when the groom stays away for the majority of the shower but arrives at the end to briefly greet and thank the guests. The groomal shower, labeled by Berardo and Vera (1981), occurs when the event is staged for the groom, the bride is not present, and both men and women are guests. The third shower ritual in which men become involved, the coed wedding shower, is held for the couple and includes both male and female guests. Montemurro (2005) found that in comparison to traditional bridal showers, coed showers are more likely to take place at night, involve alcohol, have less emphasis on gift opening, and follow a theme (e.g., CD shower), and the groom-to-be often takes on the role of comedian to maintain his sense of masculinity and heterosexuality.

๛ wedding customs

The rituals specific to wedding ceremonies and the associated receptions result in events that vary from socially isolated proceedings that involve only the necessitated rites to lavish, lengthy affairs. Amish couples, at one end, usually marry on a Tuesday or a Thursday in autumn with a simple ceremony that stresses dignity and devotion and reinforces community (O'Neil, 1997). On the other end of the spectrum are accounts of High Renaissance wedding festivals such as the Medici wedding of 1589 (Saslow, 1996) where the celebration associated with a single royal wedding could last up to a month.

The length of a wedding ceremony and the associated pomp and production are often used to ascribe meaning to the union. Kalmijn (2004), in a review of contemporary Western marriage rituals, contends that more elaborate wedding ceremonies are indicative of a couple's uncertainty regarding the transition to a marital role. This study is summarized in Research Roundtable, Case 2.3.

As a wedding consultant, you may specialize in weddings that cater to a particular culture or familiarize yourself with a multitude of cultures. The mixing of traditions due to the changing family will be discussed in more detail in Chapter 5.

Many ceremony-specific cultural customs reflect the religious affiliation of the bride and/or groom. The three dominant world religions are Christianity (32 percent), Islam (19 percent), and Hinduism (13 percent), and significant variation can be found within each of these; for example, over 1,000 Christian denominations exist, which can be classified into 15 groupings (Robinson, 2005).

Beyond the three dominant world religions, other religions of significance, in alphabetical order, include the Baha'i faith, Buddhism, Chinese folk religions, Confucianism, Judaism, Sikhism, and Taoism. An

wedding ceremonies and marital uncertainty

Purpose: To determine if those whose transition to the role of spouse is less drastic have less elaborate wedding ceremonies than those making a more drastic transition.

Methods: A sample of 572 respondents from The Netherlands answered questions pertaining to the nature of their wedding ceremony (e.g., size, location), transition characteristics (e.g., age when married, whether they had cohabitated before marriage, whether this was their first marriage), and social confirmation characteristics (e.g., perceived family support for marriage, whether friends were married).

Results: Respondents whose transitions to marriage were less radical because they were older and/or lived together before marriage placed less emphasis on the social components of the wedding celebration (e.g., church location, large reception) than those who were younger and whose changes in living arrangements were more drastic.

Conclusion: Those experiencing marital transition uncertainty use elaborate wedding rituals to reinforce external approval and as an orientation into new, socially prescribed roles.

Source: Kalmijn (2004).

PHOTO 2-2 (top) Readings from the New Testament are common at Christian wedding ceremonies.

PHOTO 2-3 (bottom) The kiddush cup is one of many Jewish ceremony artifacts.

estimated 12 percent of the world population indicate no religious affiliation (Robinson, 2005), which establishes the importance of having wedding ceremony sites available that are outside the religious realm.

✿ changes in identity due to marriage

The extent to which a person's identity shifts upon entering into the marital state has cultural influences. Specifically, symbolic indicators of marriage, the way people talk about the institution of marriage, the stability of the marital bond, and one's treatment in the workplace upon marriage can be impacted differently by culture. Kalmijn (2004, p. 585) states that the transition to bride and groom "serves to confirm the norms that the community holds, and this creates an incentive for the community to give approval."

Symbolic indicators of marriage send the community at large the message that a person's marital status has changed. Some symbols of the marital state remain primarily within the female domain, including "the changing of her family name to correspond to that of her husband, modifying her title (from Miss [or Ms.] to Mrs.) or, in traditional China, changing her hairstyle to indicate marital status" (Smith, 2004, p. 491). The social convention of wearing a wedding ring was traditionally carried out only by the female, but now a double-ring ceremony is commonplace in many countries. The Irish Claddagh ring, made up of heart, hands, and crown, is an excellent cultural example of symbolic change. When it is worn on the right hand with the crown and heart facing out, the ring tells that the wearer's heart is yet to be won; on the right hand facing in, one is under loves spell; whereas when worn on the left hand, with the crown and heart facing inwards, it signifies the marital state and that love has been requited (Royal Claddagh, 2006). The exchange of Claddagh rings is a timeless element of traditional Irish weddings (McCourt, 2003).

Beyond symbolic customs, a second way to understand how the marital state is perceived is to reflect on the metaphors and themes that are used when celebrating marriage. Dunn (2004) analyzed speeches given at Japanese wedding receptions and compared the dominant metaphors with ideas found in American dialogue about marriage. The three most common metaphors that surfaced were: (1) marriage is a joint creation (e.g., *katei*, making a new "home"—house and garden; (2) marriage is a union (e.g., *musubarete*, tied together); and (3) marriage is a journey (e.g., *kadode*, departure / start of a new life stage). Dunn found that the theme of working together was more central to Japanese speeches, whereas the idea of working on the relationship is more central to American discussions of marriage. Dunn contends that this distinction, though subtle, reflects the individualistic American mentality in comparison to the societal cultural framework found in Japan.

A third influence on post-wedding identity is cultural perceptions of marital bond stability. In Spain and other regions of Mediterranean Europe, factors such as strong Catholic ties, a more recent introduction of divorce, fewer women in the job market, a high proportion of extended families, and a late average age when children cease living with their parents all contribute to the fact that marriages in these regions reflect more stable bonds than those in Northern Europe and the United States (Redondo-Bellón, Royo-Vela, and Aldás-Manzano, 2001).

A final factor that influences marital identity is how an individual is treated in the workplace. Kuta and Kleiner (2001) report that on average married women make less than single women, while married men make more than single men. Factors that may explain these discrepancies include the likelihood of married women putting their careers on hold while having children and, simultaneously, the perception that married men need to stay on the promotional path more so than single men, since the married man may have a wife and children to support (Kuta and Kleiner, 2001). Political and discriminatory issues, as related to weddings and marriage, will be discussed in more detail in Chapter 5.

REFERENCES

Argetsinger, A., and Roberts, R. (2005, November 15). The reliable source: Foreign affairs. *Washington Post*, C3.

Bekker, M. H. J., Rademakers, J., Mouthaan, I., De Neef, M., Huisman, W. M., Van Zandvoort, H., and Emans, A. (1996). Reconstructing hymens or constructing sexual inequality? Service provision to Islamic young women coping with the demand to be a virgin. *Journal of Community & Applied Social Psychology* 6: 329–334.

Berardo, F. A., and Vera, H. (1981). Groomal shower: A variation on the American bridal shower. *Family Relations* 30: 395–401.

Clark, B. (2000). *Bridal Showers*. Carpinteria, CA: Wilshire Publications.

Dhesi, A. S. (2001). Expectations and post-school choice: Some data from India. *Education + Training* 43: 14–24.

Dunn, C. D. (2004). Cultural models and metaphors for marriage: An analysis of discourse at Japanese wedding receptions. *Ethos* 32: 348–373.

Heggestad, M. (2005). What is home economics? Hearth, Cornell University, available at http://hearth.library.cornell.edu/h/hearth/about.html

Holmberg, D., Orbuch, T. L., and Veroff, J. (2004). *Thrice Told Tales: Married Couples Tell Their Stories*. Mahwah, NJ: Lawrence Erlbaum Associates.

Ingoldsby, B. B. (1995). Mate selection and marriage. In B. B. Ingoldsby and Suzanna Smith (eds.), *Families in Multicultural Perspective* (pp. 143–160). New York: Guilford Press.

Kalmijn, M. (2004). Marriage rituals as reinforcers of role transitions: An analysis of weddings in The Netherlands. *Journal of Marriage and Family* 66: 582–594.

Kuta, M., and Kleiner, B. H. (2001). New developments concerning discrimination based on marital status. *Equal Opportunities International* 20: 45–47.

Leeds-Hurwitz, W. (2002). *Wedding as Text: Communicating Cultural Identities through Ritual*. Mahwah, NJ: Lawrence Erlbaum Associates.

Lom, P. (2004, March). The kidnapped bride: The story. PBS Frontline World, available at http://www.pbs.org/frontlineworld/stories/kyrgystan/thestory.html

Masquelier, A. (2005). The scorpion's sting: Youth, marriage and the struggle for social maturity in Niger. *Journal of the Royal Anthropological Institute* 11: 59–83.

McCourt, M. (2003). *The Claddagh Ring: Ireland's Cherished Symbol of Friendship, Loyalty and Love*. Philadelphia: Running Press.

Montemurro, B. (2005). Add men, don't stir: Reproducing traditional gender roles in modern wedding showers. *Journal of Contemporary* Ethnography 34: 6–35.

O'Neil, D. J. (1997). Explaining the Amish. *International Journal of Social Economics* 24: 1132–1139.

Prandy, K. (2001). An international comparative analysis of marriage patterns and social stratification. *International Journal of Sociology and Social Policy* 21: 165–183.

Redondo-Bellón, I., Royo-Vela, M., and Aldás-Manzano, J. (2001). A family life cycle model adapted to the Spanish environment. *European Journal of Marketing* 35: 612–638.

Robinson, B. A. (2005). Religions of the world. Ontario Consultants on Religious Tolerance, available at http://www.religioustolerance.org/worldrel.htm

Royal Claddagh. (2006). Tradition, available at http://www.claddagh.com

Sadiq, S. (2004, March). Interview with Petr Lom: Marriage by abduction. PBS Frontline World, available at http://www.pbs.org/frontlineworld/stories/kyrgystan/lom.html

Sandıkcı, Ö., and İlhan, B. E. (2004). Dowry: A cherished possession or an old-fashioned tradition in an modernizing society? In C. C. Otnes and T. M. Lowrey (eds.), (pp. 149–180). Mahwah, NJ: Lawrence Erlbaum Associates.

Saslow, J. (1996). *The Medici Wedding of 1589.* New Haven, CT: Yale University Press.

Smith, C. S. (2005, April 30). Abduction, often violent, a Kyrgyz wedding rite. *New York Times,* A1.

Smith, I. (2004). The foundations of marriage: Are they crumbling? *International Journal of Social Economics* 31: 487–500.

Uller, T., and Johansson, C. (2003). Human mate choice and the wedding ring effect: Are married men more attractive? *Human Nature* 14: 267–276.

review questions

1. Explain the idea of mate-choice copying and discuss why you think it does or does not apply to human mate selection.

2. Differentiate between bride price and dowry.

3. Explain what the discipline of Home Economics is and why it is now rarely offered as a field of study.

4. Discuss the relationship between marital uncertainty and elaborate wedding ceremonies.

5. Name the three dominant world religions, as well as three other religions commonly practiced.

6. Name and explain two ways in which one's change in identity is publicly reflected upon marriage.

terminology

- Home economics
- Bride kidnapping
- Bride price
- Claddagh ring
- Courtship
- Dowry
- Marital uncertainty
- Mate-choice copying

history and
hegemony

The foundations of marriage are rooted in history and hegemony. With regard to history, there is widespread support for considering the historical past and how it influences modern weddings. The concept of hegemony, however, is a contested term, and debate persists regarding the hegemonic influences on weddings. This chapter will, first, introduce the idea of hegemony; second, detail how hegemony intertwines with other social factors to influence marriage; third, offer examples of this convergence and its impact on weddings, both past and present; and finally, discuss the movement away from hegemony as pertaining to weddings both past and present by focusing on the emergence of a balance of power.

PHOTO 3-1 *(opposite) Notions of romantic love historically set up the desire to marry.*

↫ what is hegemony?

Hegemony, in its most generic form, is related to terms such as authority, domination, subjugation, order, and control. More specifically, hegemony is a process through which social order is maintained through the establishment of social norms, values, and belief structures that result in consent formation (Condit, 1994). Agencies such as education systems, the church, the media, and cultural institutions such as the family develop and maintain messages that are used to create a worldview and public vocabulary that define reality for the masses (Condit, 1994). The assumption is that the politically elite who create the messages do so to maintain power: "Although hegemony allows for the existence of alternative viewpoints, these lesser heard or marginal voices get 'drowned out' by those presented more often" (Engstrom and Semic, 2003).

Hegemony, at its worst, involves socially prescribed exclusion and violence. When considering the historical roots of marriage and weddings, evidence of hegemonic standards exist. These standards of order, power, and control maintain influence in many cultures today.

↫ hegemony and marriage

Wedding-related research "supports a dominant ideology of weddings, such as the expectation of a woman to marry (a man) and do so in a wedding with the costly pageantry associated with it, that has become so inculcated into everyday practices and values regarding social life that we do not even question them" (Engstrom and Semic, 2003). For the wedding process to become standardized to the point of hegemony, two conditions must be illustrated: (1) certain foundations must be established, accepted, and maintained; and (2) these foundations must create a power imbalance. Meeting the first condition requires the perception that there are benefits to establishing a joint household. Weiss (1997) uses an economic perspective to detail five ways in which couples can gain from the marital state; specifically, marriage (1) aids in the production and rearing of children; (2) presents a comparative advantage in terms of division of labor; (3) supports the coordination of investment activities, such as allowing one partner to work while the other is in school; (4) allows couples to share in collective goods, such as a shared home; and (5) involves the pooling of risk, as in the case of one partner losing a job but the other maintaining employment.

Smith (2004) contends that of all the ways that individuals are served through marriage, the sexual relationship is fundamental, evidenced by the fact that a marriage can be annulled if it is not sexually consummated. Smith (2004, p. 497) argues:

The notion that a couple love each other, and wish to raise a family and grow old together, offers a fine motivation for marriage but not a justification for the historical shape of the marital institution itself. . . . Marriage can be conceived as fundamentally a hierarchical governance solution to mitigate the hazards generated by asymmetric information in sexual relationships.

In other words, historically, marriage facilitated sexual cooperation by "transferring to a husband the right for sexual control over his wife" (p. 491). This leads to the second condition: a power imbalance. The transfer of sexual power to the male had inherent risks; for example, "until the mid-nineteenth century in England, a husband was legally permitted to use physical violence to secure the conjugal services of his wife. Alternatively, a wife could be jailed or confined in the matrimonial home for refusing marital rights" (p. 491). Furthermore, historically a woman's property was lost upon matrimony: "by stripping women of their property and codifying female dependence, marriage effectively solidified white male dominance" (Will, 1999, p. 100).

Under such a threat of dominance, why did women desire to marry? Researchers suggest that women were set up, so to speak, with societal messages of romantic love as a desirable outcome (Wilding, 2003, p. 382):

It could be argued that the culture industry has a particular interest in maintaining the subordination of women as a group by ensuring that they participate in their own oppression by succumbing to the "pleasures" of romantic love. It could also be argued that the culture industry manipulates the emotions of female audiences to ensure that the interests of the powerful are maintained, and that the "masses" actively refuse to recognize or critique their own relative powerlessness.

Although the foundations of this patriarchal asymmetry, which privileges men as a group and exploits women as a group (Ingraham, 1999) are increasingly being questioned and readjusted, their influence is still felt in today's marriages. Ingoldsby (1995) discusses the presence and influence of machismo in Latin American countries. He explains that the two principal characteristics of machismo are powerful masculinity and hypersexuality: "The culturally preferred goal is the conquest of women, and the more the better. To take advantage of a young woman sexually is cause for pride and prestige, not blame. . . . A married man should have a mistress in addition to casual encounters. His relationship with his wife is that of an aloof lord-protector" (p. 338).

hegemony and weddings

Hegemony as pertaining to weddings can be viewed in both the past and present. In this section, the roots of institutionalized hierarchical

relationships are considered first by reflecting on historically famous weddings and marriages. Then, overt hegemonic wedding traditions still in existence are illustrated by explaining the practices of child wedding ceremonies and the demand for virginity.

HISTORIC WEDDINGS AND MARRIAGES

Weddings and marriages of historical significance can be used to illustrate the prevalence of hegemonic principles. Five historical areas that will be used as examples include (1) the power display evident in *jus primae noctis* and related symbolic adaptations; (2) weddings that took place in an environment hostile to unions; (3) weddings that did not take place due to societal constraints; (4) fictional weddings that convey misogynistic norms; and (5) infamous royal weddings and marriages.

Evidence of *jus primae noctis*, a term referring to "one man's privilege of sexual access to a woman before another man's," dates back to 1900 BC, when despotic rulers in Babylonia enforced a custom "that all virgins who wanted to marry had to be brought to the king, who had the right to deflower them, first" (Wettlaufer, 2000, p. 112). Symbolic gestures reflecting the sexual right of the lord of the manor to his female peasants remained popular through the Middle Ages in European regions. While it is disputed whether the lords enforced sexual relations during the medieval period, widespread knowledge of the custom allowed them to at least engage in sexual harassment "as a sign of superiority over the dependent peasants" on their wedding night (p. 117).

Some historic weddings are worthy of note simply because they were permitted to take place in an environment hostile to unions. Will (1999) examined slave marriages in the antebellum South and explains that "The Southern legal system never recognized slave marriages on the grounds that property could not enter into a legal contract" (p. 100). Some slave owners forbade their slaves to wed, others disdainfully allowed the proceedings to take place, and still others approved the unions because they felt marriage strengthened the slaves' ties to the plantation, in essence, supporting the hegemony. In rare cases, the owners permitted Big House weddings, which took place in the plantation home with the support and assistance of the masters. The primary risk associated with marriage was that masters could sell one slave partner while maintaining the other. Nonetheless, the ceremonies and the commitment evidenced in slave marriages were important because, "To slaves, wedding ceremonies and receptions legitimized their personal relationships to the extent possible within the slave system" (p. 113).

PHOTO 3-2 *(opposite) Relationship expectations vary by culture.*

Weddings that did not take place can also serve as examples of the hegemonic order. Carmichael (2003) reports on an attempted same-sex wedding that was broken up by the police in April of 1953 in Waco, Texas. "A prominent Waco photographer was there to take pictures, and a duly licensed minister was on hand to perform the ceremony" (p. 32). When the police arrived, 67 men were arrested and held overnight in the county jail, and "most of the men picked up at the gathering lost their jobs and became estranged from their families" (p. 32). As will be discussed in detail in Chapter 5, same-sex commitment ceremonies and marriages are still widely condemned as undermining the prevailing social order.

Weddings portrayed in fiction often serve to evoke historic, misogynistic traditions, evidencing disdain toward females. In *Desirable Daughters*, Mukherjee (2002) relates the experiences of a 5-year-old Hindu Bengali girl on the day of her wedding. While being transported to the wedding, the groom receives a fatal snakebite. The bride is blamed, as the hostile relatives of the groom scream, "Your happiness-wrecking daughter is responsible." "Hang a rope around her neck!" "May she have the good sense to drown herself!" (pp. 11–12). The devastated father reflects that his daughter's life is ruined, "She was a person to be avoided. In a community intolerant of unmarried women, his Tara Lata had become an unmarriageable woman" (p. 12). As discussed in the next section of this chapter, child wedding ceremonies are still a common occurrence in India.

Historic royal weddings and marriages offer a glimpse of the treatment of women associated with hegemonic decision making. The classic case is that of Henry VIII, who was so obsessed with having a son that he secretly divorced his first wife, Catherine of Aragon, because she was unable to conceive a son and then beheaded his second wife, Anne Boleyn, when she also failed to produce a male heir (McCoy, 2001). Henry ultimately had six wives but reportedly only truly loved the third, Jane Seymour, who gave birth to his only son. She died shortly thereafter from complications, and Henry is buried with her. Another case in distant history was the Medici wedding of 1589 alluded to in Chapter 2. It was arguably the most famous wedding festival of the Italian Renaissance, uniting Grand Duke Ferdinando I de' Medici and French princess Christine de Lorraine, who was the niece of King Henri III (Saslow, 1996). While Christine was a member of royalty, she "was little more than a pawn in a high-stakes game of dynastic marriages played by her powerful older relatives" (Saslow, 1996, p. 17). However, Ferdinando and Christine were well suited, and "political motivations notwithstanding, the marriage appears to have turned out remarkably well for such arranged affairs, and it became a genuine love match" (p. 18).

In more recent history, the wedding of Princess Diana and Prince Charles offers another example of the power and influence of societal expectations. The fairytale courtship and ceremony that were suggested to the world at large overshadowed the reality of a woman who was at the point of breakdown prior to the wedding because of a distant fiancé, coupled with extraordinary public scrutiny of each element of the wedding plan (Morton, 1997). Personal interviews with Diana revealed that she had not been emotionally prepared for the relentless media attention during the wedding and marriage, and that role anxiety coupled with jealousy stemming from her husband's ongoing relationship with Camilla Parker-Bowles led to years of bulimia and multiple suicide attempts (Morton, 1997).

Another current royal marriage of note is that of Crown Princess Masako of Japan, who was educated at Harvard and Oxford, is married to Crown Prince Naruhito, and has a young daughter. In 2004, she excused herself from royal duties to recover from the accumulated stress of attempting to produce a male heir to the throne (Joyce, 2004). Many people in Japan believe that she now suffers from severe depression brought on by her inability to conceive a son. Although females were once permitted to rule, a 1947 law specified that only males could assume the throne (Talmadge, 2004). While some Japanese favored changing the law, others felt that Crown Prince Naruhito should take a concubine (i.e., mistress) in order to produce a male heir (Argetsinger and Roberts, 2005). The succession crisis was temporarily averted in November 2005, when a government panel concluded that the emperor's firstborn child, regardless of sex, should be next in line for the throne, paving the way for Princess Aiko, the 3-year-old female child of the couple, to be the first female monarch since the late 1700s (The Japan Times, 2005). Princess Aiko became "the cause celebre of reformists seeking an end to the male-only policy" (Faiola, 2006, p. A10). However, the debate reopened when the announcement was made that Prince Akishono, the brother of Crown Prince Naruhito, and his wife Princess Kiko were expecting a third child (their first two children are girls). The birth of their son, Hisahito, in September 2006 caused lawmakers to indefinitely shelve the proposed legislation that would have allowed a female heir to ascend the throne (Faiola, 2006).

CHILD WEDDING CEREMONIES AND THE DEMAND FOR VIRGINITY

Some controlling practices supported by the social order are still practiced today. Two examples that have commanded international attention are child wedding ceremonies and the demand for proof of virginity at the time of marriage.

Child wedding ceremonies are technically illegal in India, as the minimum age for marriage is 18 for women and 21 for men. However, this form of marriage is still widely practiced in some states (Washington Report, 2002). In 2002, over 200 children, some under the age of 1, were married in two mass wedding ceremonies in Rajasthan (Washington Report, 2002). The children seldom understand the meaning of the ceremony and later resent the match made by their parents or elders. For example 22-year-old Savita Chaudhry was wed to her husband at the age of 3 in a group ceremony and then remained with her parents hundreds of miles away until she reached adult age, when she was asked to join her husband (Lancaster, 2005). When she resisted, the leaders of her caste threatened her family with excommunication from the caste, which would destroy their social standing (Lancaster, 2005).

The demand for proof of virginity at the time of marriage, as introduced in Chapter 2, is an example of an overt, sexist double standard, for it is a requirement for females but not for males. For women residing in permissive environments who experiment sexually and are later confronted with an arranged marriage, a host of problems including "loneliness, social isolation, depression, despair, suicidal feelings, identity problems and serious conflicts with parents" arise (Bekker et al., 1996, p. 330). These women, in fear for their lives, will undergo surgical hymen reconstruction or will try to persuade medical doctors to provide a false virginity certificate (Bekker et al., 1996).

⚕ a balance of power

Although hegemonic practices are still evident in modern times, they are becoming less prevalent. In Chapter 5, a discussion of the influences of the changing family on wedding traditions will illustrate how many of these dominant social norms are increasingly being questioned and how a new conceptualization of women and men is prevailing in many countries and cultures. This questioning has historical precedent. Specifically, as early as the fifteenth century, women were praised during their wedding ceremonies for their beauty and cognitive abilities. As summarized by D'Elia (2002), speeches known as wedding orations delivered during courtly weddings in fifteenth-century Italy went against the prevailing power imbalance by focusing on five positive attributes of weddings and marriage: (1) the celebration of physical beauty; (2) the joys and uses of sex; (3) the importance of mutual affection; (4) the political and economic benefits of marriage; and (5) the praise of the intellectual woman.

First, marriage orators praised the beauty of both the bride and the groom. This was viewed as an important task in aristocratic society because often the couple had not met prior to the wedding. Thus, the oration could be used to reassure the appropriateness of the match while reflecting beauty as "inspiring awe" (D'Elia, 2002, p. 406) and operating as an incentive to be virtuous and faithful. Similarly, sex and

PHOTO 3-3 *(opposite) Weddings today highlight the balance of power between women and men.*

passion were viewed positively in wedding orations, and "orators sought to excite groom and bride to the sensual pleasures of the wedding night" (p. 411). Third, the ideals of mutual affection and romance were perceived as positive societal forces. Fourth, wedding orators shamelessly praised the importance and practical advantages of wealth. Finally, the intelligent woman was viewed with respect, as "wedding orators often present wisdom and learning as ideals in prospective brides" (p. 416).

Therefore, although much historical evidence suggests that hegemony influenced both weddings and marriage, these dominant messages that result in power imbalances have consistently been challenged. As a wedding consultant, you gain a better appreciation of evolving culture by understanding the past and how it continues to influence weddings and marriages today.

REFERENCES

Argetsinger, A., and Roberts, R. (2005, November 15). The reliable source: Foreign affairs. *Washington Post*, C3.

BBC News. (2006, February 7). Japan's Princess Kiko "pregnant," available at news.bbc.co.uk

Bekker, M. H. J., Rademakers, J., Mouthaan, I., De Neef, M., Huisman, W. M., Van Zandvoort, H., and Emans, A. (1996). Reconstructing hymens or constructing sexual inequality? Service provision to Islamic young women coping with the demand to be a virgin. *Journal of Community & Applied Social Psychology* 6: 329–334.

Carmichael, B. (2003). A gay wedding (almost) in Waco. *The Gay & Lesbian Review* 10: 31–32.

Condit, C. M. (1994). Hegemony in a mass-mediated society: Concordance about reproductive technologies. *Critical Studies in Mass Communication* 11: 205–230.

D'Elia, A. (2002). Marriage, sexual pleasure, and learned brides in the wedding orations of fifteenth century Italy. *Renaissance Quarterly* 55: 379–433.

Engstrom, E., and Semic, B. (2003). Portrayal of religion in reality TV programming: Hegemony and the contemporary American wedding. *Journal of Media and Religion* 2: 145–163.

Faiola, A. (2006, September 6) Japan's Princess Kiko gives birth to a male heir. Washington Post, A10.

Ingoldsby, B. B. (1995). Poverty and patriarchy in Latin America. In B. B. Ingoldsby and Suzanna Smith (eds.), *Families in Multicultural Perspective* (pp. 335–351). New York: Guilford Press.

Ingraham, C. (1999). *White Weddings: Romancing Heterosexuality in Popular Culture.* New York: Routledge.

The Japan Times. (2005, November 25). Female monarchs get green light, available at http://www.japantimes.com

Joyce, C. (2004, July 31). Crown Princess is "mentally ill." Telegraph, available at http://www.telegrapgh.co.uk

Lancaster, J. (2005, September 5). A young woman says "no" to rural India's child-marriage tradition. *Washington Post*, A27.

McCoy, D. (2001). *The World's Most Unforgettable Weddings: Love, Lust, Money, and Madness.* New York: Citadel Press.

Morton, A. (1997). *Diana: Her True Story.* New York: Simon & Schuster.

Mukherjee, B. (2002). *Desirable Daughters.* New York: Hyperion.

Saslow, J. (1996). *The Medici Wedding of 1589.* New Haven, CT: Yale University Press.

Smith, I. (2004). The foundations of marriage: Are they crumbling? *International Journal of Social Economics* 31: 487–500.

Talmadge, E. (2004, April 23). Japan's Crown Princess crumbles. CBS News, available at http://www.cbsnews.com

Washington Report. (2002). Mass child wedding in India. *The Washington Report on Middle East Affairs* 21: 41.

Weiss, Y. (1997). The formation and dissolution of families: Why marry? Who marries whom? And, what happens upon marriage and divorce? In M. R. Rosenzweig and O. Stark (eds.) *Handbook of Population and Family Economics* (pp. 81–123). Amsterdam: Elsevier.

Wettlaufer, J. (2000). *The jus primae noctis* as a male power display: A review of historic sources with evolutionary interpretation. *Evolution and Human Behavior* 21: 111–123.

Wilding, R. (2003). Romantic love and "getting married": Narratives of the wedding in and out of cinema texts. *Journal of Sociology* 39: 373–389.

Will, T. E. (1999). Weddings on contested grounds: Slave marriage in the antebellum South. *The Historian* 62: 99–119.

review questions

1. Explain what hegemony is and how it influences marriages and weddings.

2. Using an economic perspective, name three ways in which couples benefit from the marital state.

3. What was the significance of slave weddings in the antebellum South?

4. Describe two historical weddings of prominence and how they reflected hegemonic ideals.

5. What two hegemonic practices related to weddings are still being practiced today?

6. How did historic wedding orations challenge the prevailing power imbalance?

terminology

- Hegemony

- Machismo

- Misogynistic norms

- Patriarchy

- Wedding orations

PHOTO 4-1 *The diamond engagement ring is an invented tradition.*

the mediated *construction of weddings*

The progressive advent of print, film, televised, and computer-generated media has greatly expanded the ability to structure, create, and recreate the meaning of weddings as well as the manner in which these events take place. This chapter will look at five ways in which the media has shaped the construction and implementation of weddings: (1) invented traditions; (2) celebrity weddings; (3) portrayal of weddings in film; (4) reality television; and (5) the Internet.

✿ invented traditions

Media framing involves the ability of a media presentation to define a situation (Tankard, 2001). In the case of weddings, mass communication operates to frame specific views or traditions to the extent that they become so expected and dominant that people accept them without thinking and seldom pause to reflect on their origins. Three commonly accepted Western wedding traditions with invented roots that were largely framed by the media are the diamond engagement ring, the double-ring ceremony, and the white wedding gown.

The fact that "the American diamond engagement ring sector is a keystone to the worldwide natural diamond market" (Fram and Baron, 2004, p. 340) is due solely to very successful marketing initiatives. The royal beginning of the story occurred when Archduke Maximilian of Austria reportedly gave Mary of Burgundy the first diamond engagement ring in 1477. However, diamonds as the stone of choice did not become a preferred option until much later.

The legal precursor of the modern engagement ring was the Breach of Promise Action. Brinig (1990) explains that from the mid-1800s to the early 1900s, this action entitled a woman whose fiancé had broken off the engagement to sue him for economic damages as well as personal damages for embarrassment, humiliation, and loss of other marriage opportunities. Most women who sought such damages had also lost their virginity, as a woman was supposed to remain chaste until the time of engagement, but it was common for intimacy to occur during the engagement period. Thus, Breach of Promise Actions where intimacy had occurred resulted in more substantial damages than in cases where it had not. By the 1940s, Breach of Promise Actions became known as "legally sanctioned blackmail" (p. 205). Though largely abolished by the 1970s, this law still exists in some jurisdictions.

While Breach of Promise Action lawsuits declined, the sale of diamonds began to take off, made possible by the discovery of the South African diamond mines during the 1870s and 1880s, which emerged just as supplies in India and Brazil were diminishing (Ingraham, 1999). De Beers Group was formed in 1888 to protect diamond mine investors. In its early years, De Beers produced over 90 percent of the world's diamonds and thus completely controlled pricing (Fram and Baron, 2004). De Beers remains the largest supplier of uncut diamonds in the world (De Beers Group, 2006).

Before the Depression, diamond rings were available but not an essential element of engagement (Brinig, 1990). National advertising for them was largely regarded as vulgar. During the Depression, supply exceeded demand as new diamond sources were discovered. Diamonds were stockpiled so there would not be a perceived glut. To stimulate the market, De Beers formed an alliance with a prominent New York advertising agency, N. W. Ayer. In 1939, the famous "A Diamond Is Forever" slogan, combined with diamonds being worn by

Hollywood stars, energized this created tradition (Howard, 2003). De Beers also popularized the "Two Months' Salary" tradition to suggest how much a man should pay for the engagement ring. By the end of World War II, the diamond engagement ring had become the ring of choice in America and by 1965, 80 percent of couples chose the diamond engagement ring (in Brinig, 1990).

An equally invented tradition with historic roots similar to the diamond engagement ring is the double-ring ceremony, as explained by Howard (2003). The impetus for the double-ring ceremony was the failed campaign for a male engagement ring. During the late 1800s, the growth of mail-order catalogs and large department stores put the jewelry retailers at risk, and they searched for new customs to broaden the market. "In 1926, manufacturers and retail jewelers launched a major campaign to popularize the custom of male engagement or betrothal rings" (p. 838). Jewelers had to counteract widespread beliefs that jewelry was a female domain and that "engagement was something that happened to women" (p. 840). Despite concerted marketing efforts, the campaign failed.

By the late 1920s, jewelers changed tactics and began focusing on the male wedding band rather than the male engagement ring. Prior to this time, wedding bands for men were not a common Western tradition. The success of the groom's ring was sealed in the 1940s, when "wedding consumption became a patriotic act" during World War II (Howard, 2003, p. 847). Images of soldiers wearing wedding bands were used to illustrate emotional bonds of commitment from afar. After the war, when marriage rates soared, the groom's ring became a symbol of the masculine ability to support a wife and children. Interestingly, this invented tradition affected the church: the popularity of the double-ring ceremony led to the transformation of the religious legislation, as the wording of the ring blessing had to be changed from singular to plural.

A third, created Western tradition is that of the white wedding gown. Prior to 1840, the common color was red or another bright color. Queen Victoria's marriage to Albert of Saxe in 1840 changed this tradition when she wore what was considered a flamboyant white gown (McCoy, 2001). The wealthy immediately copied this statement of class and style, and so the tradition spread. The white dress had nothing to do with being virtuous at the time. It was an extravagant sign of being able to afford a gown that you would likely never wear again, as cleaning techniques were not sophisticated. During the Depression, simple white dresses were chosen that could be dyed and worn again, or brides just wore the best dress they owned. After World War II, royalty and movie stars were seen wearing extravagant white gowns and the tradition was set.

Photograph by www.adrevey.com

PHOTO 4-2 *The white wedding gown is an invented tradition that began in 1840.*

celebrity weddings

Celebrities have always captured the attention of the media, with their weddings being of particular interest. From classic movie stars such as Grace Kelly to modern pop singers such as Pink, the design choices of celebrities are sure to be discussed and mimicked by their fans. Security measures employed by celebrities to protect their privacy are extreme, which simply heightens the intrigue of the event as well as the public's desire to know the specifics of the ceremony and reception.

Media outlets disseminate the details of celebrity weddings, and retail outlets hasten to offer knock-offs of items chosen by the rich and famous. For example, the 2005 special issue of *People* Magazine entitled "I Do! The Great Celebrity Weddings" focused on celebrity weddings that took place between 2000 and 2005. This synopsis illustrates the power of the stars to set trends, such as: (1) a movement away from diamond engagement rings, evidenced by Nicole Richie's pink sapphire; (2) gowns that experiment with color, seen with Gwen

Stefani's pink attire, Kelis Rogers' green gown, and Julianne Moore's light purple; (3) use of different gowns for the ceremony and reception, such as was done by Melania Knauss and Britney Spears; (4) the bride carrying or being surrounded by dark flowers, such as Carmen Electra, Courteney Cox, Heather Mills, Shanna Moakler, and Britney Spears; and (5) participation of animals in the ceremony, such as Adam Sandler's dog, Meatball, and Tori Spelling's two dogs. By and large, however, the choices made by the couples exhibited standard traditions, with white dresses, flowers, and cakes being balanced by black tuxes.

The issue also highlighted changing social trends, such as the increasingly mainstream nature of interethnic weddings (e.g., Heidi Klum to Seal, Tiger Woods to Elin Nordegren, and Benjamin Bratt to Talisa Soto) and the growing acceptance of same-sex weddings (e.g., Melissa Etheridge to Tammy Lynn Michaels, Rosie O'Donnell to Kelli Carpenter, and Elton John to David Furnish). Finally, the open discussion of brides being pregnant, such as Jennifer Garner, Gwyneth Paltrow, and Kacie Searcy, suggests that the shotgun wedding stigma has been lifted.

Celebrity weddings have increased the exposure and status of wedding planners, with the five most dominant "marital masterminds" being Preston Bailey, Marcy Blum, Colin Cowie, Sharon Sacks, and Mindy Weiss (Muhlke, 2005, p. 57). These planners work with average budgets between $100,000 (Bailey) and $500,000 (Cowie), have been in business for an average of 20 years, plan between 6 (Cowie) and 100 (Bailey) weddings a year, work primarily with celebrities and the "richest of the rich" (p. 57), and have their own lines of housewares (Cowie), clothing (Sacks), and books (Bailey and Blum). The over-the-top events orchestrated by these planners have generated tremendous press, making them celebrities in their own right as their famous clients set trends with ideas inspired by the planners.

portrayal of weddings in film

While famous individuals influence wedding decisions based on their real lives, modern filmgoers are also influenced by how romance, weddings, and marriage are portrayed in cinematic texts. Recent films such as *The Wedding Planner*, *My Best Friend's Wedding*, *My Big Fat Greek Wedding*, and *Wedding Crashers* comically portray the nuances of wedding planning and implementation.

Wilding (2003) analyzed four films to illustrate how the implicit and explicit fictional messages influence real couples' wedding plans. To gauge the media's influence she then interviewed 16 couples who were preparing to marry. The films investigated include *Father of the Bride* (United States), *Muriel's Wedding* (Australia), *Four Weddings and a Funeral* (United Kingdom), and *The Wedding Singer* (United States).

Each of these films is saturated with wedding imagery, with elements such as cakes, dresses, flowers, stationery, bridal parties, and reception entertainment on display for the viewing audience to interpret as desired (e.g., Mackey, 2001).

Wilding (2003) suggests that the plots in these films indicate three themes: (1) weddings are indications of a person's change in social status; (2) weddings are a signifier that true romantic love has been achieved; and (3) true romantic love can be differentiated from sexual attraction in that true love "is always the culmination of a difficult journey" (p. 377). However, the narratives of the couples interviewed were not clearly patterned after what was exhibited in film. Couples' discussions of falling in love indicated transcendence, spontaneity, and irrational thought, whereas commentary about getting married and wedding planning focused on pragmatic concerns and rational decision-making processes. Wilding concludes by asserting that cinema texts contribute to thoughts and choices related to weddings and marriage but do not necessarily determine specific actions.

While film can be used to reinforce traditions, it can also be suggestive of changing customs. Karena (2003) explores how modern influences impact a traditional Indian arranged marriage in *Monsoon Wedding*. This film "not only provides a window into the community but also challenges our assumptions about Indian culture" (p. 117). Western influences are seen in the choice of clothing, dance moves, expressions, access to cable and cell phones, forthright women, and extramarital affairs. Simultaneously, the film showcases the stunning decorations, jewelry, tents, dance, music, and dress customary to traditional Indian weddings. The film grants access to "a contemporary India usually not seen on the big screen" (p. 117) and offers a balanced view of old values and new.

Finally, nonfiction film can be used to examine how weddings in everyday life can illustrate the challenges facing a particular culture. Smaill (2003) offers a synopsis of "A Wedding in Ramallah," in which a Palestinian living in exile in the United States returns to the West Bank city of Ramallah for his arranged marriage. This documentary highlights the impact of Israeli occupation on the lives of Palestinians, as checkpoints, struggle, hardship, and gunfire blend with daily tasks as the bride runs errands such as preparing her papers in anticipation of moving to America. The groom, who had "spent 3 years in an Israeli prison accused of being an activist," must return to the United States after the wedding and leaves his bride with her new in-laws until her papers are processed. This film uses the context of a wedding to explore "the more complex and localized effects of the Palestinian's ongoing struggle for autonomy and recognition" (p. 79).

PHOTO 4-3 *(opposite) The trend toward dark wedding bouquets was inspired by celebrities.*

⚙ reality television

Television is another mediated channel that has framed how the public views weddings. The recent popularity of reality programming has brought this medium from fiction to fact. Three programs that have depicted reality weddings include the The Learning Channel's *A Wedding Story*, the Today show's *Hometown Wedding* series, and Style Network's *Whose Wedding Is It Anyway?*

A Wedding Story involves a narrative, noninterventionist approach, and each 30-minute episode follows a similar format, where the audience is able to view (1) the bride and groom individually giving an account of the relationship prior to the wedding; (2) pre-wedding tasks and the rehearsal; (3) wedding day preparations; and (4) footage from the wedding and reception (Engstrom and Semic, 2003). Engstrom and Semic conducted a research study of the religious images found in episodes of *A Wedding Story*, the results of which are summarized in Research Roundtable, Case 4.1.

Hometown Wedding employs an audience participation model for wedding planning, in which couples enter a contest and are selected "to receive an all-expenses-paid wedding planned entirely by the morning show audience" (Roberts, 2005, p. C1). The *Hometown Wedding* series has had a tremendous influence on dictating trends and has catapulted the careers of vendors chosen by the viewers. For each wedding element, four options are presented, and viewers vote online for their favorite. The Web site also includes more information about each of the options, operating as free publicity for the vendors. "Virtual discussions sprang up, and message boards debated the options. . . . Voters really try to make the best choices for each bride and groom. They care whether the bridesmaids wear Vera Wang or J. Crew. They care deeply" (p. C1). There is a tradeoff, however: the couple has no input and no privacy as millions watch as they exchange vows (Partlow, 2005).

Whose Wedding Is It Anyway? focuses on the wedding consultant, illustrating once again the status that is now associated with the career. In this series, cameras follow expert planners across the United States as they assist their clients in planning weddings at every budget level. Viewers are given an inside perspective of how consultants operate to design weddings for their clients. Simultaneously, practitioners and the general public can benefit from the many tricks of the trade that are highlighted.

⚙ the internet

Nothing has fueled the wedding frenzy of the past five years more than the Internet. All of the above-mentioned media outlets (i.e., print, television, and film) are represented on the Internet. Web sites asso-

reality tv weddings

Purpose: What recurring images of religion are depicted in the marriage stories of *A Wedding Story*?

Methods: A sample of 85 episodes of *A Wedding Story* were content-analyzed. The following information was documented or estimated: demographics (bride and groom's age, race, and religious affiliation), ceremony site, bridal escort, officiant, mention of religious terms, wording of vows, exchange of rings, other rituals, and overall religiosity of the ceremony.

Results: Over 70 percent of the brides and grooms were under 30 and Caucasian. The majority of ceremonies were held in a church, with the father of the bride acting as escort. Sixty percent of the ceremonies appeared to be Christian and were performed by a minister or priest. Other affiliations represented were Baha'i, Hindu, Jewish, and Native American. Sixty percent of the weddings included traditional vows, while others included some nontraditional wording or were completely written by the couple. Observed religious rituals included those such as the unity candle, breaking the glass, and chanting of prayer.

Conclusion: The researchers found that 34 percent of the episodes were devoid of religiousness, 57 percent were somewhat religious, and 9 percent were very religious. The authors found "religion, its rituals and its symbols as stylized and of secondary importance" (p. 158).

Source: Engstrom and Semic (2003).

ciated with The Knot, The Wedding Channel, Brides, and InStyle Weddings are just a few of the countless Internet sites devoted to weddings and wedding planning.

The Knot has arguably brought wedding planning to the forefront. Vendors and planners clamor to be featured on the Web site, and television programs team up with The Knot to create wedding specials. The Knot Web site offers instant advice relating to all elements of wedding planning, while steering the customer to featured vendors and advertisers. The Wedding Channel and Brides sites follow a similar format; however, both The Knot and The Wedding Channel have television links, while Brides focuses on its related magazine. InStyle Weddings is unique in that this site focuses on celebrity weddings, offering an overview of recent weddings, classic historical weddings, and trends set by the stars. The site also offers fashion, beauty, and planning tips, while highlighting specific vendors and advertisers.

The abundance of information available on the Internet can overwhelm a prospective bride and groom. While some suggest that the proliferation of material available on Web sites negates the need for a wedding consultant, quite the opposite is true. A wedding consultant can help the couple sort through the information and determine what is relevant. Furthermore, the consultant will have firsthand knowledge of local vendors, which will help the couple avoid being misled or sidetracked by the inundation of paid advertising on these sites.

REFERENCES

Brinig, M. F. (1990). Rings and promises. *Journal of Law, Economics, & Organization* 6: 203-215.

De Beers Group. (2006). Welcome to the De Beers Group, available at http://www.debeersgroup.com

Engstrom, E., and Semic, B. (2003). Portrayal of religion in reality TV programming: Hegemony and the contemporary American wedding. *Journal of Media and Religion* 2: 145-163.

Fram, E. H., and Baron, R. (2004). Are natural diamond engagement rings forever? *International Journal of Retail & Distribution Management* 32: 340-345.

Howard, V. (2003). A "real man's" ring: Gender and invention of tradition. *Journal of Social History* 36: 837-857.

Ingraham, C. (1999). *White Weddings: Romancing Heterosexuality in Popular Culture.* New York: Routledge.

Karena, C. (2003). Monsoon wedding: Raining of tradition. *Australian Screen Education* 33: 117-119.

Mackey, J. A. (2001). Subtext and countertext in Muriel's Wedding. *NWSA Journal* 13: 86-104.

McCoy, D. (2001). *The World's Most Unforgettable Weddings: Love, Lust, Money and Madness.* New York: Citadel Press.

Muhlke, C. (2005, January 16). The wedding banners. *New York Times,* Section 6, 57.

Partlow, J. (2005, September 17). Morning vows, before millions of viewers. *Washington Post,* B3.

People (2005). I do! The great celebrity weddings. New York: Time Inc. Home Entertainment.

Roberts, R. (2005, August 9). A Maryland couple finds a way to beat the high cost of marriage. *Washington Post,* C1; C7.

Smaill, S. (2003). The home front: A wedding in Ramallah. *Metro Magazine* 135: 76-79.

Tankard, J. W. (2001). The empirical approach to the study of media framing. In S. D. Reese, O. H. Gandy, and A. E. Grant (eds.), *Framing Public Life: Perspectives on Media and Our Understanding of the Social World.* Mahwah, NJ: Lawrence Erlbaum Associates.

Wilding, R. (2003). Romantic love and "getting married": Narratives of the wedding in and out of cinema texts. *Journal of Sociology* 39: 373-389.

review questions

1. What is a Breach of Promise Action?

2. Explain how the diamond engagement ring, the double-ring ceremony, and the white wedding dress became invented traditions.

3. What are three recent trends that have emerged because of celebrity influences?

4. What three themes that have emerged from plots of films contain an abundance of wedding imagery?

5. How have reality television and the Internet influenced wedding planning?

terminology

• Breach of Promise Action

• De Beers

• Mary of Burgundy

• Media framing

• Queen Victoria

PHOTO 5-1 *Second marriages are a common occurrence.*
© 2006, The Washington Post Writers Group, Reprinted with Permission

the changing *family, politics, and law*

Expanding parameters of what constitutes "family" and the evolving expectations of each member therein have led to considerable political and legal upheaval. Horn (2001) explains that the past four decades have evidenced an extraordinary shift in cultural norms concerning sex, marriage, and child bearing. Factors such as the availability of effective birth control, the entry of more women in the workforce, and the increasing acceptability of cohabitation, divorce, and child bearing out of wedlock have lessened social pressure to get and stay married. Five trends that will be reviewed in this chapter, each with underlying implications for weddings and wedding planning, are (1) female workforce dynamics; (2) the missing male; (3) rates of cohabitation and divorce; (4) same-sex relationships and unions; and (5) a growing number of intercultural and interfaith marriages.

༺ female workforce dynamics

The gradual acceptance of women in the workforce has accompanying stressors. Longitudinal studies reflect changing life-cycle trends. For example, Putney and Bengston (2005) studied and compared five generations of women: 1920s Women (born 1900–1915), Depression Era Women (born 1916–1930), Silent Generation Women (born 1931–1945), Baby Boom Women (born 1946–1964), and Gen X Women (born 1965–1978). Women's increased education level and participation in the workforce were clearly evidenced in this study, as were higher stress levels and lower psychological functioning due to work–family conflicts. The most recently labeled generation, the Echo Boom Women (born 1979–2002), comprises children of the Baby Boomers (Fairchild Bridal Group, 2005). The oldest members of this group, also labeled as Generation Y and Millennials, have recently reached marriage age. Echo Boomers are more highly educated than their predecessors, and their economic and residential independence is predicted to further delay the average age that women enter into their first marriage (Fairchild Bridal Group, 2005).

These findings are not unique to the United States or other Western countries. In assessing comparative labor force participation rates in Hong Kong, researchers found that a similar percentage of women and men who have never married are in the workforce; however, there is a marked discrepancy between the percentages of married men and married women who continue to work (Lo, Stone, and Ng, 2003). The career-minded woman in Hong Kong, faces significant work–family coping issues if she chooses to marry, in particular because Hong Kong largely remains a gender-stereotyped society where women get little to no support from their husbands with domestic duties and childcare is prohibitively expensive (Buckley, 2004).

Interestingly, the career-oriented woman in Hong Kong should not expect support from anyone in the workplace, even from a female manager, as "women managers in various industry sectors feel that marriage and motherhood are personal choices and decisions and, as such, individual women should themselves be responsible for solving work–family conflicts, rather than demanding that their work organizations adopt policies and practices that help ease their role conflicts" (Lo, Stone, and Ng, 2003, p. 188). Thus, women with career expectations are putting off marriage or opting out all together. Similar work–family conflicts are occurring in Singapore and Japan (e.g., Kim and Ling, 2001), so much so in Japan that women are increasingly choosing dogs over marriage and children. This trend has caused a boom in Japanese dog ownership and, simultaneously, a sharp decline in the birth rate (Buckley, 2004).

In Egypt, women entered the workforce in record numbers during the twentieth century. Mostafa (2003) contends that the fact that Egypt followed this universal trend is surprising, as Arab societies tend to be particu-

egyptian attitudes toward women in the workforce

Purpose: Do attitudes toward women in the Egyptian workforce vary by age, sex, and religious affiliation?

Methods: A sample of 217 participants responded to a scale that measured aversion to women who work. Approximately half were university students, while the other half were nonstudents whose ages ranged from 40 to 60.

Results: College students' views were not found to be different from those of older generations. Egyptian females had more favorable attitudes than Egyptian males. No differences were found when comparing the attitudes of Muslims and non-Muslims.

Conclusion: Although a gender gap in attitudes persists, a moderate change in restrictive attitude towards women who work in Egypt is occurring. However, the liberal views found in this study "should by no means be interpreted as Egypt moving away rapidly from a patriarchal and traditional society" (p. 262).

Source: Mostafa (2003).

larly reluctant to abandon their traditional views on women. Accordingly, Mostafa measured aversion levels toward women in the workforce to determine if attitudes differed based on characteristics of the respondents. This study is summarized in Research Roundtable, Case 5.1.

☞ the missing male

A second factor that is influencing changing family dynamics is the diminishing role of males in many households. Starting in the 1970s, women's enrollment in institutions of higher education slowly but surely caught up with and then passed men's. "Where men once dominated, they now make up only 43% of students at American institutions of higher learning" (Gurian, 2005, p. B1). This trend has a direct impact on wedding and marriage statistics, as individuals without a college degree are twice as likely to be divorced and are five times as likely to be involved in criminal activities (Gurian, 2005). Men without degrees who work in low-paying jobs are "staying out of the long-term marriage pool because they have little to offer to young women" (p. B4).

The breakdown of family structure is a severe problem in low-income African American communities in the United States. In 1950, married couples comprised 78 percent of African American families; however, by 1999 this figure had dropped to 48 percent (Shulman, 2001). As a result of this dramatic decline, single women are increasingly the only parental influence for young African Americans, as "half of the nation's 5.6 million black boys live in fatherless households" (Fletcher, 2006, p. A10). The lack of two parents leads to a family income shortage, which necessitates welfare dependency. Welfare reform legislation is targeting antimarriage policies and focusing on ways to promote marriage, as "communities with higher marriage rates evidence fewer social pathologies, including crime, educational failure, and poverty, than do those with lower marriage rates" (Horn, 2001, p. 40). For example, in an analysis of male juvenile criminals in African American communities, Carney (2005) found that "Most come from families living at or near the poverty line. All but a few are being raised by their mothers with limited, if any, involvement from their fathers. Quite a few of these boys are on track to become second- or third-generation felons. Without male role models, they turn to their peers for guidance" (p. 107). African American women are left with "a relative shortage of marriageable men" (Shulman, 2001, p. 1010), pronounced rates of marital breakup, and low rates of remarriage (Bramlett and Mosher, 2002; Britt, 2006).

Financial problems are also influencing the marital opportunities of young men in developing regions with limited economic opportunities. In these areas, "young men without the means to marry find themselves condemned to a kind of limbo life" (Masquelier, 2005, p. 60). For instance, in traditional societies such as those found in rural

Niger, where women generally stay at home and bridalwealth payments are expected, women are likened to race horses searching for men who can provide for them, and men who cannot marry due to economic restrictions are socially disgraced (Masquelier, 2005). Thus, spiraling wedding expectations and costs, combined with economic fluctuations, have led to a marriage crisis in developing countries. In Taiwan, for example, increasing male unemployment has been linked to marital breakup that "has affected children, financial security, labor supply decisions [and] human capital investment" (Hsing, 2003, p. 613).

❧ cohabitation and divorce

A third trend that has led to changing family dynamics is the increasingly commonplace nature of cohabitation and divorce. In Western countries, rates of cohabitation have increased dramatically since the 1970s. For example, in Great Britain, cohabitation rates for single women rose dramatically between the 1960s and 1990s. Specifically, in the 1960s approximately 5 percent of women reported living together with their first husband before marriage; by the late 1990s, the number had risen to 77 percent (Haskey, 2001). Simultaneously, a considerable shift in attitudes toward cohabitation has taken place, with the number of adults indicating that "living together outside of marriage is always wrong" (p. 6) plummeting within the same time frame. Haskey explains the trend (p. 11):

> Increasingly, couples who have started to live together do not place a high priority on marrying, though they intend to do so; many view the cost of a "proper wedding" as very expensive, particularly in the early days of a partnership when setting up home, and housing costs, can be demanding, even on two incomes. There perhaps has been a tendency for couples to defer considering when to marry until they feel they can afford it, when domestic arrangements have been settled and when they are ready for the large social occasion they wish it to be.

Couples are also increasingly having children outside of marriage. The proportion of births occurring outside of marriage in Great Britain increased from 6 percent in 1960 to 40 percent in 2001 (Kiernan and Smith, 2003), so couples will often defer marriage longer than they wait to start a family. In this study, even births in areas that were economically advantaged had over a 20 percent chance of being with a cohabiting couple.

Rates of cohabitation are also on the rise in the United States. By the late 1990s, 10 percent of single women reported cohabitating, and 31 percent of married women indicated that they had cohabitated at some point before marriage (Bramlett and Mosher, 2002). In Asian countries, the rates are significantly lower. For instance, in Japan, the percentage of single women who had ever cohabitated remains under 3 percent (Atoh, 2001). In China, cohabitation occurs almost exclusively in the major cities such as Beijing and Shanghai and is primarily done on a platonic basis to save money and avoid psychological isolation (Rucai, 2004).

While the social acceptability of cohabitation is on the rise, unmarried couples have historically been at financial risk. As explained by Scott (2005), "Although many cohabitees believe they have 'common law' rights equivalent to those of married couples, in reality unmarried partners have no right to financial support from a partner or entitlement to their assets on death unless stipulated in a will; nor do they benefit from the same tax advantages available to spouses, regardless of how long they have lived together."

Divorce trends also vary significantly by country and are strongly influenced by divorce legislation. In the United States, divorce rates increased sharply between 1970 and 1975, as no-fault divorce laws were introduced and it became easier to obtain a divorce (U.S. Census Bureau, 2005). Prior to this legislative change, there had to be evidence of "fault," such as cruelty, adultery, abandonment, or imprisonment for a divorce to be granted (Grossman, 2004). This made it extremely difficult for couples who had simply fallen out of love or gone in separate directions to be granted a divorce. Prior to the 1970s, cases of collusive adultery, where infidelity had not truly taken place but the couple would set up a fake adultery so that they could divorce, became notorious and created confusion and anxiety as couples were essentially forced to lie in court to obtain a divorce (Grossman, 2004). Once no-fault divorce laws were enacted, divorce rates spiked, but then evened out once the new legislation had stabilized and have remained relatively flat since (U.S. Census Bureau, 2005). Similarly, in Taiwan, a legislative amendment of the Civil Code in 1996 that was intended to protect married women also facilitated divorce and has caused an increase in the divorce rate (Hsing, 2003). In historically ultraconservative Chile, divorce was legalized in 2004 after a five-year debate (Campbell, 2003; Reel, 2005). The shifting cultural landscape in Chile is also reflected in the 2006 election of Chile's first woman president, Michelle Bachelet, who is a socialist and single mother (Reel, 2006). Only two countries, Malta and the Philippines, do not recognize divorce, and the issue is widely contested in both locations. Generally speaking, countries that are either culturally conservative, such as Japan and Mexico, or have particularly restrictive laws, such as Italy, have lower divorce rates.

As divorce has become more commonplace, so too have second marriages. First marriages that end in divorce last an average of eight years in the United States, and over half of divorced individuals will remarry within 3.5 years (U.S. Census Bureau, 2005). The result is that

the wedding of diane and joe: blending families

The Couple: Both Diane and Joe are in their late 40s, have been married before, and have teenaged children. They wanted a very private and no-stress event to commemorate their newly combined family but also wanted to celebrate with a special group of supportive friends. In order to achieve both goals, they decided to have two separate events. The first was a wedding and dinner that only included immediate family members. Two days later, the couple had a reception that included both family and their circle of friends.

The Family Wedding and Dinner: The couple was married on an early June evening in a quaint historic 200-year-old church in a rural town. Twenty family members watched as the bride's son and daughter walked her down the aisle where her groom waited with his son and daughter. The couple's respective children stood next to them during the whole ceremony. Each child also gave a reading during the service. After the ceremony and church photos were complete, the group traveled to an intimate restaurant that had been reserved for the evening. New family members got to know each other during dinner, with seating assigned to encourage conversation. Recorded music played in the background, including a CD of music that had been written and performed by the groom. Both the bride and groom's eldest child addressed the group and proposed toasts before the couple cut an elegant Italian wedding cake.

The Reception: Two days later, the couple hosted a casual cookout-style reception at a local vineyard for a group of 70 family members and friends. Tableware and floral décor reflected the vineyard theme, with wine-colored linens, roses, and candles gracing the tables. Guests could order from the tasting bar inside the winery or choose beverages iced in tubs outside on the veranda while hors d'oeuvres were served. The vineyard offered ongoing tours of the facility and wine tastings. The tables scattered along the lawn overlooked the vines. A second wedding cake was cut for this event. The toast was given by the groom, who thanked the crowd for supporting the couple. The couple's favorite CDs played in the background as guests talked and wandered around the grounds throughout the evening.

Case submitted by Diane Haworth

many couples are blending families when they remarry, which poses unique challenges to the wedding consultant. Culture Corner, Case 5.2 offers an example of how one couple approached the complexity of a wedding where it was the second marriage for both bride and groom. Similar to first marriages, "Women who live in communities with higher male unemployment, lower median family income, higher poverty and higher receipt of welfare are more likely to experience a second marital breakup" (Bramlett and Mosher, 2002, p. 3).

same-sex relationships and unions

Arguably, the most controversial topic relating to weddings and marriage pertains to same-sex relationships. Opinion, policy, and legislation on this issue vary dramatically, with change evidenced continually but inconsistently, as some political entities grow more open while others make statements and pass laws to limit the rights of same-sex partners.

In the United States, the only state that allows same-sex marriage is Massachusetts, and that right is under attack, as gay-rights advocates have filed a lawsuit to block a proposed constitutional amendment that would end same-sex marriage (Rights Activists, 2006). Same-sex marriage affords couples the same rights, benefits, and responsibilities as heterosexual couples (Alm, Badgett, and Whittington, 2000; National Center for State Courts, 2005). Connecticut passed a law that went into effect in October 2005 allowing for same-sex civil unions, which are also legal in Vermont (Connecticut Justices, 2005). The benefits attached to civil unions are similar to those granted to married couples; however, federal law does not recognize civil unions, and the benefits are not necessarily transferable to other states (National Center for State Courts, 2005). Domestic partnership registries are available in the states of California, Hawaii, Maine, and New Jersey and allow unmarried same-sex couples to receive limited rights and benefits, such as those related to property, hospital visitation, inheritance, and domestic violence protection (Human Rights Campaign Foundation, 2004). These registries can also be found in local municipalities (i.e., cities and towns) throughout the United States as well as the District of Columbia (Jenkins, 2006a).

Voters in Texas, on the other hand, passed a constitutional ban on same-sex marriage in November 2005, the nineteenth state to do so, while another 12 states have constitutional amendments under consideration (Cillizza, 2005). Close to 40 states have what are known as Defense of Marriage Acts (DOMAs), which explicitly stipulate that marriage is between one man and one woman (Alliance Defense Fund, 2006). These statistics are continually changing, as states move back and forth on their views of same-sex relationships. For example, neighboring states Virginia and Maryland made politically opposite statements in early 2006, with Maryland moving to amend a constitutional ban on same-sex marriage based on a ruling that the state statute is discriminatory (Mosk and Wagner, 2006; Otto, 2005), while simultaneously Virginia leaders advanced an amendment to ban same-sex marriage. Although Virginia state law already bans same-sex unions, "supporters of the constitutional amendment say it's necessary to clarify that Virginia is not compelled to recognize same-sex marriages or civil arrangements permitted in other states" (Jenkins, 2006b, p. B1).

Internationally, same-sex marriages are legal in Belgium, Canada, The Netherlands, Spain, and, as of late 2005, South Africa, while civil unions exist in all or part of over a dozen other countries, such as Australia, Brazil, and Denmark (Timberg, 2005). South Africa is the first country in Africa to permit same-sex marriage, "on a continent where homosexual activity is widely condemned and often outlawed" (Timberg, 2005, p. A16). The United Kingdom's Civil Partnership Act became law in December 2005 and was heralded by Elton John's union to David Furnish, with a ceremony and lavish reception that took place on the first day the law went into effect (Jones and Collinson, 2005; Jordan, 2005).

Those who support same-sex marriage and unions see the issue as one of discrimination, and many lawyers, politicians, religious leaders, and civil rights groups have joined to send a message of tolerance while simultaneously organizing programs designed to influence organizational and public policy (e.g., Bolte, 1998; Gebremeskel and Kleiner, 2002; Landrum, 2006; McCrummen, 2006; Wildman, 2004). Those in opposition, including politicians and religious leaders who wish to sway policy in the opposite direction, contend that same-sex relationships are immoral and undermine marriage and family values (e.g., Gowen, 2005; Jones and Collinson, 2005).

Same-sex commitment ceremonies, whether legal or symbolic, are increasingly taking place all over the world. As a wedding consultant, you will need to determine if this is a niche market you would like to pursue. Most wedding-related vendors are not in the business of turning away clients, and same-sex ceremonies and receptions tend to be as extravagant and planning intensive as those of heterosexual couples. However, if this is not within your comfort zone, you should become familiar with wedding consultants in your area who regularly work with same-sex couples so that you can make referrals as necessary.

intercultural and interfaith marriages

The changing family, demographic shifts, expanding ethnic and religious tolerance, widespread access to transportation, and the influences of a global economy have led to a dramatic increase in intercultural and interfaith marriages since the 1970s (Lee and Edmonston, 2005; Nelson and Otnes, 2005). This growth is particularly noteworthy, as miscegenation laws, defined as statutes prohibiting interracial marriage, existed in the United States for over 300 years (Pascoe, 2004). The first miscegenation law was passed in the colony of Maryland in 1664, and, by the Civil War, similar laws were passed through much of the South and Midwest and were continuing to move west (Pascoe, 2004). Civil rights groups began to openly challenge the laws in the 1920s, and in 1967 the United States Supreme Court declared all remaining state miscegenation laws unconstitutional in the landmark case *Loving v. Virginia* (U.S. Supreme Court, 1967).

An understanding of the historic struggles endured by many interracial and interfaith couples sheds light on why the blending of wedding traditions can cause stress and emotional conflict, in particular if different beliefs are ignored, misunderstood, or not respected. Cross-cultural ambivalence is defined as "the emergence of mixed or multiple emotions that arise from conflict among values, norms, traditions and practices of different cultures not found within the same society" (Nelson and Otnes, 2005, pp. 89–90). For example, "90% of marriages in Northern Ireland are between Catholics or between Protestants, there is a small minority which are joined across the religions frontier, that is between a Catholic and a Protestant" (Stringer, 1994, p. 71). Couples who cross this boundary may be socially estranged from family members and friends who are opposed to the match (Stringer, 1994). Thus, because of historic and social distinctions, the practice of creating a new identity as a couple can pose considerable difficulties for intercultural or interfaith couples.

When acting as a consultant for weddings with blended traditions, you will benefit from considering the following six suggestions (González, 2005; Nelson and Otnes, 2005; Stringer, 1994):

1. Be certain to involve both families in the decision-making process, so that elements of the ceremony and reception do not inadvertently offend the beliefs and traditions of either family. Encourage the couple to communicate openly with one another and their parents to create a supportive environment and so that arrangements do not come as a surprise to anyone.
2. Respect the customs of both families by finding out how the rituals are observed and helping the couple make sure that they are carried out properly. If the ceremony is going to be held at a place of worship, communicate with the individual who will be leading the ceremony to determine the rules and restrictions specific to the religious site.

PHOTO 5-2 *(opposite) Marriage allows couples to create a shared identity.*

3. Discuss the notion of time carefully with the couple. Different cultures have dramatically varying perspectives of the definition of being "on time." For example, if the wedding invitation states 3:00 P.M., in some cultures the bride and groom may not arrive until 5:00 P.M. For a wedding consultant and guests who are not in tune with the custom, they may assume that the wedding was canceled.

4. Consider a neutral site and leader for the ceremony if tensions arise due to religious differences. Alternatively, for example, if a wedding is between a Protestant and a Catholic and it is being held in a Protestant church, a priest from a Catholic church can be invited to concelebrate. However, some religions do not permit co-leaders from different places of worship or the offer could be rejected, so this option should be approached with caution.

5. Appreciate the multilingualism that accompanies many cross-cultural marriages. Translations can be incorporated in stationery elements such as invitations and ceremony programs, readings and toasts can be performed in more than one language, and music from both cultures can be played.

6. Ultimately, some couples will not feel comfortable abandoning cultural norms or having a hybrid ritual. In cases where the customs are appreciably different or the extended families live in two different countries, couples may opt for two separate wedding events. This doubling process increases planning time as well as costs but ensures that the sacred rituals of both cultures are upheld.

Blended traditions add to the uniqueness and beauty of weddings and are reflective of the evolution of society and family. Incorporating elements of dress, food, entertainment, and ceremonial traditions that reflect the different backgrounds of the couple enhances the celebration of diversity.

REFERENCES

Alliance Defense Fund. (2006). DOMA watch, available at http://www.domawatch.org

Alm, J., Badgett, M. V. L., and Whittington, L. A. (2000). Wedding bell blues: The income tax consequences of legalizing same-sex marriage. *National Tax Journal* 53: 201–214.

Atoh, M. (2001, June). Why are cohabitation and extra-marital births so few in Japan? Paper presented at the 2001 EURESCO Conference.

Bolte, A. (1998). Do wedding dresses come in lavender? The prospects and implications of same-sex marriage. *Social Theory and Practice* 24: 111–131.

Bramlett, M. D., and Mosher, W. D. (2002). Cohabitation, marriage, divorce, and remarriage in the United States. Centers for Disease Control and Prevention: Vital and Health Statistics Series 23, Number 22.

Britt, D. (2006, June 9). To have and to hold, but with higher standards. *Washington Post*, B1; B9.

Buckley, S. (2004, September 28). Japan's women wary to wed. BBC News, World Edition, available from http://news.bbc.co.uk

Campbell, D. (2003, August 28). Church mounts rearguard action as Chile votes to allow divorce. Guardian, available from http://www.guardian.co.uk/international

Carney, M. P. (2005, December). Don't hurt me, I'm just a kid. *Washingtonian*, 105–111.

Cillizza, C. (2005, November 9). Corzine defeats Forrester to become N.J. governor: Bloomberg wins easily; Texas passes gay-marriage ban. *Washington Post*, A18.

Connecticut justices gear up for gay civil unions. (2005, September 25). *Washington Post*, A10.

PHOTO 5-3 *(opposite) Intercultural weddings allow for blended traditions.*

Fairchild Bridal Group. (2005). The American wedding 2005. Microsoft PowerPoint research presentation.

Fletcher, M. A. (2006, June 2). Being a black man: At the corner between progress and peril. *Washington Post*, A1; A10–A12.

Gebremeskel, D., and Kleiner, B. H. (2002). New developments concerning marital status discrimination. *Equal Opportunities International* 21: 51–58.

González, I. C. (2005, June 23). Down the aisle, into the melting pot. *Washington Post*, H1; H5.

Gowen, A. (2005, November 15). Arlington's pastor's protest: Wedded bliss for all or none. *Washington Post*, B1; B4.

Grossman, J. (2004). Will New York finally adopt true no-fault divorce? Recent proposals to amend the state's archaic divorce law. FindLaw: Legal News and Commentary, available at http://writ.news.findlaw.com

Gurian, M. (2005, December 4). Disappearing act. *Washington Post*, B1; B4.

Haskey, J. (2001). Cohabitation in Great Britian: Past, present and future trends—and attitudes. *Population Trends* 103: 4–25.

Horn, W. F. (2001). Wedding bell blues: Marriage and welfare reform. *Brookings Review* 19: 39–42.

Hsing, Y. (2003). Impact of institutional and socioeconomic changes on marital relationship. *International Journal of Social Economics* 30: 613–618.

Human Rights Campaign Foundation. (2004). Relationship recognition law, available from http://www.hrc.org

Jenkins, C. (2006a, January 26). Gay marriage ban advances toward Virginia referendum. *Washington Post*, A1; A6.

Jenkins, C. (2006b, January 14). Gay marriage ban advances in Virginia. *Washington Post*, B1; B2.

Jones, R., and Collinson, P. (2005, July 2). Another step forward for same-sex couples. Guardian, available from http://money.guardian.co.uk

Jordan, M. (2005, December 22). Elton John, "Single Man" no more. *Washington Post*, C1; C7.

Kiernan, K., and Smith, K. (2003). Unmarried parenthood: New insights from the Millennium Cohort Study. *Population Trends* 114: 26–33.

Kim, J. L. S., and Ling, C. S. (2001). Work–family conflict of women entrepreneurs in Singapore. *Women in Management Review* 16: 204–221.

Landrum, J. (2006, January 22). Black gays ask clergy for tolerance. *Washington Post*, A17.

Lee, S. M., and Edmonston, B. (2005). New marriages, new families: U.S. racial and Hispanic intermarriage. *Population Bulletin* 60: 1–38.

Lo, S., Stone, R., and Ng, C. W. (2003). Work-family conflict and coping strategies adopted by female married professionals in Hong Kong. *Women in Management Review* 18: 182–190.

Masquelier, A. (2005). The scorpion's sting: Youth, marriage and the struggle for social maturity in Niger. *Journal of the Royal Anthropological Institute* 11: 59–83.

McCrummen, S. (2006, January 23). Church ceremony celebrates gay pairs. *Washington Post*, B1.

Mosk, M., and Wagner, J. (2006, January 21). Judge strikes down Md. ban on gay marriage. *Washington Post*, A1; A10.

Mostafa, M. M. (2003). Attitudes towards women who work in Egypt. *Women in Management Review* 18: 252–266.

National Center for State Courts. (2005). Same-sex marriage, available from http://www.ncsconline.org

Nelson, M. R., and Otnes, C. C. (2005). Exploring cross-cultural ambivalence: A netnography of intercultural wedding message boards. *Journal of Business Research* 58: 89–95.

Otto, M. (2005, August 31). Suit to allow gay marriage in Maryland argued. *Washington Post*, B3.

Pascoe, P. (2004). Why the ugly rhetoric against gay marriage is familiar to this historian of miscegenation. History News Network, available from http://hnn.us/articles/4708.html

Putney, N. M., and Bengston, V. L. (2005). Family relations in changing times: A longitudinal study of five cohorts of women. *International Journal of Sociology and Social Policy* 25: 92–119.

Reel, M. (2005, December 10). Female, agnostic and the next presidente? *Washington Post*, A1; A17.

Reel, M. (2006, January 16). Chile elects first female president. *Washington Post*, A1.

Rights activists sue to protect same-sex marriage in Massachusetts (2006, January 4). *Washington Post*, A18.

Rucai, L. (2004). Let's be lodgers! Urban China's new wave of platonic cohabitation. China Today, available from http://www.chinatoday.com.cn/English/e2004/e200403/p28.htm

Scott, M. (2005, July 3). Married rights without the rites. Guardian, available from http://money.guardian.co.uk

Shulman, S. (2001). Family structure, Afro-Euro inequality and economic justice. *International Journal of Social Economics* 28: 1003–1024.

Stringer, P. (1994). Cross-community marriage in Northern Ireland: Social support and social constraints. *Sexual and Marital Therapy* 9: 71–123.

Timberg, C. (2005, December 2). S. Africa's top court blesses gay marriage. *Washington Post*, A16.

U.S. Census Bureau. (2005). Number, timing, and duration of marriages and divorces: 2001. *Current Population Reports*, Household Economic Studies. Report Number P70-97.

U.S. Supreme Court. (1967). *Loving v. Virginia*, 388 U.S. 1: Appeal from the Supreme Court of Appeals of Virginia No. 395, available from http://caselaw.lp.findlaw.com

Wildman, S. (2004). Wedding-bell blues. *The American Prospect* 15: 39–40.

review questions

1. What are some of the outcomes that have resulted from changing female workforce dynamics?

2. Explain the phenomenon of the "missing male" and give two examples of related impacts.

3. Give three examples of cultural differences as associated with cohabitation and divorce.

4. Explain the differing legal stance that various states and countries have taken on same-sex partnerships.

5. Name three suggestions that consultants should consider when helping plan weddings with blended traditions.

terminology

- Blended traditions
- Civil unions
- Cohabitation
- Commitment ceremonies
- Cross-cultural ambivalence
- Defense of marriage acts
- Domestic partnership registries
- Echo boomers
- Miscegenation laws
- No-fault divorce
- Same-sex marriage

SO MY PARENTS ACTUALLY SAID, "WE'D RATHER NOT PAY FOR A LAVISH WEDDING WHEN THE IMPORTANT THING ISN'T THE WEDDING, IT'S THE MARRIAGE." CAN YOU BELIEVE I CAME FROM THESE PEOPLE?

PHOTO (comic) 6-1 *The consumerist mentality that accompanies weddings is often the subject of humorous critique.*
© 2006, The Washington Post Writers Group, Reprinted with Permission

weddings and
consumerism

Consumerism suggests that an ever-expanding purchase of goods is advantageous to an economy. The consumptive mentality that grabs hold of many couples during the wedding planning process has been a common subject of critique, with self-absorbed Bridezillas and Groomonsters acting as easy targets for those who sense that the commercialization of weddings is overtaking the sanctity of marriage vows. Bridezilla has become a mainstream term, so much so that Women's Entertainment television created the popular show *Bridezillas* to showcase how and why some women turn their nuptials into a nightmare for all involved. This chapter analyzes the consumerism that is evident in many facets of wedding planning by considering (1) the urge to consume; (2) the quest for perfection and associated expectations; (3) sponsored weddings; and (4) planning anticonsumptive and conservationist weddings.

✒ the urge to consume

Weddings have become a year-round shopping spree, with wedding costs increasing an average of 5 percent per year over the past 15 years (Fairchild Bridal Group, 2005). The pressure and emotions inherent to ritual-related consumption can stress both personal finances and relationships, in particular if the couple is not in agreement on some purchases.

Brides are more likely than grooms to consider specific wedding-related artifacts as crucial to the success of the wedding and will speak of certain items "with anticipation, rhapsody or reverence" (Lowrey and Otnes, 1994). This consumer passion or "fire of desire" (Belk, Ger, and Askegaard, 2003, p. 326) leads to impulse buying, which occurs when a consumer experiences a sudden, powerful urge to buy something immediately. This desire is complex, may include emotional conflict, and is prone to occur with a short-term disregard for the consequences (Rook, 1987). Furthermore, impulse buying is associated with the desire to fulfill a fantasy and the need to experience social gratification (Hausman, 2000).

"Despite the jading that occurs in a culture of abundance, we are still enchanted and desire to be enchanted . . . consumer desires entail hope and are vitally energizing" and, conversely, can result in despair for those who cannot afford their fantasies (Belk et al., 2003, p. 347). Thus, the process of purchasing or the inability to purchase within a wedding context is also associated with disappointment, regret, and anger (Otnes, Lowrey, and Shrum, 1997). A study pertaining to the conflict and mixed emotions inherent in wedding purchases is summarized in Research Roundtable, Case 6.1.

Beyond the emotional drawbacks, the consumption patterns associated with many weddings are accompanied by wanton spending, self-centeredness, excess, and waste, and therefore are subject to critique, as evidenced in newspaper columns, cartoons, novels, prose, poetry, television, and film. Humor columnist Gene Weingarten writes in his treatise on big weddings, "My problem with big weddings is that they tend to be ostentatious, wasteful, unseemly celebrations of self in which previously sane human beings wind up developing lifelong personal enmities over ridiculously petty things" (2005, p. 40). The wit that is evident in much of the critique has a serious side; as a wedding consultant, you are likely to see friendships and family relationships become strained owing to the demands that occur during the planning process. You may even be called in to mediate very difficult situations, as evidenced in Consultant in Action, Case 6.2.

conflict and wedding purchases

Purpose: To determine the conflict and emotional outcomes associated with wedding purchases.

Methods: Focus groups were conducted with brides and grooms, in-depth interviews were completed with brides, and researchers accompanied brides during shopping trips to florists, caterers, and formal wear vendors. In all, over 40 individuals participated in the study.

Results: The researchers identified four problem areas and associated coping strategies. First, consumers' product and vendor expectations were not always met in reality; coping occurred through returning merchandise, changing vendors, putting up with undesirable vendors, or using assertiveness to get what they wanted. Second, feelings of overload were associated with being ill prepared for the number of purchases; coping strategies included simplifying the wedding, seeking assistance from friends and relatives, and broadening the information search. Third, conflict occurred with family and peers who were trying to influence purchase decisions; coping included resignation to pleasing others and compromise. Fourth, custom and value conflict occurred with perceived mandated purchases; coping included resistance to custom and conformity and "defiant nonpurchase of sanctioned items" even when they knew guests would be disappointed.

Conclusion: Social and cultural mandates cause conflict and necessitate purchase modifications, resulting in a mixture of happiness, stress, anxiety, and regret.

Source: Otnes et al. (1997).

the wedding is called off

It is 5:00 P.M., just two hours before the evening ceremony when Susan, who is the mother of the groom, pulls you aside. She just spoke with her son, who said he is fed up with the bride and is calling the wedding off; he simply cannot go through with it. Susan said that she tried to calm him down, but there was nothing she could say or do to change his mind.

Susan and her husband helped pay for the lavish ceremony and reception, which are at the same exclusive hotel, and she is insistent that they still throw the party since the money is already spent.

The bride is dressed and relaxing in one of the hotel rooms. Susan wants you to tell the bride that the ceremony will not take place, but that Susan is planning on starting the reception early and hosting the party. Susan also wants you to coordinate with all the vendors so that the tone of the evening changes from a wedding reception to a party.

What do you do?

Source: Adapted from Yabroff (2005).

☞ the quest for perfection and associated expectations

The urge to splurge is driven by the quest for the perfect wedding. This perfectionism has ballooned into a wedding obsession craze that has become the latest cultural contagion (Horyn, 2004). From an early age, many women fantasize about their dream wedding, with ubiquitous fairy tales such as Cinderella, Snow White, and Beauty and the Beast feeding young imaginations that translate into adult purchase decisions (Otnes and Pleck, 2003). The lavish wedding allows for a temporary escape from a world of imperfection, as "the magic invoked by a performative spectacle and symbolic objects becomes a key means of generating a rite of passage through a public display of success" (Clarke, 2005, p. 350).

The pursuit of perfection is fueled by the commercialization of the white wedding which started in the mid-1800s, where not only the bride was dressed in white, but the bridesmaids as well (Penner, 2004). Weddings held during this period included an obsessive public inspection of the presents and the trousseau. "It became common practice to set aside one room or apartment for this purpose.... A card accompanied each present indicating its donor's name" (Penner, 2004, p. 11). This ritual display was decried as loathsome because it introduced a competitive edge into gift giving, where "Wealthy families sought to outdo one another in the magnificence of their gifts, driving the prices of presents ever upward. Nuptial couples pitted gift givers against one another" (p. 15), and those who had given the most flattering gifts were, for the moment, the best friends of the couple while those of modest means were pushed to spend more than they could afford.

The desire to look perfect, be perfect, please everyone, and have celebrity-like events leads brides to take extreme measures such as undergoing liposuction or having their jaws wired shut to ensure that they will reach their desired dress size. The quest for perfection has also fueled a quickly growing market of male grooming products and has pushed couples to make extravagant purchases that lead to long-term debt. The competitive edge that accompanies many weddings has reached such heights that even vendors and planners lament that couples sometimes behave like "spoiled brats" in the pursuit to be original (Horyn, 2004). The goal that drives this consumer mentality is that "for one day, couples become wealthy nobles—they are at the very center of an opulent and grand existence" (Lewis, 1997, p. 173) regardless of their true economic status. A true Bridezilla can strike fear in the hearts of planners and wedding vendors, as suggested in Consultant in Action, Case 6.3.

The spending spree does not end with the wedding, as retailers are using direct marketing tactics to lure newlyweds to participate in

oy, vey!

It is two hours before the casual reception of a middle-aged couple, Clarisse and Ben, who have been a challenge to work with, to say the least. A first-time bride at the age of 43, Clarisse is definite in her demands and fully intends to have the perfect party to celebrate her nuptials. The fearful staff members at the hotel have nicknamed her Bridezilla and are doing everything in their power to stay out of her line of fire. You are protecting the staff from her wrath as much as possible. As the crew finishes setting the hotel banquet room for the event, you go to the kitchen to find the cake that has been delivered by the upscale bakery selected by the bride.

As you approach the counter, your eyes locate the large box consistent with the oversized sheet cake that was ordered by the bride and received by the hotel staff at 3:00 P.M. You open the lid and are repelled in horror as you see "Mazel Tov David" chiseled into the sugary concoction, and realize that the wrong cake has been sent. It is 6:00 P.M., the bakery has closed, and the reception starts at 8:00 P.M.

What do you do?

Case submitted by Diane Haworth

completion programs to set up their perfect households. Completion programs are special discounts on unfulfilled registry items and other housewares for a given period of time after the wedding date. These aggressive sales tactics "are part of a growing trend among national and regional retailers to court newlyweds in hopes of snagging them as loyal customers" (Groer, 2005, H1; H5).

sponsored weddings

Rather than foregoing dreams they cannot afford, couples often search for innovative ways to fund their fantasies. The latest trend, and one that has been the target of much ridicule, is the sponsored wedding. In return for free goods and services, sponsors create contracts that both parties sign, guaranteeing marketing exposure such as (Gaudette, 2006; Leonard, 2005; Martin, 2005; Rowan, 2005):

- A list of sponsors' names included in the invitations and thank-you cards
- Full-page advertisements in the wedding programs
- The sponsors' business cards and discount vouchers placed on the tables at the reception
- The couple thanking sponsors during their wedding speeches
- Photographs with the couple using the sponsors' products
- Signs at the reception designating what each sponsor had donated
- T-shirts as favors that include all of the sponsors' logos
- A wedding Web site that includes links to all of the sponsoring agencies

A tradeoff is time, with between 3,000 and 6,000 requests by telephone and e-mail needed to sponsor a single wedding (Leonard, 2005; Martin, 2005; Rowan, 2005).

Sponsored weddings are seen as primarily an American phenomenon, with some experts from other countries calling the practice a fresh idea and others reviling it as vulgar, a corporate jamboree, and tacky (Leonard, 2005; Martin, 2005). Contests such as "Bridal Survivor," where seven brides lived in a storefront for nine days, forming alliances, withstanding humiliating competitions, and voting brides out, all for the chance to win a $16,000 wedding package, illustrate the lengths couples will go to have an outsider pay for their wedding (Gaudette, 2006). Similarly, in a "bling backlash" (Megna, 2005, p. 28), hundreds of couples vied for free weddings held at Dunkin' Donuts and Ikea.

While the novelty of sponsored weddings will soon wear off, it is currently a tactic that even the rich and famous have exploited to pay for their weddings. Stars such as Britney Spears and Tori Spelling accepted wedding gifts and discounts in exchange for publicity. Most notably, Star Jones, who even had an official airline for her wedding, was criticized heavily for using *The View* as an avenue for promoting her sponsors (Rowan, 2005; Thomas, 2004). Also condemned was "runaway bride" Jennifer Wilbanks, who made up an abduction story when she could not go through with her April 2005 wedding, prompting a nationwide search (Hart, 2005). When her lie was discovered, she received probation and had to pay approximately $15,000 in fines; in return, she received a $500,000 movie deal for the rights to her story (Kurtz, 2005).

🐇 planning anticonsumptive and conservationist weddings

Many couples embrace the consumptive mentality when planning their weddings, and others reject it; yet, they still may wish to celebrate their transition to marriage. In expressing why they are "tied in knots" (Toerien and Williams, 2003, p. 435) over how to forge a union, one couple from the United Kingdom suggests, "A commitment ceremony might be nice, as long as it is non-traditional, non-heterosexist, non-religious, non-sexist, non-expensive and compromises no components derived from exploitive relationships with workers or the environment!" (p. 425). While written with humorous intent, this passage reflects some of the difficulties in planning anticonsumptive, conservationist weddings.

The extreme anticonsumptive approach is participating in a mass or collective wedding. This approach has become popular over the past decade in Islamic countries, where government institutions organize public events for those who otherwise would not be able to afford to marry (Toameh, 2005). Mass weddings have become the norm in countries such as Iran, Jordan, Malaysia, Pakistan, Sudan, Syria, and Yemen (Salleh, 2005; Toameh, 2005).

A second, common means to reduce consumption is to forego certain traditions. For example, many cross-cultural couples use their differences as an excuse to avoid some of the materialistic mandates of their individual cultures, as summarized in Research Roundtable, Case 6.4. Couples who wish to release their guests from the burden of wedding gifts will make a request for no gifts in their invitations or ask that, in lieu of gifts, guests make a contribution to a charity if they feel the need to commemorate the occasion. For example, couples can register with "Good Gifts," which allows guests to give funds that result in the donation of a camel to poor nomadic tribes in countries such as Somalia and Ethiopia or trees to areas affected by deforestation (Siegle, 2005).

Some anticonsumptive choices are not necessarily cost-effective, but are practiced for ethical or conservationist reasons or to promote one's local community. A simple wedding practice that most couples

consumer coping strategies of cross-cultural couples

Purpose: To determine the consumer conflicts experienced and decision strategies employed by cross-cultural couples.

Methods: Interviews and e-mail surveys conducted with 26 cross-cultural couples who represented a total of 23 different national cultures.

Results: Three themes emerged from the study. First, although the appreciation of cultural differences was strong, couples actively rejected or modified some practices that resulted in nonpurchase of traditional items. Second, there was a prevalent rejection of American/Western materialism evidenced in the deviation from common Western ring selection, wedding attire, and gift registry. Rings were not necessarily diamonds, dresses were more likely to be ethnic rather than white, and registries were thought to be inappropriate or vulgar. Third, couples expressed fears about where to host the wedding and how to meet the needs of their culturally diverse audiences, with decisions often based on economic practicality.

Conclusion: "Being different" gave cross-cultural couples freedom to deviate from prescribed cultural customs and dominant white wedding norms. Active modifications were generally nonmaterialistic.

Source: Nelson and Deshpande (2004).

PHOTO 6-2 *Selecting edible favors that are produced locally is a mindful practice that supports a couple's community.*

can consider pertains to the selection of favors. Rather than purchasing a favor that guests are unlikely to ever use, some couples forego favors altogether. Alternatively, couples can select organic favors or those produced locally that have a clear use such as fruit from a farmer's market; seeds or flower bulbs; locally made chocolate or candles; pottery from a nearby artist; or organic soap.

Other mindful practices might include wearing dresses made of recycled material, using stationery elements made from recycled paper, renting rather than purchasing dresses and tuxes for the bridal party, using an organic caterer, and making sure the selected reception venue recycles materials that are commonly used such as glass bottles and aluminum cans. Amnesty International (2006) promotes buying conflict-free diamonds and explains that conflict diamonds are those sold in order to fund armed conflict and civil war. This human rights group explains that concerned consumers should ask jewelers to see a written guarantee that the diamonds are conflict-free. As a consultant, you should forge relationships with vendors who offer local, organic, and recycled goods so that you can assist couples who wish to take a conservationist approach to planning their wedding.

REFERENCES

Amnesty International. (2006). Conflict diamonds, available at http://www.amnestyusa.org/diamonds/index.do.

Belk, R. W., Ger, G., and Askegaard, S. (2003). The fire of desire: A multisided inquiry into consumer passion. *Journal of Consumer Research* 30: 326–350.

Clarke, A. (2005). The globalization of feminine consumption. *Current Anthropology* 46: 349–351.

Fairchild Bridal Group. (2005). The American wedding 2005. Microsoft PowerPoint research presentation.

Gaudette, K. (2006, January 21). Two brides-to-be with true grit. *Seattle Times*, B1.

Groer, A. (2005, November 17). Polishing off the wish list. *Washington Post*, H1; H5.

Hart, A. (2005, May 26). Runaway bride is indicted. *New York Times*, A3.

Hausman, A. (2000). A multi-method investigation of consumer motivations in impulse buying behavior. *Journal of Consumer Marketing* 17: 403–419.

Horyn, C. (2004, June 6). Recipe for the new perfect wedding: A $5,000 cake and hold the simplicity. *New York Times*, A32.

Kurtz, H. (2005, June 16). Runaway bride's dowry deal. *Washington Post*, C1.

Leonard, T. (2005, May 16). This wedding is brought to you courtesy of . . . *The Daily Telegraph*, News 5.

Lewis, C. (1997). Hegemony in the ideal: Wedding photography, consumerism and patriarchy. *Women's Studies in Communication* 20: 167–187.

Lowrey, T. M., and Otnes, C. (1994). Construction of a meaningful wedding: Differences in priorities of brides and grooms. In J. A. Costa (ed.), *Gender Issues and Consumer Behavior* (pp. 164–183). Thousand Oaks, CA: Sage Publications.

Martin, N. (2005, February 7). Today's wedding ceremony has been sponsored by . . . *The Daily Telegraph*, News 9.

Megna, M. (2005, February 13). Down the aisle: Wacky weddings. New York, *Daily News*, 28.

Nelson, M. R., and Deshpande, S. (2004). Love without borders: An examination of cross-cultural wedding rituals. In C. C. Otnes and T. M. Lowrey (eds.), *Contemporary Consumption Rituals: A Research Anthology*. Mahwah, NJ: Lawrence Erlbaum Associates.

Otnes, C., Lowrey, T. M., and Shrum, L. J. (1997). Toward an understanding of consumer ambivalence. *Journal of Consumer Research* 24: 80–93.

Otnes, C., and Pleck, E. (2003). *Cinderella Dreams: The Allure of the Lavish Wedding*. Berkeley: University of California Press.

Penner, B. (2004). "A Vision of Love and Luxury": The commercialization of nineteenth-century American weddings. *Winterthur Portfolio* 39: 1–20.

Rook, D. W. (1987). The buying impulse. *Journal of Consumer Research* 14: 189–199.

Rowan, D. (2005, January 29). Trendsurfing: Sponsored weddings. *The Times*: United Kingdom, available at http://www.davidrowan.com

Salleh, I. M. (2005, September 26). Grand wedding for 20 couples. *New Straits Times*: Malaysia, 12.

Siegle, L. (2005, February 20). With this conflict-free diamond, I thee wed. *Guardian*, 15.

Thomas, K. (2004). Star Jones says "I do" to wedding freebies. *USA Today*, 1D.

Toameh, K. A. (2005). Hamas grooms improved image by sponsoring mass weddings. *Jerusalem Post*, 1.

Toerien, M., and Williams, A. (2003). In knots: Dilemmas of a feminist couple contemplating marriage. *Feminism & Psychology* 13: 432–436.

Weingarten, G. (2005, June 5). Thinly veiled contempt: A treatise on big weddings. *Washington Post Magazine*, 40.

Yabroff, J. (2005, January 16). Witness to a wedding that wasn't. *New York Times*, Section 9, 6.

review questions

1. Explain what impulse buying is and why it is so common in the context of weddings.

2. What are two drawbacks associated with the desire to have a perfect wedding?

3. Name four possible ways in which a business can be recognized for sponsoring a wedding.

4. What are three ways to add anticonsumptive or organic practices into wedding planning?

terminology

- Anticonsumptive weddings

- Commercialization

- Completion programs

- Conflict-free diamonds

- Conservationist weddings

- Consumerism

- Impulse buying

- Perfectionism

- Sponsored weddings

PHOTO 7-1 *Weddings offer a motivation to visit new places.*

tourism and *destination weddings*

Weddings and honeymoons contribute to local economic development in a number of ways. First, couples generally use local goods and services, relying on vendors such as florists, caterers, and transportation specialists whose businesses are in close proximity to the wedding and reception. This spending fuels the economy of the community where the wedding is held. Second, weddings involve out-of-town guests who are, in essence, tourists during their stay. Their expenditures on hotels, food and beverage, gasoline, and entertainment bring new money into a region, thus enhancing the local economy. Third, most couples will celebrate their newlywed status by taking a honeymoon. Now the newlyweds are the tourists, and their spending at a chosen destination will enhance the livelihood of the local businesses where they are vacationing. This combined outlay of cash is significant, leading to fierce competition to attract engaged and newly married couples. Finally, communities that historically have served as honeymoon spots are now increasingly repackaging their services to also serve as the wedding site, giving rise to the destination wedding. This chapter will review three areas of economic development through tourism that are particularly relevant to weddings: (1) visiting friends and relatives tourism; (2) honeymoon travel; and (3) destination weddings.

visiting friends and relatives tourism

Wedding travel offers an excellent example of visiting friends and relatives tourism (VFR tourism). Historically, businesses did not take a keen interest in VFR tourism, as many believed that it had little economic value in comparison to other forms of tourism and that it could not be stimulated by marketing efforts (Seaton and Palmer, 1997). This attitude has changed dramatically, as research has shown that VFR tourism is the second most common form of travel, comprising close to 24 percent of all short-term departures, which is second only to holiday tourism (Collins and Tisdell, 2002; Seaton and Palmer, 1997). Furthermore, for many destinations, VFR is the principal form of tourism and operates as a means of generating repeat visitation over time (Cave, Ryan, and Panakera, 2003).

VFR tourism is more resilient to crisis situations than other forms of travel. For example, the September 11, 2001, terrorist airplane attacks on the Twin Towers of the World Trade Center in New York City, the Pentagon in Washington, DC, and in Somerset County, Pennsylvania, created a travel and tourism crisis in the United States (Goodrich, 2002). The repercussions severely affected the industries directly involved with tourism activities, such as airlines, hotels, and catering services, and caused significant cutbacks in orders placed to the support companies that supply goods and services to these industries (Blake and Sinclair, 2003). Vacation plans were postponed, and business travel suffered significant losses, as "firms cancelled or postponed conventions, corporate meetings, seminars, and trade shows" (Goodrich, 2002, p. 576). However, couples were still getting married, and relatives and friends were there to support them. The emotional ties inherent to VFR travel allow these trips to take place even when extenuating circumstances arise. Moreover, the extensive planning that accompanies wedding events acts as an impetus to move forward. Anecdotal evidence suggests that couples who married on September 15, 2001, which was the Saturday following the attacks, did so with the support of friends and relatives and with the strong sentiment that canceling weddings would only validate the terrorist efforts to cripple the United States.

September 11 nonetheless left a mark on wedding businesses, as illustrated on September 11, 2004, which was the first time since the attacks that the date fell on a Saturday. Although September is one of the most popular months to marry in the United States, both wedding consultants and vendors were cognizant that couples would be reluctant to celebrate on a date that is rooted in tragedy. This reluctance was evidenced by open calendars at reception halls that would generally be booked solid during this month (CBS, 2004). Couples who married on this date (many of whom were heavily criticized for doing so), did so to mark a transition out of grief, for logistical reasons, and also because they received significant discounts from vendors who were trying to book business for that date (CBS, 2004).

In times of peace and crisis, VFR remains one of the most stable forms of tourism. VFR tourism is a common form of travel for all age groups and becomes increasingly important as individuals age (Collins and Tisdell, 2002). Weddings give parents, aunts and uncles, grandparents, cousins, and siblings an excuse to travel. As families become less centralized, it is often difficult for groups to get together for holiday gatherings; however, weddings provide a motivation to travel.

Guests are a critical part of all weddings, but in the excitement of the planning process their specialized needs may be overlooked. Specifically, as guests generally include elderly relatives who may have physical impairments, their travel needs should be considered. Research Roundtable, Case 7.1, offers an overview of the travel experiences of persons with physical disabilities.

PHOTO 7-2 *Guests are a critical part of all weddings.*

travel experiences of persons with physical disabilities

Purpose: To determine the constraints to pleasure travel experienced by individuals with physical disabilities as well as the strategies commonly used to negotiate these problem areas.

Methods: Narrative accounts of travel experiences written by 23 individuals with physical disabilities were analyzed. The stories, known as "Travel Tales," were read and categorized in order to find patterns of travel constraints and negotiation strategies. A total of 1,065 statements within the narratives were coded and sorted based on similarities.

Findings: Three themes of constraints and associated negotiation strategies were found: (1) intrapersonal, which included physical/sensory issues, emotional barriers, and knowledge gaps; (2) interpersonal, which pertained to interactions with travel companions, service providers, and strangers; and (3) structural, which involved transportation, facilities, environmental areas, and financial considerations. Of the three overall themes, structural statements were the most common.

Conclusion: Travelers with physical disabilities have to overcome a significant number of obstacles to have successful leisure travel experiences. They must face their own limitations and fears, find supportive travel companions and service providers, and consistently overcome difficulties related to transportation, lodging, dining, and sightseeing.

Source: Daniels, Rodgers, and Wiggins (2005).

PHOTO 7-3 *Unique wedding venues may not be easily accessible for guests with disabilities.*

honeymoon travel

Honeymoon travel, as we know it today, came about as accommodations, services, and transportation became formalized in the early 1820s and 1830s (Towner, 1985). Prior to this time was the period of the Grand Tour, which lasted from 1500 to 1820 (Fridgen, 1996). Travel during the Grand Tour period was physically punishing and often dangerous; hence, it was primarily completed by young, male aristocrats for the purposes of education, curiosity, cultural enrichment, and career development (Towner, 1996).

Transportation enhancements during the industrial age, including travel by stagecoach, ship, and train, allowed tourism to become a commercial business and increased opportunities for individuals to travel purely for leisure and pleasure (Weaver and Lawton, 2002). Luxury commercial sea tours to destinations across the globe became available by the late 1800s (Fridgen, 1996). The emergence of the automobile and airplane, coupled with shorter workweeks, longer vacation times, increased income, and decreased family size, opened up the door to mass tourism (Weaver and Lawton, 2002). Today the

PHOTO 7-4 *Honeymoon destinations offer opportunities for cultural enrichment.*

honeymoon is an expected and anticipated travel experience that most Westernized couples employ to launch their new life together.

Newlywed American couples spend an estimated $7 billion a year on honeymoon travel (Fairchild Bridal Group, 2005). The top 10 destinations for Americans in order of popularity, based on a travel agent study conducted by Modern Bride (2005), were: Hawaii, Italy, Tahiti, Anguilla, Fiji, St. Lucia, Mexico, St. Barths, Jamaica, and France. Honeymoon destination preferences will differ by culture, in large part based on geographical proximity. For example, the most popular honeymoon destinations for Koreans are quite different from American choices; specifically, Korean newlyweds traveling overseas were found to prefer Thailand, Japan, the United States, and France, in that order (Kim and Agrusa, 2005). Regardless of country of origin, couples appear to be seeking similar attributes in a honeymoon destination: good (typically warm) weather, a romantic image, shopping opportunities, and a wide range of activities, including those that are beach/water based and cultural/historic in nature.

PHOTO 7-5 *Beach resorts are popular honeymoon destinations.*

Despite the pervasiveness of honeymoon travel, there are potential associated drawbacks if the vacation is not planned carefully. Weddings tend to be very public occasions, where couples are surrounded by their closest friends and family members who envelop them with support and create a stimulating environment. Honeymoons, on the other hand, emphasize isolation in remote places. While this seclusion allows the couple to decompress and reconnect, it may also lead to feelings of loneliness and strain (Medved, 1996). These feelings are likely to be exacerbated if the honeymoon destination is more to one person's liking than the other's or if there are not enough activities to keep the couple busy. Kim and Agrusa (2005) state that beach resorts in particular need to offer honeymooners programs that allow them to become actively engaged in the novelties of an exotic culture so that they can feel involved with the community rather than experiencing "the inevitable feeling of boredom that comes with a beautiful beach or tropical scenery with nothing else to do except sit in the sun" (p. 901). Some couples become so disenchanted with their honeymoon that they cut the stay short. They become anxious to return to their social networks, enjoy their new gifts, and review pictures and video clips from the wedding day. The decision to leave the honeymoon destination early can be a stressful one, for it may be accompanied by feelings of guilt or the sense that the marriage did not start off on the right note. Increasingly, couples are waiting a few days, weeks, or even months to take their honeymoon vacations, allowing them to soak up the wedding moments and then pull away at a later date.

As a wedding consultant, you may be asked to assist with honeymoon planning. Rather than simply directing couples to a travel agent or handing them a list of top destinations, help them to carefully consider their activity preferences and, in particular, what they like to do together. Communicate with them openly about the timing of the honeymoon and present different leave-taking scenarios that will broaden their sense of options.

destination weddings

The destination wedding occurs when a couple decides to hold their wedding in a location where neither one of them resides. Generally,

PHOTO 7-6 *Destination weddings are usually held at popular tourism locations.*

an exotic or popular tourism destination is chosen, and the wedding often merges into the honeymoon. The joining of these two events creates what is popularly called the WeddingMoon, a term coined by Sandals Resorts, which specializes in Caribbean destination weddings and has partnered with celebrity planner Preston Bailey to create four WeddingMoon packages (Sandals, 2006). Destination weddings are increasing in popularity, with 86 percent of couples considering a destination wedding, while 16 percent actually have one (Fairchild Bridal Group, 2005; Forrest, 2006). Beyond Caribbean locations such as Jamaica, St. Lucia, and the Virgin Islands, other major players in the destination wedding business are Walt Disney World, which has wed over 22,000 couples since 1991 (Horyn, 2004), Las Vegas, where the Viva Las Vegas Weddings (2005) offers over 30 themed wedding packages from which to choose, and Hawaii, which has capitalized on its popularity as a honeymoon destination by offering wedding services.

Couples choose to have a destination wedding for a number of reasons. They tend to be intimate affairs with only the closest of friends and family members in attendance, as associated travel costs can be considerable. Because of the distance, stressful haggling over guest lists dissipates and reception costs decrease dramatically, which allows for considerable overall savings of money and sanity. Destination weddings are frequently all-inclusive, so the planning process becomes streamlined. Furthermore, couples will not experience the dramatic separation anxiety that can be associated with honeymoons, as many of the guests stay with the couple for an extended vacation (Ingraham, 1999). On the other hand, couples who envision a large affair with all of their friends and family members in attendance are likely to be disappointed and should therefore not seriously consider a destination wedding.

As a consultant, you will eventually have the opportunity to work with couples who elect to have destination weddings. Most likely they will want you to be in attendance to make sure that their events run smoothly. When creating a contract for a destination wedding, be certain that your costs for transportation, lodging, and meals are written in as additional expenses that are separate from your base consultant fee. While the destination wedding is a vacation for the couple and their guests, you will be there to work and should be compensated accordingly. Some planners do not accept destination weddings because they do not like to be taken away from their own families and other clients, but others thoroughly enjoy the challenge and travel.

If you live in an area that is known for destination weddings, such as a beach or mountain resort community, you should be prepared to market your services to visitors who are looking to get married on

your home turf. For example, if a couple from Pittsburgh plans to marry in Seattle, it may be more practical for them to hire a knowledgeable Seattle planner rather than pay for the travel costs of a consultant from Pittsburgh. The destination wedding market is yet another avenue through which you can build your business.

REFERENCES

Blake, A., and Sinclair, M. T. (2003). Tourism crisis management: U.S. response to September 11. *Annals of Tourism Research* 30: 813-832.

Cave, J., Ryan, C., and Panakera, C. (2003). Residents' perceptions, migrant groups and culture as an attraction—the case of a proposed Pacific Island cultural centre in New Zealand. *Tourism Management* 24: 371-385.

CBS News. (2004, September 9). Getting married on Sept. 11? available at http://www.cbsnews.com/stories

Collins, D., and Tisdell, C. (2002) Age-related lifecycles: Purpose variations. *Annals of Tourism Research* 29: 801-818.

Daniels, M. J., Rodgers, E. B. D., and Wiggins, B. P. (2005). "Travel Tales": An interpretive analysis of constraints and negotiations to pleasure travel as experienced by persons with physical disabilities. *Tourism Management* 26: 919-930.

Fairchild Bridal Group. (2005). The American wedding 2005. Microsoft PowerPoint research presentation.

Forrest, K. (2006, June). The bride wore flip-flops. *Washingtonian* 41: 150-156.

Fridgen, J. D. (1996). *Dimensions of Tourism.* East Lansing, MI: Educational Institute.

Goodrich, J. N. (2002). September 11, 2001 attack on America: A record of the immediate impacts and reactions in the USA travel and tourism industry. *Tourism Management* 23: 573-580.

Horyn, C. (2004, June 6). Recipe for the new perfect wedding: A $5,000 cake and hold the simplicity. *New York Times* Section 1: 32.

Ingraham, C. (1999). *White Weddings: Romancing Heterosexuality in Popular Culture.* New York: Routledge.

Kim, S. S., and Agrusa, J. (2005). The positioning of overseas honeymoon destinations. *Annals of Tourism Research* 32: 887-904.

Medved, M. (1996). Banish the honeymoon! The American Enterprise, available at http://www.taemag.com/issues/articleid.16350/article_detail.asp

Modern Bride. (2005). The world's 50 best honeymoons, available at http://www.modernbride.com/travel/top50/?full_list.html

Sandals. (2006). Weddings at Sandals, available at http://www.sandals.com/general/wedding.cfm

Seaton, A. V., and Palmer, C. (1997). Understanding VFR tourism behaviour: The first five years of the United Kingdom tourism survey. *Tourism Management* 18: 345-355.

Towner, J. (1985). The Grand Tour: A key phase in the history of tourism. *Annals of Tourism Research* 12: 297-333.

Towner, J. (1996). *An Historical Geography of Recreation and Tourism in the Western World 1540-1940.* Chichester, UK: John Wiley & Sons.

Viva Las Vegas Weddings. (2005). Viva Las Vegas Wedding Chapel, available at http://www.vivalasvegasweddings.com/live_internet_wedding_links.htm

Weaver, D., and Lawton, L. (2002). *Tourism Management,* 2nd ed. Milton, Australia: John Wiley & Sons.

PHOTO 7-7 *(opposite) Consultants who reside in tourism areas can market to couples who wish to have destination weddings.*

review questions

1. As a consultant, what advice would you give to couples who were considering marrying on September 11?

2. What three attributes do most couples look for in a honeymoon destination?

3. What advice would you give to a couple considering leaving for their honeymoon directly after their wedding reception?

4. What are the pros and cons of destination weddings?

5. Would you like to plan a destination wedding if it meant being on site for seven days?

terminology

- Destination weddings
- Grand Tour
- VFR tourism
- WeddingMoon

section two

PRACTICE

having gained an understanding of the historical, cultural, and social underpinnings of weddings, you are fully prepared to move to the second section of this book, which explores the practice of wedding consulting. in the following 14 chapters, you are given the opportunity to examine the individual elements that together lead to the design and implementation of weddings. from determining the vision through assessing the satisfaction level of your clients, the second section will focus on the fundamentals of planning a wedding.

The critical steps of determining the budget, timeline, and vision for the wedding will be explored in CHAPTERS 8, 9 AND 10. CHAPTER 11 offers an in-depth discussion of food, beverage, and the wedding cake. Wedding attire and the ceremony will be examined in detail in CHAPTERS 12 AND 13. From there, you will learn about the intricacies of floral décor, photography, and entertainment options in CHAPTERS 14, 15, AND 16. Rentals and site layout, followed by stationery elements and transportation, will be covered in CHAPTERS 17, 18, AND 19. This section concludes with a discussion of wedding day details followed by post-wedding evaluation in CHAPTERS 20 AND 21. At the end of each chapter in this section, you will find a consultant checklist and reminders that can be used for quick reference.

As you will find, beautiful weddings don't just happen. They are the culmination of hundreds of hours of planning and management. In order to be a wedding consultant with a successful practice, you must be well versed in each of these areas so that you can effectively communicate and coordinate with your clients and vendors.

PHOTO 8-1 *Popular ceremony venues are often booked a year or more in advance.*

wedding
timelines

Timelines allow wedding consultants, vendors, and their clients to stay organized, on-track, and realistic. While each couple's timeline is unique to their wedding, there are certain commonalities to all weddings that will help you in assisting your clients set priorities as they plan and prepare.

t he average length of engagements has stretched out over time, and now couples typically have 17 months to prepare for their weddings (Fairchild Bridal Group, 2005). However, 17 months is an average, which means that some couples will take longer to plan while others will move more quickly. Accordingly, there is not one sure-fire time period from which to operate. Thus, it is appropriate to think about wedding timelines in terms of phases.

The seven phases of wedding timelines are: (1) research; (2) design; (3) coordination; (4) legal issues; (5) confirmation and details; (6) implementation; and (7) wrap-up and evaluation. As illustrated in Table 8.1, you will often find that some of the phases overlap. As a consultant, you may offer your clients guidance throughout the whole process, or you can be brought in to assist during a single phase. Use the items in each of these phases as a checklist and reminder of what needs to be done next. As each task is accomplished, indicate the associated date. Over time, you will notice consistencies in the region where you live that will help you streamline the planning process and adjust the order of the task list to fit your target market. This list will also act as a guide when considering the questions you need to ask your clients.

research

The first phase involves research, which starts shortly after a couple becomes engaged. One of the first things a couple needs to do is estimate the number of guests to be invited, for this will influence many other decisions, in particular, the location of the ceremony and reception. For example, historic venues create a magnificent backdrop for a wedding and reception but are often limited in their capacity. Location assessment will in turn influence the wedding date options, as popular venues are often booked a year or more in advance. A venue may take precedence over an ideal date, and more couples are opting to get married on Thursdays, Fridays, and Sundays in order to get their desired sites.

The research phase is also the time to start a list of the types of vendors to be included in the wedding planning process. A list of the vendors commonly involved in weddings is provided in Table 8.2. A vendor is any individual or entity that is receiving payment for goods or services that pertain to implementation of the wedding. The order of vendors is based on a typical booking necessity. This does not mean that the top vendors are the most important; rather, it shows that some vendors, such as photographers, can only be present at one wedding per day, while vendors such as pastry chefs can handle multiple weddings on any given day. Based on the estimated budget, which should be determined at this time, a realistic feasibility analysis can occur by having columns of "must haves" versus "include if budget permits" where, for example, a couple who loves music may state that having a string quartet is essential but will cut out the limousine if the budget gets tight.

design

The second phase of wedding planning timelines is wedding design. Discussion of design options will frequently take place during the

TABLE 8.1   The Seven Phases of Wedding Timelines

Phase	Task	Start Date
Research	• Estimate number of guests to be invited • Assess potential location for ceremony, reception, and honeymoon • Identify wedding date options • Identify potential vendor • Determinate budget • Conduct feasibility analysis	12–24 months before or As soon as possible
Design	• Develop theme and vision • Conduct site inspections • Select date and book venues • Contact and visit potential vendors • Determine wedding party members • Finalize list of guests to be invited • Consider desired styles of formalwear for couple and attendants	10–18 months before
Coordination	• Select and book vendors, sign contracts as needed, and make down payments • Select formalwear for couple and attendants • Select and book honeymoon destination • Mail save-the-date cards • Develop draft of production schedule • Develop draft layout of ceremony and reception sites • Prepare gift registry • Reserve block of hotel rooms for out-of-town guests and wedding night location • Take engagement photos • Mail invitations	6–12 months before 4–8 months before 2–6 months before
Legal Issues	• Review contract legalities for final payments and accountability • If marrying out of resident country, determine documentation requirements (can take a year or longer) • Obtain passports, if applicable • Complete blood tests, if required • Apply for and obtain marriage license • Obtain name-change forms	1–3 months before (longer if marrying out of resident country)
Confirmation and Details	• Finalize production schedule • Finalize layout of ceremony and reception sites • Finalize seating assignments, create escort cards and place cards • Finalize confirmed guest list • Determine security plan • Confirm with vendors • Prepare gifts, favors, and on-site stationery elements • Update gift registry • Finalize hotel block and wedding night location • Confirm honeymoon details • Send newspaper announcement	1–6 weeks before
Implementation	• See Table 8.3 for sample production schedule	1–3 day period, sometimes longer
Wrap-up and Evaluation	• Send thank-you cards • Solicit and compile feedback from couple • Solicit and compile feedback from vendors • Prepare and file wedding summary	1–6 weeks after

TABLE 8.2 Common Wedding Vendors in Timeline Order

Wedding consultant
Ceremony and reception venues
Celebrant
Caterer
Photography
Videography
Musician/Disc jockey
Wedding attire
Florist
Honeymoon site
Dentist
Web site designer
Transportation
Rentals
Invitations
Pastry chef
Jeweler
Lighting
Hair stylist
Makeup artist
Dance instructor
Special effects (e.g., butterfly release)
Ice sculptor
Chocolate fountain
Favors and other gifts
Clerk of court's office
Local newspaper

research phase, so considerable overlap between these two stages is common. The initial design consideration is developing the theme and vision for the wedding. (Vision determination is discussed thoroughly in Chapter 10.) Also during the onset of the design phase, clients need to inspect possible ceremony and reception venues and book their choices, which will occur simultaneously with determining the wedding date. Some couples give the date precedence over the venue and will only consider venues available on their chosen date, while others feel the venue is more important than the date.

Chances are that your clients may only have one or two vendors in mind that they must have; you have been hired to help them with the rest. Thus, during the design phase you will present your clients with a list of two to four vendors in each vendor category. Part of your job is to know your area and a variety of vendors in each category so that you can match your client to the most suitable vendors and make the contacts that will get the wedding planned. Consultants will typically offer options in the low, medium, and high-price range for each area, which will allow couples to decide where and how they want to target their budgets. During this phase, the list of guests to be invited should

Photograph by www.RodneyBailey.com

PHOTO 8-2 *During the design phase, couples should select their wedding party.*

be finalized. In addition, the couple should determine who will be in the wedding party and start considering the desired formalwear that will work with their theme and vision.

coordination

Now that all of the background research has been completed and the design elements have been chosen, the third phase, coordination, will move into full swing. As a consultant, you will help your clients make final vendor selections and walk them through the associated contracts and down payments. Formalwear for the couple and the attendants will be selected. The honeymoon destination should be selected and booked, and save-the-date cards should be mailed, in particular if the couple has decided on a destination wedding or if the wedding date is over a holiday weekend such as Memorial Day or Labor Day.

This is also the time for you to initiate the first draft of the production schedule, which includes everything that will take place during the

implementation of the wedding. Simultaneously, you should prepare a draft site layout of the ceremony and reception.

During the latter part of the coordination phase, the couple should prepare their gift registry, reserve a block of hotel rooms for out-of-town guests, and have engagement photos taken. Many top photographers choose two weekends out of the year when they take all of their clients' engagement photos. Be certain to check with the selected photographer about these dates and then inform your clients so they can have engagement photos taken if desired.

legal issues

Once the coordination is well under way, the fourth phase, legal issues, must be considered. The legal issues become more involved if the wedding is to be held outside the resident country of the couple. The Bureau of Consular Affairs with the United States Department of State (2006) outlines the requirements that must be followed when U.S. citizens are married abroad. As the specifics vary from country to country, it is recommended that the embassy or tourist information bureau of the country where the marriage will be performed be contacted. Blood tests and documentation such as passports and birth certificates are frequently required and may have to be authenticated. The Department of State emphasizes that the process can be time consuming, so it is essential to start early if a couple wishes to marry abroad. Locations that specialize in destination weddings are able to expedite the documentation process.

Even when marrying in one's country of residence, blood tests may be required. In the United States, blood test requirements are determined at the state level and for the most part have been eliminated. Many of the state blood test laws were initiated in the 1930s before the advent of penicillin and other antibiotics, to check for syphilis and other venereal diseases that could be transmitted through sexual contact as well as other diseases that could be passed on during pregnancy (Franks, 2003). Currently, only Connecticut, the District of Columbia, Mississippi, and Montana still require blood tests before a marriage license can be obtained (Nolo, 2006).

As for the marriage license itself, you need to inform your clients about the rules of their state in terms of waiting period and expiration. For over half of the United States, there is no waiting period between applying for and receiving a marriage license. For those states that do have a waiting period, it varies between one and five days and applies either to the period between applying for and receiving the license or

PHOTO 8-3 *(opposite) Prepare a draft layout of the ceremony site during the coordination phase.*

the period between receiving the license and the actual wedding date (Nola, 2006). Most states have an expiration provision that varies from 30 days to one year; therefore, the marriage license should not be applied for too early, as it may expire before the wedding day (Nola, 2006).

To apply for a marriage license, some form of identification is necessary for proof of age, such as a valid driver's license, birth certificate, passport, or military identification. Social security numbers and place of residence for both parties will be requested. State residency is not required, but the license must be purchased and filed in the state where the ceremony is taking place. If either individual was previously married, proof of divorce may be required. Both parties must be present at the time of application, and it may be necessary to have a witness. The cost of the marriage license typically ranges between $30 and $100. As the regulations vary considerably, you should be familiar with the process in the counties where the majority of your clients reside.

Finally, if one or both parties, most typically the bride, opts for a name change upon getting married, forms can be obtained in advance that will apply to documents such as the driver's license, social security card, health insurance card, workplace identification card, and credit cards. While the forms should not be submitted until after the wedding date, as a copy of the marriage license may be required, it will save valuable time in the long run to obtain these forms in advance. When applying for the marriage license, the bride must know the name she intends to use once she is married.

confirmation and details

The fifth phase of the wedding planning process involves confirmation and working out the final details. At this point the production schedule and site layout should be completed, and the guest list should be confirmed. Site layout is described in detail in Chapter 17. A security plan should be in place, which may be as straightforward as determining who will be responsible for transporting the gifts but may include a complete security staff if the wedding is high profile.

At this point, it is essential that a final confirmation occur with each vendor. Many consultants prepare partial production schedules or timelines for each vendor. The vendors do not need the entire production schedule but can benefit from the specifics that pertain to their individual roles. The more detailed or particular the needs of the couple, the more important it becomes to provide the vendors with targeted production schedules. For example, if the couple wants their chocolate fountain to come out with no announcement or if there is to be no father-daughter dance, the DJ should be given specific instructions on an individualized timeline so announcement errors that would be disappointing to the couple will not be made.

Other details that should be attended to at this point include the final preparation of favors and on-site stationery elements such as seating assignments and escort cards. The couple should also be advised to consult their registry to determine if it needs to be updated. The hotel block should be confirmed, as should the honeymoon details. Finally, if the couple wishes to have their wedding details published in their local newspaper in a timely fashion, the announcement generally needs to be submitted a minimum of 10 days prior to publication.

implementation

Wedding implementation occurs smoothly if the planner has a comprehensive production schedule. Also known as a build-out schedule, the production schedule is a timeline that offers a detailed plan of the specific tasks that pertain to the actual implementation of an event (Goldblatt, 2005). For wedding events, this schedule generally includes the rehearsal, day-of, and day-after the wedding. The production schedule is your primary tool that ensures the wedding implementation will go smoothly. The first page of the production schedule includes day-of contact information for all key parties involved in the process. Following the contact sheet is a detailed agenda that includes each task, start time, the point-of-contact for the task, and any details or notes. A full production schedule sample is given in Table 8.3.

Keep in mind that the day-of activities can vary significantly by culture. Culture Corner, Case 8.1, gives a timeline synopsis of the typical day-of activities for weddings in China.

wrap-up and evaluation

After the implementation of the wedding, the consultant's contact with the couple will generally continue for a short time so that wrap-up and evaluation can take place. As a consultant, you should solicit feedback from the couple. Furthermore, if any of the vendors are new to you, it would be helpful to request commentary and suggestions from them as well. (The specifics of evaluation are covered in Chapter 21.) This information should be compiled so that a final summary of the wedding can be filed for future reference.

Ad hoc services may also continue after the end of the wedding. For example, some couples have luncheons the day after their weddings, which gives them an opportunity to unwind with their families and

TABLE 8.3   Sample Production Schedule

Page Kramer/Jamie Faden Wedding
Saturday, October 18, 2008
Wedding Implementation Points of Contact

Ceremony Location	Star of the Sea Chapel	Phone number
	123 Main Street	
Ceremony Time	2:00 P.M.–3:15 P.M.	
Pre-reception	4:00 P.M.–5:30 P.M.	
Gathering	Jackie and Bill Faden personal residence	Phone number
	456 Oak Avenue	
Reception Location	Magnolia Estate and Gardens	Phone number
	789 Magnolia Way	
Reception Time	Cocktails: 6:00 P.M.–6:45 P.M.	
	Dinner Dance: 7:00 P.M.–11:00 P.M.	
Bride and Groom	Bride: Page Kramer	Phone number
	Groom: Jamie Faden	Phone number
Parents	Bride: Doris and Paul Kramer	Phone number
	Groom: Jackie and Bill Faden	Phone number
Wedding Consultants	Natalie Bernard	Phone number
	Jake Pennington	Phone number
Officiant	Reverend Franklin	Phone number
Caterer	Sarah Mahmud: Elegant Cuisine	Phone number
Florist	John Fortune: Fortune's Flowers	Phone number
Lighting	Riley Kerr: Dramatic Lighting	Phone number
Photographer	Lexi Sunshine: Sunshine Photos	Phone number
Ceremony Music	Angel Peterson: Angelic Strings	Phone number
Recessional Music	Bagpiper: Seamus Mitchell	Phone number
Reception Music	Courtney Madison: Grand Marnier	Phone number
Transportation	Janis Jones: Black Tie Limousine	Phone number
Wedding Cake	Rabi Townsend: Cakes by Rabi	Phone number
On-site Stationery	Trevor Hayword: Signature Stationery	Phone number
Elements		
Rentals	Kimmie King: A+ Rentals	Phone number
Hair Dresser	Tony Vigiani: Up-Dos by Tony	Phone number
Makeup Artist	Maxine L'Oreal: Makeup by Maxine	Phone number

Agenda
Thursday, October 16, 2008

Start Time	Task	Point of Contact	Details and Notes
4:00 P.M.	Try on and pick up tux	Jamie Faden	Drop off at parents' house
5:00 P.M.	Pick up menus, seating chart, table numbers and placards	Doris Kramer	Get from Signature Stationery

Agenda
Friday, October 17, 2008

Start Time	Task	Point of Contact	Details and Notes
10:00 A.M.	Bring 14 guest welcome baskets to Tradewinds Hotel	Jackie Faden	Jackie will leave with reception desk
1:00 P.M.	Hay delivered to Estate	Paul Kramer	
6:00 P.M.	Rehearsal, Star of the Sea Chapel	Rev. Franklin	
7:30 P.M.	Rehearsal Dinner: River Front Inn	Shelby Kenton	Phone number

TABLE 8.3 *(Continued)*

Agenda
Saturday, October 18, 2008

Start Time	Task	Point of Contact	Details and Notes
6:30 A.M.	Groom, fathers, and groomsmen depart for golf course; brunch afterwards		Jamie will travel with his father
8:30 A.M.	Hair and makeup for bride and bridesmaids at Kramer residence	Doris Kramer	Tony Vigiani, two assistants, and Maxine will arrive at Kramer residence
12:00 noon	Page dresses at Kramer residence	Doris Kramer	Doris Kramer and Janet Blohm will assist
12:00 noon	Jamie returns with father, dresses at Faden residence		
12:30 P.M.	Personal flowers delivered, wreaths installed at church	John Fortune	Ribbons only for hanging wreaths
12:30 P.M.	Wedding consultants arrive at church	Natalie Bernard Jake Pennington	
12:45 P.M.	Limo arrives at Kramer residence for bridesmaids, departs for church	Black Tie Limo	
1:00 P.M.	Bridesmaids, groom, groomsmen, and parents arrive at church		Jamie will travel with best man, Cole Faden
1:00 P.M.	Photographer arrives Officiant arrives	Lexi Sunshine Rev. Franklin	
1:15 P.M.	Boutonnieres pinned on men Bouquets and corsages distributed	Natalie Bernard Jake Pennington	
1:15 P.M.	Musicians arrive	Angelic Strings	
1:30 P.M.	Bentley arrives at Kramer residence, takes Page and Paul Kramer (father) to church	Black Tie Limo	No pre-ceremony pictures
1:40 P.M.	Prelude music begins Guests begin to arrive Groomsmen seat guests and hand out programs	Angelic Strings	
1:45 P.M.	Page arrives, waits in Bentley with father	Paul Kramer	
1:45 P.M.	Groom and groomsmen join Rev. Franklin in anteroom		
	Rest of wedding party gathers in room at the back of the church	Natalie Bernard	
1:50 P.M.	Bride and father join wedding party	Natalie Bernard	
1:55 P.M.	Wedding party lines up	Jake Pennington	Natalie leaves for reception site; Jake stays for ceremony

Ceremony

2:00 P.M.	Seating Music "Ode to Joy" (Beethoven) Seating of Tim and Rosemary Mohl (groom's grandparents) Seating of Jackie and Bill Faden (Jamie's parents)	Angelic Strings	
	Seating of Doris Kramer (Page's mother)		Page's Uncle Ted will seat Doris
	Rev. Franklin walks to front of altar		

(Continues)

TABLE 8.3 *(Continued)*

Ceremony			
2:05 P.M.	Processional Music: "Canon in D" (Pachelbel)	Angelic Strings	
	Jamie and groomsmen file in:		Men stand outside on right. (Al will stay with women and Jack and will hand off Jack to the sitter and then take his place).
	Jamie Faden (groom)		
	Cole Faden (best man)	Brother of groom	
	Mac O'Leary	Friend of groom	
	Duarte Cabrera	Friend of groom	
	Al Blohm	Brother-in-law	
	Bridesmaids walk to front:		Women stand outside on left
	Patricia Weaver	Friend of bride	
	Lorna Mueler	Cousin of bride	
	Mary Ellen Bailey	Friend of bride	
	Janet Blohm (matron of honor)	Sister of bride	
	Ringbearer, Jack Blohm, walks to front	Nephew	Al Blohm will escort Jack
	Flower girls, Allyce and Cassie Weaver, process side by side	Nieces	
2:10 P.M.	Procession of the bride	Angelic Strings	
	Music: "Jesu, Joy of Man's Desiring" (Bach)		
	Page Kramer (bride) escorted by Paul Kramer (father)		
2:15 P.M.	*Liturgy of the Word*		
	Opening prayer	Rev. Franklin	
	First reading	Linda Borosky	Friend of the Bride
	Song of Songs 2: 8–10, 14, 16		
	Responsorial Psalm	Doug Michel	Uncle of the Groom
	Psalm 145: 8–9, 10, 15		
	Second Reading	Carla Davis	Cousin of the Bride
	Colossiams 3: 12–17		
	Gospel Acclamation	Rev. Franklin	
	1 John 4:16		
	Gospel	Rev. Franklin	
	Matthew 7:21, 24–29		
	Homily	Rev. Franklin	
2:45 P.M.	*Rite of Marriage*		Bagpiper will arrive during this time and will be waiting outside
	Exchange of Vows	Page and Jamie	
	Blessing/Exchange of Rings	Page and Jamie	
	Prayer of the Couple	Rev. Franklin	
	Prayer of the Faithful	Congregation	
	Lighting of the Unity Candle	Page and Jamie	
	The Lord's Prayer	Congregation	
	Nuptial Blessing	Rev. Franklin	
3:00 P.M.	*Concluding Rite*		
	Final Blessing	Rev. Franklin	
	Call for applause	Rev. Franklin	
	Recessional Music: "Four Seasons"	Angelic Strings	

TABLE 8.3 *(Continued)*

Ceremony		
3:05 P.M.	*Recessional and Leave-taking* Page and Jamie walk down aisle, wait in room at back of church Bridal party walks down aisle, groomsmen return to escort guests Bagpiper begins to play as guests exit	Seamus Mitchell
3:15 P.M.	Guests depart for party at Faden's house. Directions and invitations handed out as they depart.	Jake Pennington
	When church is clear, Jake will get bridal party for 15 minutes of photos	Jake Pennington
3:40 P.M.	After photos, bridal party gets in limos and goes to Faden's party	
	Page and Jamie ride in Bentley to DC monuments for photos	Black Tie Limo Lexi Sunshine
	Remove wreaths and bring to Magnolia Estate	Jake Pennington

Reception		
2:00 P.M.	Groom's cake arrives	Alexandria Pastry Shop
2:45 P.M.	Consultant arrives at Magnolia Estate	Natalie Bernard
3:00 P.M.	Begin lighting install (wagon first)	Dramatic Lighting
3:15 P.M.	Rentals arrive	A+ Rentals
	Begin floral installation	John Fortune
	Harvest cart set up and decorated	Natalie Bernard
	Sign-in framed photo set up	Natalie Bernard
	Escort table set	Natalie Bernard
4:30 P.M.	Bride and groom arrive	Lexi Sunshine	Sunset is at 4:55 P.M.
	Take outdoor photos	
4:45 P.M.	Bride bustled	Natalie Bernard
	Jake arrives, gives wreath to florist for installation	Jake Pennington
	Linens set and chairs placed	A+ Rentals
	Menus and seating chart set	Jake Pennington
	Table numbers and head table placards set	Jake Pennington
	Wedding cake arrives	Cakes by Rabi
	Florist adds flowers to cake	John Fortune
5:45 P.M.	Room check	Natalie Bernard Jake Pennington
6:00 P.M.	Cocktail music begins	Grand Marnier
	Bars open	Elegant Cuisine
	Cocktails and hors d'oeuvres passed	
	Guests arrive	
	Page and Jamie join guests	
6:45 P.M.	Guest invited to be seated for dinner	Elegant Cuisine
	Straighten and stand by escort table	Jake Pennington
	Guest pick up escort cards	

(Continues)

TABLE 8.3 *(Continued)*

Reception			
7:00 P.M.	Lights are brought up	Dramatic Lighting	
	Wedding party is introduced and proceeds to head table	Grand Marnier	
7:05 P.M.	Bride and groom introduced	Grand Marnier	Introduce bride as
	Lights dim slightly	Dramatic Lighting	Page Kramer-Faden
	They proceed to dance floor and dance to "It's Your Love"		
	They dance entire length of song		
7:15 P.M.	Welcome and blessing	Rev. Franklin	
	Lights dimmed for dinner	Dramatic Lighting	
	Guests begin to eat plated salad	Elegant Cuisine	
7:30 P.M.	Tables invited to food stations	Elegant Cuisine	
8:15 P.M.	Lights brought up slightly	Dramatic Lighting	
	Father/daughter dance: "Because You Loved Me"	Grand Marnier	
	Mother/son dance: "You Raise Me up"	Grand Marnier	
	All guests invited to dance	Grand Marnier	
	Harvest cart is set and ready	Natalie Bernard	
9:00 P.M.	Guests seated		Have DJ invite guests to be seated. No announcement of chocolate fountain.
	Champagne poured	Elegant Cuisine	
	Chocolate fountain starts		
9:15 P.M.	Cakes brought to middle of dance floor	Elegant Cuisine	DJ announces cake
	Lights brought up slightly	Dramatic Lighting	
	Cake cutting	Page and Jamie	Natalie Bernard assists
	Cakes taken to kitchen for plating	Elegant Cuisine	
	Place slices on cake table	Elegant Cuisine	
9:30 P.M.	Father toast	Paul then Bill	Use DJ microphone
	Best man toast	Cole Faden	
	Maid of honor toast	Janet Blohm	
	Lights dimmed for more dancing	Dramatic Lighting	
10:15 P.M.	Bar closes	Elegant Cuisine	No bouquet or garter toss
	Photographer departs	Lexi Sunshine	
	As guests leave they are invited to help themselves to favors on the harvest cart		Jake Pennington stands by to assist with harvest cart
10:30 P.M.	Bride and groom depart		DJ announces
11:00 P.M.	Music ends	Grand Marnier	
	Good-nights and final guests exit		
11:15 P.M.	Signed picture and gifts removed	Natalie Bernard	Put in Kramer's van
	Extra favors boxed up	Jake Pennington	
11:30 P.M.	Lighting removed	Dramatic Lighting	
12:15 P.M.	Final walkthrough	Natalie Bernard Jake Pennington	

Monday, October 20, 2008		
9:00 A.M.	Rentals picked up	A+ Rentals
10:00 A.M.	Floral rentals removed	John Fortune
11:30 A.M.	Hay picked up and donated to Happy Trails Ranch	Cole Faden

wedding timelines in china

2–3 weeks prior	The couple will go to the wedding bureau, file for, and receive the government's wedding certificate. Generally, no church ceremony takes place. The "ceremony" includes all of the ritual preparations on the wedding day.
Wedding Day 6:00 A.M.	The bride goes to the hairdresser/makeup artist in preparation for the day's events. Usually the bride's sister or closest friend will accompany her.
8:00 A.M.	The groom's family gathers at the hotel where the wedding reception will be held. They gather there for breakfast and to make sure that everything is prepared for the reception.
9:00 A.M.	The bride arrives back home where her immediate family has started to gather for breakfast. The bride's mother, sister, and friends help the bride to get dressed in her Western-influenced white wedding dress as well as pack up the other wedding dresses for the reception. The bride will have at least one traditional red Chinese wedding dress as well as many others to change into during the reception.
	The hair, makeup, and dressing of the bride at her home are based on family tradition and represent the ceremonial elements of the day, which symbolically prepare the bride for leaving her parents' home and becoming part of the groom's home and family. In the more rural areas of China, the local brides will wear special clothes handed down from mother to daughter or made by the mother. A bride is only allowed to wear these garments upon getting married.

(Continues)

11:00 A.M.	The groom's family leaves for the bride's home while the groom waits at the hotel. In some cities this is reversed, and the groom goes to the bride's home while his family waits at the hotel. In either case, whoever goes travels in an entourage of cars decorated with red flowers.
11:30 A.M.	At the bride's home, the groom's family will knock on the door wanting entrance, but the bride's family will not let them in until the groom's family presents a red envelope containing 600 Renminbi (RMB, equal to about $75US), or a multiple thereof depending on the affluence of the groom's family. The envelope is given to the youngest male of the bride's family. Once this ritual has been completed, the groom's family members are welcomed into the home. Pictures are taken for about 10 minutes, and then everyone gathers their things and departs for the wedding reception.
11:30 A.M.	The invited guests start arriving at the hotel. Only immediate family members are invited to attend the private events earlier in the day; however, other guests are invited to attend the reception and arrive early to await the bridal party.
12:00 noon	As the bride's car pulls up to the hotel, the groom comes out to greet her, and hotel staff members light firecrackers to chase away any evil spirits. However, before the groom can open the car door, the bride's youngest male relative will block the groom's path until the groom gives him another red envelope, again containing 600 RMB. The groom is then allowed to open the bride's door, help her out of the car, and escort her into the wedding reception.

The Reception, Stage 1: The Announcer 12:15 P.M.	An announcer states the arrival of the bridal party to the guests by first, introducing the groom's immediate family; second, introducing the bride's immediate family; and finally, introducing the bride and groom. The couple may be asked to try to eat an apple together without using their hands. The announcer will then share a funny story about the couple and ask the couple to show their wedding certificate to the gathering to clearly illustrate to the crowd that they are now legally married. Then the announcer might do an exchange of rings ceremony. Until recently, displays of wealth such as rings were discouraged; however, today rings and ring exchanges are very much in style. Once the rings have been exchanged, the announcer will again formally introduce the couple to the gathering. This concludes the announcer's work, and he departs.
The Reception, Stage 2: Introductions 12:45 P.M.	The groom takes his new wife over to his immediate family and formally introduces each member of his family to his wife. Each member of the groom's family will tell the bride how she can now address him or her. Once completed, then the bride takes the groom over to her family and goes through the same process.
The Reception, Stage 3: The Feast 1:15 P.M.– 4:00 P.M.	The bride now changes into one of her many wedding reception outfits, each of which is to be worn at some point during the rest of the day. The first outfit is usually the high-collared, red, traditional Chinese wedding dress. During the wedding feast, the groom and bride do not sit down, as they must go and visit every guest at every table. After greeting each guest, a few words are exchanged and then the bride offers to light the guest's cigarette if that person smokes or

(Continues)

feed the guest a bite of food or toast the guest with a small shot of the alcohol being served. The frequent changing of clothes gives the bride short breaks from the toasting. At the same time, guests are toasting the couple and their families. As people toast the groom, they hand him a red envelope containing money. The Western approach of giving a gift rather than cash is catching on in China, so either is acceptable. There is usually no dancing during the wedding feast. It is a sit-down affair with everyone at round tables and a "lazy-susan" in the middle. At each place setting there is a small gift basket including chocolates and sweets, as well as a pack of good cigarettes and a lighter or matches.

Case submitted by Yao and David Wosicki

out-of-town guests and often acts as a forum to open wedding gifts. As a consultant, you may be called upon to coordinate such events and tie up other loose ends such as the preparation of thank-you notes. Therefore, your timeline should take into account all services from start to finish.

REFERENCES

Bureau of Consular Affairs with the United States Department of State. (2006). Marriage of United States citizen abroad, available at http://travel.state.gov

Fairchild Bridal Group. (2005). The American wedding 2005. Microsoft PowerPoint research presentation.

Franks, R. (2003, July 11). New law may threaten marriage mecca. The Catoosa County News, available at http://www.catt.com

Goldblatt, J. (2005). Special Events: Event Leadership for a New World, 4th ed. Hoboken, NJ: John Wiley & Sons.

Nolo. (2006). State marriage license and blood test requirements, available at http://www.nolo.com

Consultant Checklist and Reminders for Timelines

- ☐ Include names and contact information for all key parties.

- ☐ Indicate who is responsible for each task.

- ☐ Give partial production schedules to all vendors.

- ☐ Add all details that might be overlooked by a vendor (e.g., no bouquet toss).

- ☐ Include drop-off and pick-up times for equipment and supplies.

- ☐ Know the earliest time that you and the vendors will have access to venues.

- ☐ Generally do hair before makeup.

- ☐ Know rules of floral installation and removal at the venues (e.g., if the ceremony site is a place of worship, it is common for altar flowers to be donated).

- ☐ Include what will be done with a large gap of time between the ceremony and reception.

- ☐ Know the time of sunset: check out the Web site timeanddate.com for assistance.

- ☐ Indicate who is responsible for security and transportation of gifts.

- ☐ Include a post-reception agenda.

review questions

1. Name the seven phases of wedding timelines.

2. Explain two tasks that occur in each of the seven phases.

3. What are two of the issues related to obtaining a marriage license that vary from state to state?

4. What are four key elements of wedding production schedules?

5. What are two unique elements associated with wedding timelines in China?

terminology

• Feasibility analysis

• Marriage license

• Production schedule

• Timeline phases

• Vendor

PHOTO 9-1 *The reception and rentals take up 40 percent of the average wedding budget.*

wedding budgets

Over the past 20 years, considerable shifts have taken place in terms of wedding budgets. As evidenced in Chapter 1, wedding costs have increased dramatically, and a significant number of couples spend more on their weddings than originally planned. Simultaneously, as discussed in Chapter 5, the changing family and in particular women's increased educational and career opportunities have led to a delay in marriage, which allows more couples to contribute to the cost of their weddings. Therefore, couples are more likely to pay for the entire wedding themselves, which occurs 27 percent of the time, rather than the bride's parents financing the wedding, which still happens an estimated 25 percent of the time (Fairchild Bridal Group, 2005). A combination of contributions from the couple and both sets of parents represents the most common scenario.

t he average wedding in the United States is estimated to cost $26,000, but significant variations exist. For example, weddings held in Southern states such as Mississippi ($14,000) and New Mexico ($17,000) are on average considerably less expensive than those held in the Northeast, such as Connecticut ($31,000) and New Jersey ($34,000) (McMurray, 2005). Moreover, within any given state there are distinct differences. For instance, while the average wedding budget in Richmond, Virginia, is $22,000, the budget in Greenway, Virginia, is $124,000, which is an enormous difference. The useful online resource costofwedding.com allows you to enter in any zip code to get an estimate of the average budget. This tool will help you get a sense of the average budget in your target market.

Regardless of the total outlay, the categories of spending are consistent. The purpose of this chapter is to outline the primary budget categories that emerge in most weddings while offering tools to assist you in presenting organized and realistic budget information to your clients. Understanding the percentage generally allocated to each budget category will allow you to help your clients make informed expenditure decisions.

wedding budget categories

There are many ways to organize wedding budgets, but couples can more readily make rational decisions if the categories are presented in a logical manner. Use a spreadsheet and include columns for each of the following seven areas: (1) the category names and specific items in each; (2) a means of determining whether or not a given element will be included; (3) an indication of estimated cost; (4) the total final cost; (5) the down payment amount; (6) the date when the final payment is due; and (7) notes pertaining to each area. Table 9.1 offers a sample of how this information can be compiled, using reception and rentals, which is the most expensive wedding category, as an example.

By learning the common expenditure areas in each category, you can readily apply these same seven ideas to all budget categories and items. Table 9.2 presents the 13 common categories of spending, the average percentage of the budget allocated to each category, and the common associated items.

budget summaries

Although you will need a detailed budget for the planning process, once a wedding is complete, it is useful to have a summary budget so

TABLE 9.1 Wedding Budget Categories and Details: Reception and Rentals Shown as Sample

Category Name/ Specific Items	Included?	Estimated Cost	Final Cost	Down Payment Amount	Final Payment Due Date	Notes
Reception and Rentals (40%)						
Site rental fee	yes/no					
Tent rental fee	yes/no					
Food	yes/no					
Alcohol	yes/no					
Other beverages	yes/no					
Tables	yes/no					
Chairs	yes/no					
Dance floor	yes/no					
Lighting	yes/no					
China	yes/no					
Linens	yes/no					
Flatware	yes/no					
Glassware	yes/no					
Other decorations (e.g., ice sculpture)	yes/no					
Tips (e.g., wait staff, coat check)	yes/no					
Other	yes/no					

TABLE 9.2 Budget Categories and Related Areas of Expenditure

Reception and Rentals (40%)
- Reception site rental fee
- Tent rental fee
- Food
- Alcohol
- Other beverages
- Tables
- Chairs
- Dance floor
- Lighting
- China
- Linens
- Flatware
- Glassware
- Specialty decorations (e.g., ice sculpture)
- Tips (e.g., banquet manager, wait staff, valet, coat check)
- Other

Photography and Videography (10%)
- Engagement photos
- Photographer ceremony/wedding: time and album package
- Additional photos for family/friends
- Videographer ceremony/wedding: time and package

(*Continues*)

TABLE 9.2 (*Continued*)

Wedding Consultant (10%)
- Consultant package
- Ad hoc services

Wedding Attire (8%)
- Bridal dress and alterations
- Headpiece/veil
- Shoes
- Lingerie
- Purse
- Jewelry
- Groom's formalwear
- Groom's accessories

Floral Décor (7%)
- Bridal bouquet
- Bridesmaids' bouquets
- Groom's boutonniere
- Groomsmen's boutonnieres
- Parents of couple (corsages/boutonnieres)
- Grandparents of couple (corsages/boutonnieres)
- Other family members
- Flower girl (flowers and basket)
- Ringbearer (boutonniere and pillow)
- Readers, soloist, other
- Ceremony flowers, wreaths, and bows (altar, pews/chairs, doors)
- Ceremony special elements (e.g., chuppah décor)
- Reception (cake, cake table, centerpieces, serving table, other)
- Packing and delivery

Music and Other Entertainment (7%)
- Ceremony musicians
- Cocktail hour musicians/band/DJ
- Reception musicians/band/DJ
- Other music/entertainment (e.g., soloist, bagpiper, drummers, dancers)

Wedding Rings (excluding engagement ring) (4%)
- Bride's wedding ring
- Groom's wedding ring

Stationery Elements (3%)
- Save-the-date notices
- Invitations (invitation card, reception card, reply card)
- Calligrapher
- Ceremony programs
- Specialized ceremony elements (e.g., ketubah, pew cards)
- Guest book
- Seating chart
- Escort, table, and place cards

TABLE 9.2 *(Continued)*

- Table card holders, stands, or frames
- Menus
- Personalized table or cake napkins
- Personalized boxes, bags or matches to accompany favors
- Wedding announcements
- Thank-you notes

Gifts (3%)
- Bride's attendants
- Groom's attendants
- Parents of bride
- Parents of groom
- Other bridal party members (e.g., readers)
- Wedding favors

Transportation and Lodging (3%)
- Transportation for bride and groom
- Transportation for wedding party
- Transportation for guests
- Parking fees
- Hotel room/s for couple, night prior
- Hotel room for newlyweds, wedding night
- Tips for transportation and lodging

Wedding Cake and Other Pastries (2%)
- Wedding cake (including delivery)
- Groom's cake (including delivery)
- Cake cutting fee
- Other pastries (e.g., cookies or biscotti)

Ceremony and Legal Issues (2%)
- Ceremony site rental fee
- Officiant fee/donation
- Marriage license
- Blood tests, if applicable
- Ceremony special elements (e.g., unity candle, chuppah rental, broom, crowns)

Wedding Day Preparation (1%)
- Bridal hair trial run
- Bridal hair day-of
- Bridal makeup trial run
- Bridal makeup day-of
- Bridal manicure/pedicure
- Groom's hair
- Groom's manicure/pedicure
- Tips for stylists, makeup artists, manicurists

PHOTO 9-2 *Floral décor purchases add up to 7 percent of the average budget for weddings.*

that quick comparisons can be made over time. Furthermore, when helping new clients get started, it is easier to give them a summary budget that allocates by overall category percentages rather than overwhelming them with potential costs for each and every item. Table 9.3 uses a budget of $26,000 to highlight the amount available per category based on average expenditures. Note that the engagement ring, rehearsal dinner, and honeymoon are not included, for these are considered outside of the wedding day itself. However, these elements represent considerable areas of expense that should not be forgotten. For example, the average engagement ring in the United States costs $3,500, and couples spend an average of $3,750 on their honeymoons (McMurray, 2005).

It is important to convey to your clients that, although your consultant fee is 10 percent of the overall budget, this payment is easily recouped because of the savings you are passing onto them through your negotiating skills and through your relationship with vendors,

PHOTO 9-3 *(opposite) Allow 2 percent of the budget for the wedding cake and other pastries.*

TABLE 9.3 Sample Summary Budget

Category	Budget %	Amount ($) Allocated
Reception and Rentals	40	10,400
Photography and Videography	10	2,600
Wedding Consultant	10	2,600
Wedding Attire	8	2,080
Floral Décor	7	1,820
Music and Other Entertainment	7	1,820
Wedding Rings (excluding engagement ring)	4	1,040
Stationery Elements	3	780
Gifts	3	780
Transportation and Lodging	3	780
Wedding Cake and Other Pastries	2	520
Ceremony and Legal Issues	2	520
Wedding Day Preparation	1	260
Total	100%	$26,000

which often results in discounts that are passed along to the couple. Furthermore, not only do your professional relationships save the couple money, but you are saving them an enormous amount of time and stress by facilitating the planning, design, and implementation of the wedding.

As discussed in Chapter 8, an open discussion of budget issues early on will help your clients complete a feasibility analysis. Couples often feel overwhelmed and experience "sticker shock" as they start to realize the number of purchases that accompany their wedding day. You can help them approach the often emotional process of decision making rationally and calmly.

Organization is absolutely critical to budgets. You can assist your clients by encouraging them to keep all of their contracts and receipts in one folder. Some consultants have personalized folders that they give to their clients for this very purpose. The day of the wedding, you should have the folder close by in case any payment issues arise. A misplaced receipt can cause havoc on the day of the wedding, as evidenced in Consultant in Action, Case 9.1.

Finally, it is a good idea to encourage your clients to put aside a slush fund of 5 to 10 percent of the overall estimated costs. At times, unforeseen expenses arise, and if the extra money is in place, it can be used for emergencies. For example, perhaps the best man lives out of town, unexpectedly loses his job, and reports to the groom that he cannot travel because of his strained financial situation. The couple may decide to fly the best man out and pay for his hotel.

rental refusal

The reception venue that your clients have chosen is an historic site with very strict regulations. There is only one rental company in town that carries the chairs that are permissible. At 10:30 A.M. on the wedding day, you are setting up the place cards at the site when the chair company arrives, as scheduled. However, the company representative, Claire, refuses to unload the truck until final payment is made. According to your records, the groom, Matt, made the final payment a week previously. You call Matt, who is in the middle of getting his hair trimmed in preparation for the 1:00 P.M. wedding, and he verifies that he made the payment and that the receipt is probably somewhere on his desk at work. Claire firmly states that she has no record of the payment, and her crew cannot unload without being paid the balance due.

What do you do?

They can do this without breaking the bank because they were pre-pared. If the slush fund is not needed, then the couple can spend the money as they see fit, perhaps treating themselves to new furnishings or putting it toward a house savings fund. They will feel pleased because their wise spending habits allowed for a post-wedding benefit.

Although wedding finances can become complicated, a pragmatic approach taken by the consultant can ease the process. Encouraging your clients to keep track of their expenditures will help them stay within their budgets. While some couples have the luxury to spend freely, most will appreciate budget guidance that will keep them from having long-term wedding debt.

REFERENCES

Fairchild Bridal Group. (2005). The American wedding 2005. Microsoft PowerPoint research presentation.

McMurray, S. (2005). The Wedding report: 2006 wedding statistics & market estimates US and 50 states, available from http://www.theweddingreport.com

Consultant Checklist and Reminders for Budgets

- ☐ Discuss the anticipated budget early on in the planning process.
- ☐ Encourage the couple to clearly delineate who will be contributing to the budget.
- ☐ Discuss tipping etiquette with the couple, as they may not realize they should factor this into their budget.
- ☐ Have the couple or the party responsible for the particular budget item make all down payments.
- ☐ Keep clients aware of final payment dates so they are not charged late fees or denied service on their wedding day.
- ☐ Give clients a folder to organize all of their contracts and receipts.
- ☐ As the consultant, make sure you receive your final payment at least two weeks prior to the wedding day.
- ☐ Remind the couple to have cash for tips on the wedding day, which you can distribute on their behalf as applicable.

review questions

1. Name the seven columns that you should include on a spreadsheet to streamline the presentation of wedding budgets.

2. Name five of the thirteen common categories contained in wedding budgets.

3. What percentage of a wedding budget is generally allocated to reception costs? to photography? to wedding cakes and other pastries?

4. What are three areas of significant expenditure related to weddings that are generally not included in the day-of budget?

terminology

- Site fee
- Spreadsheet
- Sticker shock
- Wedding budget categories

determining
the vision

A wedding vision is an imaginative conception of the event that encompasses all five senses: sight, sound, smell, taste, and touch. As a consultant, the goal of discussing vision with your clients is to determine their ideal day and then move to the pragmatics of making that vision a reality. This chapter presents the tools that will aid you and your clients in establishing a focused vision that will be accompanied by theme, destination, and site selection.

PHOTO 10-1 *(opposite) A color scheme can dictate the vision for a wedding.*

✒ vision determination

When you have an initial consultation with a couple, before you can start on your checklist of things to do, before you can book a venue or hire a photographer, you have to find out a little bit about the couple's vision. In order to meet their expectations, it is your responsibility to figure out what makes them tick and how that can be expressed in their wedding. This should be handled through a series of open-ended questions asked during a client interview, as presented in detail in Chapter 24. You can also ask the primary point of contact, generally the bride, to bring pictures and samples of ideas that she likes. These materials do not have to be wedding specific; they can include almost anything, for example, the shape of a plate, a swatch of fabric, or a photo that brings back a favorite childhood memory.

It is important that you meet with the couple, or at least the primary point of contact, in person. While many of the wedding particulars can be handled by e-mail or telephone, a face-to-face meeting will help you understand the styles and personalities of the individuals, which will typically be translated during their wedding. For example, you can expect different visions from brides who dress in a tailored fashion versus those who wear cutting-edge, fashion-forward clothing versus those who discuss the wicking ability of the latest outdoor hiking gear. Be careful not to overgeneralize based on appearance; rather, use this information in conjunction with other data provided. The bottom line is to gather a breadth of information that you can draw upon when executing a vision.

Most importantly, as a consultant you have to remember you are not planning your own wedding; you are planning your clients' wedding. So when they tell you, for example, that they got engaged at a popular historic theme park and want a cotton candy machine at the reception, you need to make that happen. When you are trying to uncover your clients' vision, you must actively listen while looking directly at them. Really listen. Don't get overly caught up in taking notes or talking about your experience. Don't say, "Oh well, when I did that wedding...and when I did that wedding." You are there to learn about this couple and their desired wedding day.

✒ wedding themes

In the process of learning about a couple's vision, thematic ideas are likely to emerge. Wedding themes can vary from subtle to dramatic and generally feed into destination and site selection as well as influencing other elements such as floral décor and favors. A common starting place is a favorite color. A color scheme can be the impetus for the entire framework of a wedding. Consider the Consultant in Action, Case 10.1, to see the influence of color on wedding planning.

140

color composition

Your client is a huge Julia Roberts' fan and absolutely loves the movie, *Steel Magnolias*, so much so that she wants her theme to be based on the colors Roberts' character had for her wedding: blush and bashful (i.e., light pink and dark pink). You compliment your client for having this creative idea and explain that a choice of colors will aid in the overall design of the wedding. Using blush and bashful as an example, determine the following elements:

1. Month of year: Jan   Feb   Mar   Apr   May   June

   Jul   Aug   Sep   Oct   Nov   Dec

2. Ceremony time of day: Morning   Afternoon   Evening

3. Reception location: Hotel   Historic Estate   Museum
   Garden   Country Club   Resort

4. How the colors can be incorporated into clothing:

5. Two ideas for favors:

6. One other effect:

Complete the same activity using the following colors:

- Electric blue and black

- Champagne beige

- Tangerine orange

A second thematic category pertains to seasons and holidays. Seasons often coincide with colors, with pastels working best in the spring, bright colors coordinating with summer, muted tones favored in the fall, and festive shades and darks working well in the winter. Considering the calendar year, some popular holidays that coincide with wedding themes include New Year's Eve, Valentine's Day, St. Patrick's Day, Easter, Memorial Day, Fourth of July, Labor Day, Halloween, Thanksgiving and Christmas. Holiday weekends are popular because they generally allow guests to have more travel time; however, because of their popularity, prices tend to be higher during these periods. A specific aspect of a season or holiday period can be used to dictate the thematic elements; for instance, a harvest wedding can include a hay wagon, mums, pumpkin centerpieces, a cider-based signature drink, and favors such as baskets of pumpkin bread or candied apples.

For those with an appreciation of the past, a wedding theme based on a specific historic period may be appealing. Renaissance and Victorian periods as well as eras such as the Roaring 1920s and the Big Band 1930s and 1940s lend themselves to specific musical genres as well as clothing styles. A related theme involves drawing on a specific culture or subculture. This may be based on the experiences or heritage of the bride and/or groom or on a particular interest or borrowed culture. For example, a couple may wish to have an Ascot-themed wedding, based not on a British heritage but on their love of horses. Another couple, equally passionate about horses, may opt for a more casual Country Western theme. A subculture theme can even be based on a career; for instance, military weddings have specific associated customs and protocol embedded within the ceremony.

Couples with an interest in outdoor activities may decide to have a beach, mountain, garden, or park theme. Gazebos, atriums, resorts, and estates lend themselves to outdoor themes. A related thematic area is comprised of earth and celestial elements, which can be tied into conservationist weddings as well as those using stars, planets, the moon, or angelic features.

A final, broad, theme pertains to popular culture, with couples frequently drawing on books, theatre, and film to inspire their weddings. Plot lines, time periods, characters, and music associated with stories such as Alice in Wonderland, Camelot, Cinderella, Romeo and Juliet, Star Wars, and The Great Gatsby fuel the imagination.

When choosing a theme, it is important to consider the knowledge base of the guests. If the couple wishes to incorporate Scottish elements into the wedding based on the bride's heritage, it will be helpful to explain the significance of the unique features in the wedding program so that the cultural experience will not be lost on guests who are not of Scottish descent. In addition, the comfort level of the guests

Photograph by www.RodneyBailey.com

PHOTO 10-2 *The theme can be tied into a wedding cake design.*

must be kept in mind. A couple with a Country Western theme might like to offer their guests the option of a horseback ride between the wedding and the reception, but they need to offer transportation alternatives for those who might not want to participate in this activity.

destinations and sites

Wedding destinations and sites can be chosen based on the theme of the wedding. For instance, a Great Gatsby-themed wedding could be held at the Great Gatsby Estate located on the Island of Martha's Vineyard, Massachusetts, or at the Rosecliff Mansion in Newport, Rhode Island, which was the setting for the film. Similarly, an Italian Renaissance-themed wedding could take place at the James Leary Flood Mansion in San Francisco, California, as the architects who designed this building employed this classical style (Flood Mansion, 2006). For those with an interest in United States history and politics, the National Park Service allows wedding ceremonies to take place at two sites along the National Mall: (1) at the Tidal Basin west of the

Jefferson Memorial, and (2) at an area between the World War I Memorial and World War II Memorial (Ford, 2006). Furthermore, as discussed in Chapter 7, destination weddings allow many couples to live out their dream themes; for example, Walt Disney World has custom packages that can even include Cinderella's carriage (Disney Weddings, 2006).

In many cases, it is not feasible for couples to choose a destination and site based on the wedding theme. Accordingly, the site can be transformed to reflect the theme and/or destination. For example, many couples who desire to have a beach theme do not live near an ocean or lake. However, the theme can still be established through stationery selections, favors, music, and other specific elements. Similarly, many couples get engaged while traveling and may want to incorporate elements of those memories in their weddings. For example, a bride and groom who became engaged in Paris at the Eiffel Tower are not likely to return to Paris for their ceremony, but they can readily include Parisian elements to impart a French flavor to their day.

While the destination is the broader geographical area such as a city, the site is the specific physical venue as well as the placement within that venue. For example, most major hotels have multiple-function spaces where a wedding and reception can take place, with options such as a courtyard, ballroom, or conservatory being quite common. Each of these spaces has a different feel, thus allowing for a wide range of themes.

Many wedding ceremonies take place at a house of worship, and then the couple and their guests often move to a separate location for the reception. Alternatively, many sites can accommodate both the ceremony and the reception. Some common reception venues include aquariums, atriums, ballrooms, country clubs, gardens, historic estates, hotels, inns, museums, park facilities, plantations, and resorts.

Many of your clients will not have a clear vision of their day and may rely on you to help construct a theme and then indicate the appropriate destination and site to carry out the theme. When this occurs, you have to gently lead your clients by the hand. Taking classes in design and floral décor as well as keeping up with the latest wedding trends will help you hone your creative skills and enable you to assist each couple in determining a unique style.

When selecting a wedding venue, you should pay particular attention to the following issues: (1) capacity; (2) rental costs and/or cost per person; (3) taxes, service charges, and other fees; (4) restrictions and special requirements; and (5) setup time. First, capacity will dictate whether a given facility is feasible and practical. Many historic homes, garden sanctuaries, and smaller museum sites have capacities limited

PHOTO 10-3 *Estates are popular venues that can accommodate the wedding and reception.*

to 150 or fewer persons; therefore, for large weddings, clients are better served with major hotels that can often handle as many as 3,000 guests. By the same token, a grand ballroom reserved for a 50-person reception would feel cavernous, so a couple planning an intimate wedding should select an equally personal setting.

Second, rental fees will differ significantly from property to property. For some hotels, there are no rental fees and pricing is based per person for food and beverage. In other cases, venues can charge $15,000 or more simply to reserve the space, which buys your clients nothing but the privilege of using the space for a certain number of hours.

When calculating costs, it is important to remember the third consideration: taxes, service charges, and other fees. For example, if a hotel using a per-person structure gives a reception estimate of $100 per person for 150 guests, the immediate assumption might be to budget $15,000. However, this estimate can be misleading if it is exclusive of tax and service charge. If the tax is 7 percent and the service charge is 18 percent, that adds an additional 25 percent to the bill, and the

PHOTO 10-5 *Small receptions should be held in venues that feel personal and intimate.*

reception actually costs $18,750, which may be out of the couple's budget range. When you are showing your clients three different proposals from three different venues, you are going to want to compare apples to apples. If one venue is including everything and one is not, the one that is incomplete will look less expensive, so you have to peel away the layers and make sure that the information provided is consistent and complete. Be mindful of other fees such as those pertaining to cake cutting, beverage corkage, and overtime.

A fourth consideration when selecting a venue is restrictions and special requirements. Some facilities, such as historic chapels in academic settings, private country clubs, and famous cathedrals, are only available to those who belong to the associated communities. While nominal membership fees may be paid to gain access to some such venues, in other cases it is cost prohibitive or impossible to secure usage privileges. Some venues are only available if the bride, groom,

PHOTO 10-4 *(opposite) Ballrooms make for dramatic ceremony settings.*

or an immediate family member has an established relationship created through ongoing and noteworthy financial contributions.

Special requirements also refer to what can and cannot occur at the given facility. Many historic buildings have policies that are in place to maintain the integrity of the building and its artifacts. Some common wedding elements that may be prohibited because of their ability to stain or cause damage include red or blush wines, other red liquids such as tomato and cranberry juice, chocolate fountains, candles, and flower petals. Other restrictions often apply to the types of rentals that can be used. For instance, some rental chairs may scratch flooring and will therefore be prohibited. Venues with strict guidelines will generally provide a list of accepted vendors with whom they have cultivated a trusting relationship. For venues such as hotels that have their own catering services, you may be required to purchase their food, beverage, and even the wedding cake as part of the contract. It is important that you become very familiar with the policies and regulations of wedding sites in your area so that you can assist your clients in making informed decisions.

A final consideration is the amount of setup time available. Essentially, you need to know when the vendors can move in to prepare for the guests to arrive. This issue can be particularly problematic at popular venues that book back-to-back receptions, which may mean that one ends at 5:00 P.M. and the next starts at 6:00 P.M. As a consultant, this makes the turnaround time very, very tight. Have a candid conversation with the venue manager to determine if the staff can accomplish the following in a one-hour turn: get the previous guests out, take the gifts away, vacuum the carpet, turn the room, reconfigure the tables, replace all the linens, and clean the bathrooms. Simultaneously, you will need to time the setup of the escort card table, floral décor, food, cake, musicians, lighting, and other reception elements.

The bottom line is that a short turnaround does not allow for the emergencies, problems, and challenges that invariably arise. Generally speaking, you should look for a setup time of no less than four hours; if it has to be less, make sure that you have plenty of assistants on hand. With large weddings, it is best to advise your clients to select a venue that only handles one event per day so the stress of setup and breakdown is minimized. With setup and breakdown, you also need to be aware if the venue works with unions, as this, too, will influence time orientation. Most unions work within the exact specifics of their contracts and can actually leave if activities do not take place as scheduled.

One way to get an answer to all of the key questions pertaining to a venue is to send out a request for proposal (RFP) to the two or three venues under consideration. The RFP details the specific requirements of your client's wedding and asks potential vendors to bid based on the guidelines provided. You will send out the exact same RFP to all of the venues where you ask them to address the same issues. This way, your clients can readily compare information when making a venue decision. Decisions are not based solely on budget competitiveness; in addition, your clients should be assessing the completeness, organization, creativity, and feasibility of the proposal. As a wedding consultant, you should not blindly send out RFPs and hope for the best. Instead, you should start with a trusted list of venues and allow your clients to select the one that is the best fit.

149

REFERENCES

Disney Weddings. (2006). Disney's fairy tale weddings and honeymoons, available at http://www.disneyweddings.com/site/wed/cus/start/index.jsp

Flood Mansion. (2006) The James Leary Flood Mansion, available at http://www.floodmansion.org

Ford, E. (2006). Where to say "I do": Five little-known sites for a ceremony. Washingtonian Wedding Guide, available at http://www.washingtonian.com/weddings/06/ceremonies.html

Consultant Checklist and Reminders for Theme, Destination, and Site Selection

☐ Make sure the theme resonates with the couple.

☐ Stick to one primary theme and stay consistent in the application of the theme.

☐ Don't overdo a theme, as it can take away from the meaning of the day.

☐ Keep the guests' knowledge base and comfort level in mind.

☐ Keep the budget in mind, as the implementation of some themes can be cost prohibitive.

☐ Choose destinations and sites on the basis of the wedding theme; alternatively, transform a venue to reflect the theme.

☐ When helping your clients compare venues, be very familiar with the: (1) capacity; (2) rental costs and/or cost per person; (3) taxes, service charges, and other fees; (4) restrictions and special requirements; and (5) setup time.

review questions

1. Name three categories of themes and give examples of each category.

2. What are four common types of sites where wedding receptions are held?

3. What are five considerations to bear in mind when selecting a wedding venue?

4. Explain why it is important to keep taxes, service charges, and other fees in mind when selecting a wedding venue.

5. Name three restrictions that are common to historic buildings that influence the selection of wedding elements.

terminology

- Destination

- Rental fees

- Request for proposal

- Site

- Vision

- Wedding themes

food, beverage, and the wedding cake

Food and beverage are generally the most expensive wedding elements, taking up a significant portion of the amount allocated to the budget category of reception and rentals. Most couples are not accustomed to making detailed menu decisions or serving large numbers of people; accordingly, the guidance and advice of a wedding consultant and caterer are sought. Wedding planners and caterers work as a team. While some vendors do not like working through a liaison, others often prefer working with knowledgeable consultants. This is particularly true for caterers, who often become the planner by default if a professional wedding consultant has not been hired. Many consultants have ongoing relationships with caterers, which saves both the couple and the caterer valuable time. This chapter offers an overview of essential considerations pertaining to food, beverage, and the wedding cake.

PHOTO 11-1 *(opposite) Signature drinks are a very popular catering trend.*

food and beverage

Finding and working with a caterer is a sales process from start to finish. When helping a couple select a caterer, typically a wedding consultant first suggests a number of caterers who vary in services, style, and price. Once the group is narrowed to three or four, initial meetings take place. During the initial meeting, the caterer provides information regarding service options and packages. Some caterers focus on food and nonalcoholic beverages, but most can also provide alcohol service. Other services can include the cake as well as staffing and rentals. During this meeting, logistics such as time of day, number of guests, and the site are provided, as well as information regarding other vendors that will influence catering, such as tent rental.

Dietary restrictions and other specialized needs should be introduced during this meeting because some caterers may not be able to accommodate specific requirements. For example, it is impossible for caterers who work from set menu selections to create a menu that follows strictly kosher Jewish dietary laws, also known as Glatt kosher. Three of the many requirements for Glatt kosher are as follows: (1) shellfish, pork, and rabbit are forbidden; (2) dairy and meat cannot be eaten together; and (3) grape products, such as wine, must be produced by those who follow the Jewish faith. Couples who wish to have a Glatt kosher meal must work with caterers who are kosher certified.

Caterers may be able to address some unique dietary requests, such as specialized vegetarian meals, but will generally charge additional fees for specialized services. The wedding planner should be aware of menu restrictions in advance and can limit the initial listing of caterers to those who will be able to attend to the needs of the couple.

In some cases, the couple will have dietary requests that pertain to one or two guests, while in others, the couple may impose their preferences on all the guests. For instance, a bride who is allergic to nuts may request that no nuts or nut extracts be used in any part of the meal. A diabetic groom may have a separate sugar-free cake, or the entire wedding cake might be sugar-free. It is critical that the couple and the consultant clearly communicate special needs to the caterer in advance of the formal proposal. The consultant should determine if substitutions can be made for individuals with special dietary needs.

Importantly, the initial meeting is an opportunity for the caterer to get to know the couple and their food and beverage preferences. This information can be used to build a targeted proposal, the contents of which are well explained by Rachel Gittins, an event designer at Ridgewells, which caters events such as weddings, corporate meetings, and professional sports. One of Ridgewells' principal owners, Susan Lacz, is featured in Vendor Spotlight, Case 11.1. The catering

154

susan lacz

ridgewells

How many events does Ridgewells cater a year? An "event" to us can be a food order, a rental, and/or service. With that in mind, we are at almost 100,000 events a year.

What brought you to Ridgewells? I graduated with a marketing degree and sold microcomputers right out of college, and I just hated it, but I loved to sell, organize, cook, plan, decorate, and design. Purple is my favorite color, and one day when I saw a purple Ridgewells truck go by, I knew I had to work for that company. It took six interviews over 18 months to convince them to hire me. They gave me a sales goal for the first year, and I reached it in three months. I progressively grew within the company and created the major events division, and now I am one of the three owners.

Ridgewells is known as a trendsetter. How do you go about generating new ideas? I provide all the event designers with a blank palette, which is their event. I provide them with what's hot in colors and materials to create their piece of art. Twice a year we add a new line of equipment and the chef simultaneously comes up with new menus, so it all evolves. I believe what I see in the fashion industry is going to be on the table tops—I look at a gorgeous gown in terms of color and style and will find that for our linens. I am always traveling, gathering ideas, and building on them by getting input from our chefs and designers. I want equipment from overseas that wouldn't be here for two years unless I go out and get it.

Web site: www.ridgewells.com

proposal is presented shortly after the initial meeting and generally includes the food costs, staff costs, equipment costs, taxes, gratuity and delivery. You should also ask if there are setup costs and overtime charges. In the proposal, the caterer sells to the desires outlined in the initial meeting. This document should be organized, accurate, and thorough and contain no grammatical or spelling errors. The names of the bride and groom, their venues, and other details given during the meeting must be correct. Notes regarding any specialized needs that were mentioned should be included.

Rachel explains that the proposal stage is an opportunity for the caterer to "wow" the couple by including special touches that signal to the couple that the company can and will treat each wedding as a unique event. For example, if the caterer learned during the initial meeting that the groom proposed in Australia and the wedding is going to have an outback theme, the caterer can suggest a signature drink called the koala café to accompany the cake. If the couple loves to garden, the proposal can be presented on elegant paper with a floral design. An outstanding proposal proves to the couple that the caterer listened during the meeting and really understood the focus of the event. Upscale caterers particularly enjoy working with what they call foodie brides—those who both understand and appreciate fine cuisine.

Even if the proposal is going to the wedding consultant instead of directly to the couple, the caterer should still include the special touches. The caterer and consultant can then coordinate and put together a global proposal that incorporates the catering elements. A consultant will be more eager to work with a caterer who was clearly listening during the meeting.

When meeting with potential caterers, it is critical that your clients taste the food they are considering, for they will not want to randomly select items that they may ultimately dislike. Top caterers host formal tastings two or three times a year, where they invite couples and consultants who have expressed an interest in their services to an event that showcases their food, presentation, and service. This savvy marketing technique exposes couples to specific hors d'oeuvres, entrées, pastries, and other items they may not have otherwise considered and also serves to highlight the caterer's newest linens and tableware in a festive atmosphere.

FOOD AND BEVERAGE TRENDS

Cutting-edge caterers are trendsetters. These trends are witnessed at weddings and other events. As suggested with the outback theme, signature drinks are particularly popular at the moment. This trend is fun and flexible, as beverages are versatile and a simple drink can have flair if given a clever name and presented in a fun glass with a unique straw or nontraditional garnish. Chocolate fountains, drinkable desserts, monogrammed tuxedo and wedding gown strawberries, and cookies with scanned, edible pictures are stylish ways to offer sweets as favors or prior to cutting the wedding cake. Edible place cards made out of white or dark chocolate are another fun and unexpected treat.

Trends are also evidenced in the style and presentation of entrées. Specialty entrées can be designed and named to fit the theme. A growing trend is to provide split entrées, which blends the diversity of the buffet with the elegance of a plated service. Sushi boats and bridges have resurfaced in popularity and allow for an Asian flair, with spectacular presentation opportunities.

Trends can also be evidenced in the equipment used by the caterer. Cutting-edge tableware can leave a lasting impression on the guests. For example, cocktail stations are a unique alternative to a traditional reception and present an opportunity to showcase unique and funky plates, bowls, and cutlery. For instance, while guests would not normally expect soup at a cocktail station, the use of stylish shot or

PHOTO 11-2 *Stylish presentation is a key factor in catering.*

PHOTO 11-3 *Shots or sips of soup offer a unique alternative for cocktail stations.*

cordial glasses readily creates this opportunity. Trends in rentals will be discussed in more detail in Chapter 17.

In general, the more upscale the caterer, the more likely that their managers can make things happen. Some caterers will have set menus with little flexibility, whereas high-end businesses will often operate a la carte. Furthermore, if a couple wants specialty equipment that the catering company does not own, the managers may buy it if they see it as cutting edge. They can then rent it to the couple and keep it as inventory for further use. High-end caterers are also more flexible in working with support caterers. For example, if the couple wants one specialty ethnic food item that the caterer does not carry, the primary caterer will work with the support caterer to obtain and showcase the food. By law, the primary caterer cannot pick something up from another restaurant and bring it to the reception; however, if that restaurant delivers the item to the site, the primary caterer will present it in a consistent manner. This flexibility allows the couple to know that the caterer will make the effort to ensure that their food and beverage are perfect.

PHOTO 11-4 *Cutting-edge tableware makes for an elegant presentation.*

TYPES OF SERVICE

The type of service used during the main meal is dictated by the food choices, the formality of the occasion, and the reception site. Three primary types of service presentation are buffet, plated, and French. The necessary wait staff skills vary significantly based on the type of service. Buffet service is less formal and is chosen by couples who value offering a variety of foods from which their guests can choose. The servers are skilled in maintaining the cleanliness of the buffet and making sure that dishes coming close to empty are quickly changed. The caterer does not want guests to look at a chafing dish and be embarrassed to select what looks like the last one of any item or, if standing back a few spots, fear that a given dish will run out before they reach it. The goal for a well-presented buffet is for each guest to see it looking full and beautiful, as if it was in the original state. The buffet style is not convenient to all venues, however. For example, if the reception is held in an historic house that has numerous small rooms with tables situated throughout, negotiating the guests back and forth to a buffet line would cause considerable confusion. For venues such as this, plated service would be recommended.

The majority of the work for plated service is done behind the scenes in the kitchen. Plated service allows for an elegant arrangement of food, where each plate is quickly but carefully prepared and then covered. At the moment the meal is ready to be served, the cover is removed, any sauce that is accompanying a dish is added, and the servers proceed with their plates. Using a technique called a sweep, two or three waiters may work each table to get all the plates out as quickly as possible. This type of service is common to formal weddings but may still be impractical for some venues. For instance, if a site layout is such that the kitchen is on a different level from the dining area and each staff member needs to carry four plates at a time, a considerable amount of movement back and forth would have to occur. If the site is not conducive to plated service, and yet a formal atmosphere is still desired, then French service would be the suggested alternative.

French service is the least common of the three service styles and requires significant skill among the wait staff. With French service, the entire meal for everybody at one table is brought out and served from a single large dish or platter. Each server is white gloved and has to be able to operate a fork and spoon with considerable dexterity. The server must be able to maneuver the platter, utensils, and the food skillfully so that each element of the meal is presented in an attractive manner. This type of service is not very common in the United States because even when carefully done, it is difficult to get the presentation effects that are possible with plated service. However, French service allows each guest to receive individualized attention.

When considering service, it is important to ask the caterer the staffing ratio. At premier venues, you can expect a 1 : 8 or 1 : 10 ratio, which means there will be one server for every 8 to 10 guests. At venues that are less customer-oriented, you are likely to have a 1 : 12 ratio or higher. Buffet meals will require fewer servers than plated or French service. If there is a cocktail hour, often servers will be on hand to pass hors d'oeuvres. For this service, a 1 : 30 or even 1 : 35 ratio is acceptable. In some cultures, food service for weddings is an all-day affair. Countries such as Portugal are famous for their bountiful wedding feasts, as illustrated in Culture Corner, Case 11.2.

FOOD AND BEVERAGE COSTS

The costs associated with food and beverage vary considerably based on the quality, quantity, and variety desired and, perhaps even more significantly, the geographic location of the wedding. Cost of living in the general vicinity will affect food and beverage pricing, and customs within a given locale can dictate expectations of reception fare. For example, in West Virginia the average expenditure is $4,300 for food and service and $1,200 for beverage and bartender, while in

susanne and duarte's wedding in portugal

The Couple: Susanne grew up in Longwood, Florida, whereas Duarte was born and raised in Chaves, Portugal. They met in South Carolina where their mutual love for the outdoors brought them together. The couple chose to marry in Portugal. In recognition of the dual-culture celebration, their wedding invitation was worded in both Portuguese and English. Portuguese was printed on the front of the card and English was printed on the inside.

The Wedding Location: Quinta da Mata is a seventeenth-century manor house owned by Duarte's family and located in Chaves, Portugal. The family operates the house as a bed and breakfast for tourists and hosts weddings on the lush grounds that are situated in the hillside of the Serra da Brunheira. In Portugal, the bride and groom generally have little involvement with the planning. The wedding venue selects the colors, flowers, tableware, and other wedding elements on behalf of the couple.

The Feast: Portuguese weddings are celebrated with an abundance of food. The day began with a 9:30 A.M. bridal breakfast by the pool, where breakfast pastries called natas were served along with fresh fruit, bread, homemade jellies, cheeses, juice, and espresso. After the 12:30 P.M. wedding, the feast began with a great expanse of seafood appetizers such as bolinhos de bacalhau, which is one of over 300 ways that codfish is served in Portugal. Appetizers were followed by a traditional soup called caldo verde and a fresh salad. The next course was the main dish, which for Portuguese weddings is often a roast suckling pig known as leitão, but Susanne vetoed this choice because Susanne, being an animal lover, did not want any baby pigs to suffer for her wedding. Instead, another bacalhau dish was served. Following the lunch meal was an array of 54 mouth-watering desserts, all of which were prepared on site by local pastry chefs and decorative artists. A second stage of seafood followed, this time primarily fresh tiger shrimp and lobster, as well as

(Continues)

local cheeses and bread. The wedding cake was then served accompanied by champagne and punctuated by fireworks. The traditional final course of soup was served at midnight. Wines selected from local vineyards were enjoyed throughout the feast.

Musical Entertainment: Classical Portuguese musicians performed during the ceremony and the main lunch meal. A DJ played modern dance music until early evening. Later in the evening, Duarte's brother, Lipe, played the guitar and accompanied Duarte's godmother, who sang Fado, which is the traditional folk music of Portugal.

Case submitted by Susanne Dubrouillet and Duarte Morais

Massachusetts the cost is essentially double, with food and service averaging $8,400 and beverage and bartender $2,400 (McMurray, 2005). In general, per-person costs can range from $15 to $500 and up, so it is important to familiarize yourself with the range in your community.

For couples on a budget, there are some ways to cut reception costs. Some caterers will allow the couple to purchase the alcohol and then will just charge to pour. You will need to verify this arrangement with the caterer before advising clients to consider this route. Alternatively, your clients may opt to limit the alcohol to beer and wine; however, the price of a good wine can be more expensive than liquor and has fewer servings per bottle. Some couples forego alcohol altogether or just have a champagne toast, which is common in some regions and time frames such as afternoon receptions. A cash bar, where the guests pay for drinks containing alcohol, is another way to save on costs, but this approach may offend the guests and should only be considered if it is a common practice in the region.

If the reception includes a cocktail hour, the couple can save by having the most expensive hors d'oeuvres passed rather than set out on a

Photograph by www.RodneyBailey.com

PHOTO 11-5 *To cut reception costs, some couples will limit alcohol to a champagne toast*

table. For example, if shrimp are presented on a table with an elegant ice boat, guests will flock to the table and devour this pricey item. On the other hand, if a server is walking around with a tray of shrimp, most guests will not take more than one piece at a time. The less expensive items such as vegetables, cheese, and crackers can be set on a table for guests to graze, and considerable savings will result.

Savings should also be realized when feeding children and vendors. When you are sitting down with the caterer, your clients need to be able to estimate how many children will be in attendance. If it is a plated meal, less expensive options should be available to children, who often will not appreciate or even enjoy the adult meal. Similarly, your clients should not feel compelled to feed their vendors the same $65 meal that their guests will receive. This is not to say that they can overlook the vendors, who expect and deserve to be fed. Usually, the caterer can put together a tray of sandwiches, chips, and cookies for the vendors. Keep in mind that all the vendors will want a meal, and whether the band has 2 people or 20 people, you have to include all of them in the budget.

PHOTO 11-6   *A cocktail hour allows guests to mingle while enjoying specialty hors d'oeuvres.*

PHOTO 11-7 *Individual hors d'oeuvres can be priced at $5 per piece or more.*

Related to food and beverage are the associated rentals, which also must be considered in the reception budget. Rentals such as chairs, tableware, and linens may come from the caterer but could be significantly less expensive with an outside vendor. You will need to know the policies of both the caterer and the venue before enlisting outside vendors for these items.

Beyond feasible ways to save, there are perceived cost-cutting measures that should be avoided. Having an unlicensed caterer or a family member acting as chef or bartender may seem like a way to save money, but ultimately this is compromising the safety of the guests. Having food stations instead of a full meal may appear to be cost effective but this is not necessarily the case. Individual hors d'oeuvres can be priced at $5 per piece or more, which will quickly add up if a couple wants six different stations.

the wedding cake

The cake cutting is an anticipated reception moment. Guests love to look at the wedding cake, watch the ceremonial slicing, and determine if the cake tastes as good as it looks. When assisting a couple with the process of selecting a wedding cake, primary considerations are the icing, the flavor, the design, and the size.

The outside of the cake, including the icing and related decorative touches, is more likely to dictate the price per slice than the inside. There are two types of icing: butter cream and fondant. Butter cream is fluffy with a lightly sweet taste. Fondant, on the other hand, is the consistency of putty and therefore is very moldable, allowing for intricate designs. Fondant is heavier, more versatile, has a smooth sheen, and is considerably more expensive because it is labor intensive. For instance, a cake with butter cream icing may run $4 a slice, while the exact same cake with fondant can cost $7 per slice.

Some pastry chefs will only use fondant for wedding cakes because butter cream can and will melt. Other pastry chefs will consider butter cream but only during the cooler months of the year. A drawback of fondant is that, in comparison to butter cream, it is very sweet and not always tasty. Tom Lally of the Alexandria Pastry Shop & Catering Company recommends a layer of butter cream covered with a thin sheet (about 1/8 of an inch) of fondant that can be molded and decorated. This allows couples to have the taste of butter cream and the elegance of fondant. You can read more about Tom in Vendor Spotlight, Case 11.3.

A second decision pertains to the inside flavor of the cake. The taste of the cake is a significant selection consideration, and couples enjoy the process of sampling the different flavors that pastry chefs offer prior to making a final decision. The best pastry chefs bake from scratch using butter and fresh cream, often from local dairies to ensure quality, and do not use preservatives. They also use only fresh fruit and will often import fine chocolate. As explained by Tom Lally, serving a variety of flavors encourages guests to talk about the cake as they compare notes about the various flavors. He states that this also aids in presentation once the cake is cut, as guests get to visually experience the diverse textures. However, multiple flavors can prove to be challenging if one flavor is particularly popular and runs out, potentially leaving some guests disappointed.

A third consideration when selecting a wedding cake is the design. Leslie Goldman-Poyourow of Fancy Cakes by Leslie, featured in Vendor Spotlight, Case 11.4, explains that about 30 percent of her customers come in with a picture but seldom leave wanting that exact design. A picture is an excellent starting place, and the pastry chef can then

PHOTO 11-8 *(opposite) Butter cream icing is fluffy with a lightly sweet taste.*

tom lally

alexandria pastry shop & catering company

What is your background? My degree was in food service and administration, and I have been in some form of food service ever since. After working for a number of restaurants and in bakery sales, I opened my business in 1988 and now have over 40 people on staff. On a yearly basis, we make over 100 wedding cakes and average over 145,000 customers in our shop.

How do you help couples choose a flavor? I ask what they like and encourage them to pick a variety of flavors for the different tiers. Their guests should be talking about the cake, not only how beautiful it is but how great it tastes. It should be something that they can't get just anywhere. Because we operate a pastry shop, we always have fresh samples of all of our flavors on hand for tastings.

What are your signature flavors? Our fruit Bavarian cakes and mousse cakes with fondant are very popular, as is our triple chocolate Bavarian flourless cake. Rather than a groom's cake, most couples get at least one tier that is chocolate. Almost all couples get at least one layer of fruit Bavarian. My personal favorite is milk chocolate praline mousse on a flourless chocolate cake, but I like them all.

What design suggestions do you offer? The design dimension is important, and for clients who don't come in with a firm idea, we have numerous books with pictures of cakes we have done that can spark ideas. It is important to have a good eye for lines, and I think a simple design is more elegant. Using fresh fruit and flowers brings natural scents and beauty to the cake.

(Continues)

PHOTO 11-9 *(opposite) Fondant icing is moldable, allowing for intricate designs.*

What is your greatest accomplishment? We started with nothing and worked very hard to build a successful business. I have sponsored close to a dozen people for their green cards and am proud that they learned from us and then went on to start their own businesses both here and in other countries. We have become a community institution and I enjoy making wedding cakes for brides who have been coming here with their families since they were very young.

Web site: www.alexandriapastry.com

leslie goldman-poyourow

fancy cakes by leslie

How did you get started? I have a business degree and I have always liked to bake. I worked in federal marketing for 20 years and started taking cake-decorating classes for fun and got hooked. Once people began asking for my cakes all the time, I quit my job and opened my business. I have been in business for 10 years and currently make over 400 specialty cakes a year.

What trends are you seeing in cake design? Fashion affects cake design, and there are also cultural influences, such as styles from India where you will see beadwork and vibrant colors. Each of our cakes is unique and I sit down with my clients and we plan out the design, tier by tier.

How long does it take to make a wedding cake? About 12 hours. We make everything from scratch within a day of the wedding. This time includes design, baking, icing, decorating, and delivery.

What special services do you provide? I spend time with my clients. I am almost always the person who answers the telephone because I want people to know I am accessible. Even though I now have a staff, I do the finish work on 90 percent of the cakes. I am known for my sugar flowers, which we make by hand on the premises.

What is your most popular wedding cake? I have a list a mile long of flavors, but for weddings the most popular is white cake with raspberry filling, fondant icing, and sugar flowers. With the icing, we can match any color scheme.

What is the biggest cake you have made? I made a wedding cake for 1,700 people. It was gigantic. It was for a prominent family, and Al and Tipper Gore were at the reception, as well as Hillary Rodham Clinton.

Talk about your Today *show experience.* When I was invited to submit a cake for the *Today* show's Hometown Wedding Series event being held

(Continues)

at the Chesapeake Bay Beach Club, I immediately thought of crabs. So we started making crabs by hand, and the final cake resembled a bushel of crabs. I air brushed the coloring. The second cake, which was the official wedding cake, had four tiers of chocolate fondant with pink accents. The day I won the contest, my phone rang off the hook and everyone wanted the crab cake. Since the show, I have been working double time.

Web site: www.fancycakesbyleslie.com

work with your clients to design their unique look. When setting up vendor appointments, you should schedule the meeting with the pastry chef after the couple has decided on the theme, venues, attire, invitations, and floral décor, as noted in Chapter 8. The pastry appointment should come later because one or several of the previous decisions can dictate the shape and look of the cake. For example, it has become increasingly common for brides to want their cake to reflect their wedding dress. Alternatively, the bride may want the flowers she selects for her bouquet to be mimicked by sugar flowers on the cake.

A final concern, which is related to design, is the size of the cake. This is not solely determined by the number of guests. Depending on the intricacy of the design, couples can realize enormous savings by downsizing the ceremonial cake. Once it is cut and removed to the kitchen for slicing, a sheet cake with butter cream icing can be used to serve the majority of the guests, who will never know the difference. The sheet cake is the same flavor, but does not have the labor intensity of the design or the fondant icing. Accordingly, where the ceremonial cake might cost $5 a slice, the sheet cake can be $2 a slice. Using this scenario, if you are serving 200 guests and half of them are receiving the sheet cake, that equals a savings of $300, where the total cake cost is $700 rather than $1,000. Size will also influence transportation and setup costs. Most wedding cakes are delivered already built, and a representative from the bakery is there to unload and troubleshoot as necessary. A bride and groom without access to a designer pastry chef may consider having their cake shipped from out of town, but this decision can lead to complications similar to those highlighted in Consultant in Action, Case 11.5.

Mini-cakes and cupcakes, with each guest receiving an individually decorated dessert, have risen in popularity but are quite expensive because each cake involves a significant labor investment. Mini-cakes can cost $10 to $15 per person or more. It is easier for a pastry chef to design and make a four-tier cake than 200 miniatures. Couples who love the fun and funky nature of mini-cakes will often buy them for showers or rehearsal dinners where they are only having a limited number of guests.

Timing the cake cutting is very important. Most couples will wait until the last hour of their reception, as the guests will usually stay until the cake is served and the cutting often signals that the reception is coming to an end. After the formalities, the catering staff will take the cake to the back and, if requested, box up the top layer. If the couple wants to save the top layer for their first anniversary, it is recommended that the cake be carefully sealed in wrap that will protect it from freezer burn. Most pastry chefs agree that the cake will not be as good as it tastes on the wedding day, but it should

PHOTO 11-13 *Cupcakes or mini-cakes are often served as an alternative to wedding cake.*

PHOTO 11-10 *(see p. 174) Wedding cake designs often incorporate floral décor.*

PHOTO 11-11 *(see p. 175) The cake table can establish the mood and tone of a wedding.*

PHOTO 11-12 *(see p. 176) Many couples will opt for a small ceremonial cake.*

the upside-down cake

Your client heard of a premier pastry chef who ships extraordinary wedding cakes and ordered a five-tier cake for $4,000 from this vendor, spending an additional $600 for shipping. The cake arrives while you are setting up the reception venue the morning of the wedding. As you work with the caterer to unbox the cake, you are both horrified to realize that it has been shipped upside down, causing the elaborate ribbon design along the top to be crushed. Further more, several of the stabilizing rods had shifted during shipping and the damage to the cake is beyond repair.

What do you do?

Case submitted by Patricia Borosky

be safe as long as quality ingredients have been used. Instead of trying to save the cake for a year, some couples will enjoy it a month after their wedding or will have the top layer remade for their first anniversary.

REFERENCE

McMurray, S. (2005). The Wedding Report: 2006 Statistics and Market Estimates, available from http://www.theweddingreport.com

Consultant Checklist and Reminders for Food, Beverage, and the Wedding Cake

☐ Make sure that the caterer and pastry chef are licensed and insured; permits may also be necessary when using an off-premises caterer.

☐ Bring up any dietary or menu restrictions in the first meeting with any caterer to determine if they can accommodate specialized needs.

☐ Schedule tastings with the caterer and the pastry chef.

☐ Consider a signature drink to match the wedding theme.

☐ Ask caterers to indicate the staffing ratio.

☐ Make sure that taxes, staffing, equipment, delivery, gratuity, and other fees are included in the caterer's proposal estimates.

☐ Determine how long the caterer will need for setup and teardown.

☐ Consider both the formality of the reception and the restrictions of the venue when selecting a service style.

☐ Have the most expensive hors d'oeuvres passed rather than set out on a table.

☐ Consider downsizing the ceremonial cake and supplementing with a sheetcake for cost cutting.

☐ Avoid butter cream icing during warm months due to its tendency to melt.

review questions

1. Name a minimum of four key pieces of information that a caterer must know before a formal proposal can be made.
2. What are at least three things that caterers can do to "wow" potential clients during the proposal phase?
3. Name three trends in catering.
4. Explain the difference between buffet, plated, and French service.
5. What are the four primary considerations when selecting a wedding cake?

terminology

- Buffet service
- Butter cream
- Fondant
- Foodie bride
- French service
- Glatt kosher
- Plated service
- Signature drinks
- Staffing ratio
- Sweep

wedding attire 12
and the bridal party

A woman seldom asks advice before she has bought her wedding clothes.

~ Joseph Addison, in *The Spectator*

Soon after getting engaged, a bride-to-be will begin the process of shopping for her wedding gown. This is one of the most important decisions a bride will make, and the design of the gown can set the tone for the entire wedding. Will the gown be ultraformal with a cathedral-length train, or will it be more casual with a simple colored sash? Will the gown be made of silk, organza, taffeta, lace, or satin? As for color, will it be a classic choice such as white, ivory, or champagne, or will it contain a modern flash of pink, lime, or blue? These are just a few of the many considerations that go into this important decision.

PHOTO 12-1 *(opposite) A gown can set the tone for the whole wedding*

U sually, the bride will purchase her gown without the advice of a wedding consultant; instead, she will visit bridal salons with her mother or a close friend. With that said, it is still important for consultants to be well versed in wedding attire styles and trends. Coordinating the overall look of the wedding will be an important task for the planner. Assisting the bride in matching her gown to other elements, giving advice regarding the selection of the tuxedos, offering options on the flower girl dresses, and perhaps even guiding the mothers as they select their gowns will be areas in which you may be consulted. This chapter will cover trends in bridal attire, menswear, the wedding party, and how to handle wardrobe malfunctions.

bridal attire

Wedding styles come and go, so it is important for a planner to stay on top of the trends through reading the latest trade magazines and visiting bridal fashion shows. You do not want to recommend a gown with long lacy sleeves to a client only to be told that it looks like her mother's gown from the 1970s. Fashion-forward brides look to the runways of Paris and New York for inspiration. Fashion statements made at celebrity events such as the Academy Awards are quickly copied, becoming knockoffs that mainstream retailers offer as bridal attire for the general public. Gowns adorned with lots of "bling" are turning heads on the runway, with beads, crystals, and pearls making statements. Up-to-the-moment gowns can have skirts with tiered tulle layers, voluminous bubble hems, or fabric trim designed by fashion icons such as Vera Wang. Jennifer Johnston, manager of the Vera Wang Bridal Salon at Saks Jandel, discusses the latest wedding gown trends in Vendor Spotlight, Case 12.1.

Today's brides have a wealth of options when it comes to selecting the perfect wedding gown. There are many more fabric choices today than there were even 20 years ago. Materials such as polyester, nylon, rayon, and silk can be woven into a range of stunning fabrics such as brocade, charmeuse, chiffon, crepe back satin, duchesse satin, dupioni, georgette, lace, organza, shantung, taffeta, and velvet. Synthetic materials such as nylon and polyester are more versatile and affordable than pure silk fibers, giving designers more fabric selection than ever, translating into more choices for the bride.

Although there is a vast array of contemporary styles from which to select wedding attire, many brides look back to the fashion icons of yesterday for inspiration on their wedding gowns. Probably the most

PHOTO 12-2 *(opposite) Strapless gowns remain the most popular style*

jennifer johnston
vera wang bridal salon at saks jandel

How did you become interested in wedding gowns? While studying fashion design and merchandising, I realized that my passion was sewing and designing. After attending a couture bridal sewing seminar in Baltimore led by Susan Khalje, I became fascinated with the wedding dress. This seminar challenged me to create and complete a wedding dress in two weeks. This passion for wedding style led me to the Vera Wang Bridal Salon at Saks Jandel, where I have worked for close to nine years.

Describe the Vera Wang style. The first time I saw a Vera Wang bridal gown was in the early 1990s. The model was wearing a gown with long white illusion sleeves, a high neck, and full skirt. Her jet black hair was tied simply with a bow on top of her head. It was mesmerizing and made the Vera Wang style instantly recognizable. Vera uses fabrics not often thought of as "bridal," such as mikado, zibeline, and English net, as well as the traditional duchesse, organza, and lace. Her effect of layering tissue organza and lace over duchesse and organza gives the gown a soft and romantic illusion. Her current collection offers many trim details in black velvet, a striking look against the backdrop of an ivory or white gown.

What are the latest trends in wedding gowns? The bride today is more sophisticated than a few years ago. The trend is for a mermaid style gown, which is a fitted look in the bodice and hip with a flare starting at the knee. This silhouette is a classic cut, modernized by Vera with soft overlays that create an illusion of the fit of the gown underneath. These gowns are accented with sashes of velvet in scrumptious colors of dusty rose, emerald and cobalt.

What are the most popular styles for wedding gowns? The strapless gown reigns in bridal. When Vera introduced the strapless wedding gown several years ago, it was greeted with surprise from our clients, but today it is the norm. Vera creates many other options that are not strapless, but the fit and comfort make this style most prevalent. Options for concealing the bareness of shoulders would include a bolero of lace or matching fabric or heavier veiling. The A-line style is nearly equally as popular. The fit of the bodice makes the waist look smaller, and the shape of the skirt makes the bride look taller.

In what ways do you assist a bride in deciding what style is appropriate for her wedding? Every bride has her own distinctive sense of style. We offer suggestions of dress that are flattering to her figure and that take into consideration the time and location of the wedding as well as the size of the wedding. A large wedding may dictate a more elaborate gown. A church wedding with a long aisle may beg for a more traditional lace gown. A destination wedding on a beach will lend itself to a sheath of crepe back satin with more ease of movement than a ballgown.

Any humorous anecdotes where troubleshooting was necessary? Every young woman's dream of what her wedding day will be like is different from the next, but I will never forget one particular bride who purchased a ballgown from us. When she came for her fitting, the fitter wanted to hem the skirt in the front so she could walk, as it was too long. The bride absolutely refused to allow the skirt to be hemmed and asked that we make tucks in the front of the skirt to resemble "the little birds that held up Cinderella's dress." My alterations staff and I were completely baffled, but did manage to put pinch pleats in the skirt instead of hemming. Of course, the bride was thrilled and had the best wedding day imaginable!

Web site: www.verawang.com

famous wedding gowns of the past half-century were those of Grace Kelly, Jacqueline Kennedy, Princess Diana, and Carolyn Bessette Kennedy. The Philadelphia Museum of Art (2006), current owner of Grace Kelly's wedding gown, notes that the carefully preserved gown is "one of the most popular and beloved objects in the Museum's collection as well as one of the most elegant and best-remembered bridal gowns of all time." To mark the fiftieth anniversary of Grace Kelly's April 19, 1956 marriage to Prince Rainer III of Monaco, the museum staged an enormously popular exhibit of her gown together with other elements from the wedding day including her headdress, veil, shoes, and the lace-and-pearl encrusted prayer book that the bride carried down the aisle (Philadelphia Museum of Art, 2006).

Whether a bride gets her inspiration from yesterday or today, she is not likely to consult with her wedding planner when making her dress selection. She may, however, ask for advice on the top designers or where to shop for the gown and accessories. In addition to Vera Wang, designers such as Reem Acra, Amsale, Carolina Herrera, Monique Lhuillier, and Angel Sanchez are known for bridal attire.

In any given city, there are many options for finding the perfect wedding gown, including stand-alone bridal shops, couture shops with exclusive designer labels, department stores, outlet malls, bridal chains such as David's Bridal, clothing specialists that have moved into wedding attire such as J. Crew, custom designers, and, increasingly, eBay. With more than 9,000 new and used wedding gowns listed for sale on eBay at any given time, the savvy bride can get the dress of her dreams at a reasonable price. This auction site is also an excellent resource for finding bridal accessories. Prices will vary by seller, but are usually a fraction of the retail cost.

The age of the bride will also dictate the wedding dress style. What works for a 20-something may not be comfortable for a bride in her 40s. The term *Camilla style* emerged after the wedding of Prince Charles and Camilla Parker-Bowles, based on the rave reviews the Duchess of Cornwall received for her choice of wedding outfits (BBC News, 2005). Many women have looked to the selections of famous older brides such as Camilla for tasteful and flattering guidance.

With most brides spending $1,000 and up on the dress alone, this is probably the most expensive clothing purchase the bride has ever

PHOTO 12-3 *(see p. 188) Gowns adorned with beading and embroidery make a statement*

PHOTO 12-4 *(see p. 189) Silk duchesse satin is a popular wedding gown fabric*

PHOTO 12-5 *(opposite) Brides may ask for advice regarding where to purchase shoes and accessories*

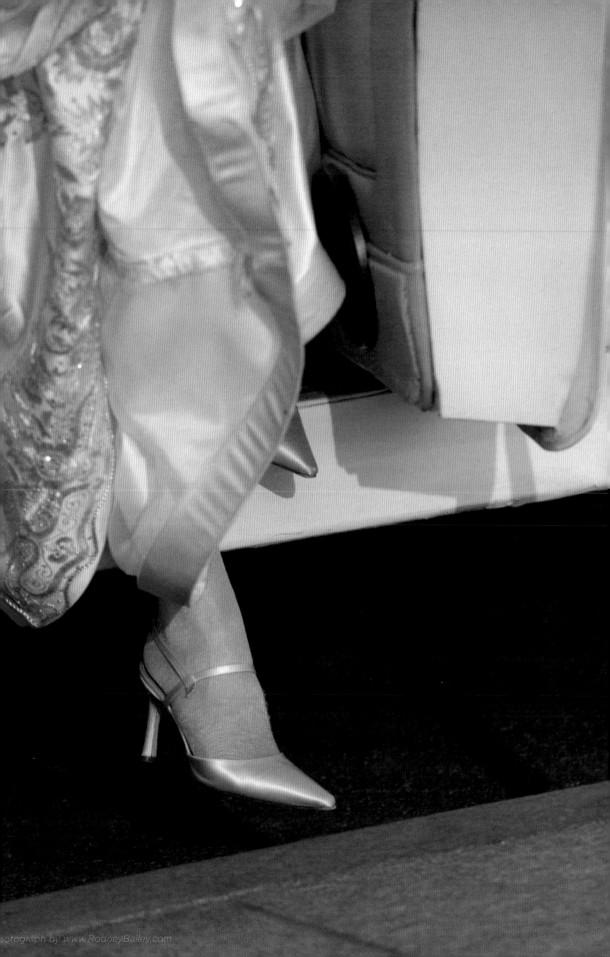

made. If your client seeks your advice on the dress purchase, you can offer the following three tips:

1. Get moving. If a wedding gown is selected less than six months prior to the wedding date, there may be a rush charge placed on the order. This charge can be as much as 25 percent of the cost of the gown.
2. Alteration fees add up. Most brides will pay $150 to $300 in alteration fees alone. Many brides do not account for this cost in the initial budget for attire.
3. Size matters. If the bride is a small size (0 to 2) or a plus size (16 or larger), there may be an extra charge of 10 to 20 percent for the gown depending on the designer. Be prepared to mention this if you know that your client falls into one of these size categories.

Jennifer Johnston explains that time is of the essence. She states that the bride often has no sense of urgency because she may not realize what is involved when starting the planning process. However, there is a rhyme and reason to creating the perfect look, and every step has to be well thought out. After choosing a gown, a bride must then consider her bridesmaids' gowns. After deciding on her hairstyle, she must then decide on hair jewelry and her veil. The veil, in particular, cannot be chosen too carefully. Most favored styles are chapel length with a blusher to cover the face and accented with lace. A lace veil can match a lace gown or complement a very simple, unadorned dress. Matching earrings, bracelet, or necklace should also be given consideration. Gloves and a wrap, either fur or matching fabric, should be considered for fall or winter weddings.

Before the fittings can begin, the bride must choose her shoes and necessary undergarments. The bridal shoes should be comfortable, first and foremost. Together, the bridal accessories complete the look.

Bridal attire and accessories vary significantly by culture. Although the white wedding gown has caught on around the globe, many cultures are still known for distinctive bridal attire. Three of these countries are India, Korea, and Japan, as highlighted in Culture Corner, Cases 12.2, 12.3, and 12.4.

Most brides do not have specific cultural traditions that influence their wedding attire; however, many wish to incorporate four elements in keeping with the sentimental phrase, "Something old, something new, something borrowed, something blue." Your clients will ask you for suggestions in each of these categories, so you can start with the ideas summarized in Table 12.1.

PHOTO 12-6 *(opposite) Lace is a popular embellishment influenced by style icons such as Grace Kelly*

bridal dress, jewelry, and makeup in india

Bridal attire in India is elaborate and stunning. Careful attention is paid to the dress, jewelry, and makeup. The bridal sari is usually made of richly woven red and gold brocade with a gold or silver belt to hold the sari in place. The bride will wear literally dozens of gold and ivory bangles on her arms, as well as richly ornamented gold earrings, necklaces, anklets, toe rings, and a nose gem. The most distinctive piece of jewelry is along the forehead, which is adorned by ornamental gold along the hairline accented by the mang-tikki, which is a round disk set with precious stones. The makeup of the bride is also stunning, with red, wax-like highlighting along the eyebrows and in the center of the forehead accompanied by small gems that are affixed to her skin. The palms of the bride are covered with intricate henna designs.

Source: Hingorani, Kaushal, and Chowdhry (2003).

PHOTO 12-7 *Cultures such as India prefer brightly colored bridal attire*

TABLE 12.1 Sentimental "Something" Selections

Something old: Items in this category usually originate from the bride's mother, grandmother, or mother of the groom. For example, the bride might wear a piece of antique jewelry that has been passed down through her family or the groom's family. Alternatively, the bride might wear a vintage dress that belonged to her mother or grandmother, or she might have lace from a vintage dress incorporated into her own dress, veil, or handkerchief.

Something new: This decision is the easiest, as the bride usually makes a number of attire purchases. However, many wish to select one of these that "counts" as filling the category. If the dress is new, this is typically the chosen representation. Otherwise, her veil, shoes, purse, lingerie, or a decorative hairpin can fit the bill for something new to be worn.

Something borrowed: A bride will often turn to a very dear friend such as the maid of honor or a close family member to borrow something for her wedding day. A bride might borrow the dress worn by a friend or use the purse that a cousin carried on her wedding day. Many brides do not have expensive jewelry, and often a close aunt or old family friend will insist that the bride wear her Tiffany necklace or bracelet.

Something blue: For brides who plan to wear a garter, it is very common to have a piece of blue silk sewn in the garter, as this is a simple way to incorporate blue. If not wearing a garter, a linen handkerchief with blue embroidery is often chosen. While a handkerchief may seem like an old-fashioned idea, it is actually quite practical. Many brides cry during their weddings, and it is nice to have something more attractive than a paper tissue close by. An embroidered handkerchief can also be a lovely keepsake. If blue is the color scheme, a blue ribbon can be used for a hand-tied bouquet. Alternatively, the bride can wear a sapphire or blue topaz bracelet or hairpin.

traditional wedding attire in korea

The earliest records of Korean wedding attire date from the Chosun dynasty, which spanned from 1392 until 1910, as summarized by Hong (2003). Traditional Korean bridal attire includes "Several kinds of underwear, a petticoat, a red skirt decorated with gold-leaf imprints, three kinds of jacket (jeoghori), and a ceremonial green robe (wonsam) or embroidered red robe (whalot). She wore a head crown with ornaments (jokduri or whakwan)" (p. 54). Before the ceremony, the bride's hair was elaborately arranged in two chignons, "the symbol of an unmarried woman" (p. 59). She also wore a headdress covered with jewelry. After the wedding, "the women arranged her hair in a chignon at the nape of her neck and maintained that hairdo for the rest of her life" (p. 59). The bride's hair was adorned with a special pin and hair ribbon. The groom wore an official's robe known as a samokwandae, which was blue or dark purple with a round neckline and wide sleeves. "Tacked to the robe, both in the front and the back, was a large square embroidered with a pair of cranes. A groom wore trousers, a jacket and a coat under his wedding wardrobe" (p. 58). Hong (2003) explains that while Western-style dress has influenced many Korean weddings, "with a recent renewed awareness of traditional Korean culture, upper class grooms and brides are increasingly returning to the more traditional Chosun dynasty wedding dress" (pp. 64–65).

Source: Hong (2003).

japanese wedding kimono

A Japanese bride is an ethereal vision in her beautiful white silk wedding kimono. This stunning garment is often handed down from generation to generation, which makes sense as a new wedding kimono costs between $10,000 and $100,000 US. In addition to the kimono, the bride will wear an elaborate hood over her head to cover up bridal horns, which are part of a headpiece worn prior to the ceremony signifying the horns of jealousy. After the wedding ceremony, the horns are removed as the new bride is freed from the jealousy. The Japanese bride's relatives will also dress in their most formal black or dark kimono for the wedding ceremony. Encircling each waist is an obi, which is a very long piece of fabric usually made of silk and highly embroidered that functions as a cummerbund or large sash to keep the kimono closed. The obi is intricately wrapped around the wearer and tied elaborately in the back. An obi can cost between $500 and $10,000 US. It is not unusual for all members of a Japanese wedding to go to professional kimono dressers in preparation for the wedding. In Japan, men and women study for years to earn a certificate to become a professional kimono dresser. As each kimono has 12 layers, it is imperative that each layer goes on as smoothly and neatly as possible. This is best accomplished with the help of a professional dresser.

PHOTO 12-8 *A Japanese bride and groom with their wedding party at the Meiji Shrine in Japan on the way to their Shinto wedding ceremony*

menswear

What should the groom wear? Do the tuxes all have to match? Can the guys wear their own tuxes? Are khakis appropriate with a navy blue blazer? Can the men wear their own blazers? Should the men's ties match the bridesmaids' gowns? Should groomsmen rent the tux in their hometown or at the wedding destination? Should the men wear white shirts if the bride is wearing an off-white gown? These are just a few of the questions you may get when the couple begins to consider menswear.

When it comes to wedding attire, the bride almost always has a clear idea of what she wants to wear, but, when it comes to the men, the

PHOTO 12-9 *(opposite) Clients will turn to consultants for advice regarding menswear*

wedding consultant will be leaned upon for advice. Educate yourself on men's formal attire by making an appointment to speak with the manager of your local tuxedo shop. Ask how the process works from measuring to ordering to picking up and what the store's policies are. You should have a good working knowledge of the details so that you can guide your clients. Also, when you attend a bridal show, pay attention to the men's fashions so you can advise your grooms on whether a vest is currently in or out and whether or not a cummerbund is passé.

Similar to bridal attire, another good place for discovering what is going on with men's formalwear is the Academy Awards telecast. Watching what the men wear on the red carpet can give you an excellent idea of what is fashionable. Rest assured, if the stars are wearing it today, your clients will be requesting it tomorrow. In some cases, it is the groom's attire that is easily recognizable based on specific cultural traditions, as evidenced in Culture Corner, Case 12.5.

The basic rule of thumb is that groomsmen and bridesmaids should look like they belong together. If bridesmaids are in summery Lilly Pulitzer shifts, the groomsmen should be in casual summer attire like khakis and navy blue blazers. If the groomsmen are in formal black tuxedos, the bridesmaids should be in formal attire as well. If the groomsmen are wearing ties, then by all means they should complement the bridesmaids' dresses. They need not match exactly, but they should work nicely together. Typically, the groom will look slightly different than his groomsmen; for example, the groom might wear a black vest, while the groomsmen have burgundy to match the bridesmaids' dresses.

the wedding party

In terms of bridesmaids' dresses, knee-length and below-knee styles are currently the most popular. Jennifer Johnston states that when designed with such fabrics as crepe back satin and chiffon, these shorter styles can be worn for both late afternoon and evening weddings. Bridesmaids' dresses generally match but need not be identical. A current trend involves selecting bridesmaids' dresses that are made of the same fabric but that come in a variety of styles to suit different body types.

The bride will usually select the attire for her bridesmaids, sometimes with their help and sometimes without any input at all. A planner is rarely consulted about this decision. However, you will probably be asked where to purchase accessories for the bridesmaids such as

PHOTO 12-10 *(opposite) Currently, cummerbunds are out of style*

the groom's attire in scotland

In Scotland, it is the groom's attire that is particularly noteworthy, including the tartan kilt, the sporran, and the dirk. The tartan kilt is an easily recognized Celtic garment, with colors and plaid patterns that represent the wearer's clan. A groom in Highland attire also wears a fur pouch, known as a sporran, and a small dirk, which is a traditional Scottish knife. The bride may wear a clan tartan shawl with her contemporary dress. Traditional Scottish dress and the romantic mood that accompanies this culture's traditions are so appealing that many couples who are not of Scottish descent have Celtic-themed weddings in order to momentarily step into the past.

Sources: Spangenberg (2001); Winge and Eicher (2003).

PHOTO 12-11 (top) Some bridesmaids' dresses are identical and chosen to echo the bride's gown

PHOTO 12-12 (bottom) Other bridesmaids' dresses are matched in terms of color and fabric but vary in design to complement various body types

shoes, wraps, jewelry, hair accessories, purses, gloves, and undergarments. Be prepared with a list of stores that you know and trust.

The groomsmen's tuxedos are usually acquired from the same location as the groom's. It is typical for the groom's tuxedo to be rented without charge if there are enough groomsmen (usually at least four) who are renting formalwear from the same store. Determine if your local tuxedo shop rents tuxedoes for infants and toddlers, as parents of the youngest of the young may want to dress their children to the nines for a formal wedding. The ring bearer in particular will need to be outfitted in a tuxedo. Similarly, the bride may wish to have a small replica of her gown made for the flower girl. Knowing a designer who specializes in this area will come in handy.

Pets are being incorporated more frequently into wedding celebrations. Just like the other members of the wedding party, they will need special attire for the wedding day. You should arm yourself with information on where to order special dog tuxes and other formalwear because sooner or later, you will be asked for a recommendation. If your local pet shop does not stock such items, there are terrific online resources such as trixieandpeanut.com that cater to chic dogs and cats alike. No detail is too small when considering wedding attire. The best wedding consultants can assist with finding appropriate wedding attire for the entire wedding party.

wardrobe malfunctions

Probably even more important than knowing where to buy or rent wedding attire is the wedding consultant's ability to fix a wardrobe malfunction on the day of the wedding. Count on something becoming undone, unfastened, unsightly, or falling apart at some point during the wedding day. It will be up to you to work your magic with the tools in your well-stocked emergency kit (the contents of which are discussed in Chapter 20). A needle and thread, a large safety pin, and baby wipes have come to the rescue at many weddings. When it comes to clothing, be prepared for a multitude of disasters from straps breaking to heels snapping off. With so many people involved in the wedding party, a wardrobe malfunction is guaranteed to happen. Two examples of attire crises are given in Consultant in Action, Cases 12.6 and 12.7.

In addition to fixing clothing problems, the most important clothing-related skills for a wedding planner to master are: (1) how to bustle a bride's train; and (2) how to knot a tie or bow tie. Bustling the bride's train is an important precaution to keep the gown from getting soiled

PHOTO 12-13 *(opposite)Pets need formal attire for the wedding day, too*

bust a gut

Your fun-loving client, Sasha, went with her mother to pick out a lovely and expensive gown eight months before the wedding. Sasha elected to purchase a size 8 instead of her normal size 10, vowing to lose the necessary 10 pounds so the dress would fit on her wedding day. Under significant work stress, she actually gained 10 pounds and during her final fitting the seamstress let out the side panels as much as possible. The seamstress suggested adding extra material, but Sasha was satisfied and didn't want to ruin the design. On the morning of the wedding, Sasha put on the somewhat uncomfortable garment, taking the teasing of her bridesmaids in stride while she "sucked-it-in" as her mother tugged up the zipper. Fifteen minutes prior to walking down the aisle, her best friend told a great joke. As Sasha erupted in laughter, her zipper busts, leaving a 6-inch split in the fabric.

What do you do?

Case submitted by Patricia Borosky

the grass is greener

Although the wedding day of your clients, Emma and Alberto, started out soggy and rainy, the weather clears two hours before the wedding, much to their delight. They are anxious to get their pre-wedding outdoor photographs taken at the nearby rose garden, as the weather is expected to turn again. They rush off to the park, where the photographer takes pictures of the couple throughout the gardens, including sitting on the famous stone walls, standing against the beautiful wrought-iron railings, and posed amidst the many gorgeous roses. As they wrap up the photo shoot, Alberto points out to Emma that the back and hem of her tailored ivory gown are now covered in mud and grass stains.

What do you do?

Case contributed by Patricia Borosky

and to keep the bride from tripping during the reception. Reviewing the bustling procedure with the bridal shop prior to the wedding day is an excellent idea because each gown is bustled slightly differently. Many bustles, if not designed correctly, will come undone during the reception. Be prepared to remedy this situation with items from your emergency kit such as a needle and thread or oversized safety pins.

Also, knowing how to knot a man's tie is a skill every wedding consultant must have. On the day of the wedding, the groom may be too nervous to knot his own bow tie, or it could be the first time many of the groomsmen have ever worn a bow tie. Make sure you can knot the tie quickly and fashionably. Similarly, the skill of being able to tie eight bridesmaids' sashes into perfect bows before they head down the aisle will carry you far in your career as a wedding consultant.

REFERENCES

BBC News. (2005, April 10). Fashionistas praise Camilla style, available at http://news.bbc.co.uk

Hingorani, J., Kaushal, N., and Chowdhry, D. (2003). The Indian bride, available at http://www.indianslivingabroad.com

Hong, N. Y. (2003). Korean wedding dress from the Chosun Dynasty (1392–1910) to the present. In H. B. Foster and D. C. Johnson (eds.), *Wedding Dress across Cultures* (pp. 53–65). New York: Berg.

Philadelphia Museum of Art. (2006, January 13). Museum Offers Rare Look at Grace Kelly's Wedding Dress April 1—May 21, 2006, available at http://philamuseum.org/press/releases/2006/492.html

Spangenberg, L. M. (2001). *Timeless Traditions: A Couple's Guide to Wedding Customs around the World*. New York: Universe Publishing.

Winge, T. M., and Eicher, J. B. (2003). The American groom wore a Celtic kilt: Theme weddings as carnivalesque events. In H. B. Foster and D. C. Johnson (eds.), *Wedding Dress across Cultures* (pp. 207–218). New York: Berg.

Consultant Checklist and Reminders for Wedding Attire

☐ Set the tone for the wedding with the wedding gown.

☐ Become familiar with wedding gown shops in your area.

☐ Make sure you are up-to-speed on current fashion trends.

☐ Educate yourself on menswear styles.

☐ See that groomsmen and bridesmaids look like they belong together.

☐ Make sure your client knows about rush charges, alteration fees, and additional charges for gowns that are smaller or larger than average.

☐ Give the bride plenty of options regarding where to purchase accessories.

☐ Don't be surprised if you are asked to order a tux for a dog or cat.

☐ Be prepared for wardrobe malfunctions.

☐ Know how to bustle a train and knot a bow tie.

review questions

1. Name three wedding gown designers.

2. Name five different types of fabric used for wedding gowns.

3. Name two style icons from the past half-century.

4. Name five places to buy a wedding gown.

terminology

- Alteration fees
- Bustle
- Camilla style
- Cummerbund
- Fashion forward
- Fashion icons
- Illusion neckline
- Knockoffs
- Princess silhouette
- Strapless gown

the ceremony

The meaning of marriage ultimately comes back to the moment when two individuals publicly pledge their commitment to one another. Therefore, planning the ceremony should be of utmost importance, as the words and symbols used represent what is internationally appreciated as a sacred union. This chapter offers an overview of the ceremony and how its inherent parts are uniquely represented in weddings around the world. Furthermore, examples of how different traditions can be blended for intercultural and interfaith ceremonies will be offered. Aspects that are present in most wedding ceremonies include (1) the celebrant; (2) readings and vows; (3) the exchange of rings and special artifacts; and (4) the ceremony program. The chapter will conclude with considerations regarding guidelines and policies.

PHOTO 13-1 *(opposite) Planning the ceremony is of utmost importance*

☙ the celebrant

The celebrant or officiant of a wedding is seen as the guiding force behind the ceremony. The necessary training needed to wed two individuals differs from culture to culture and religion to religion. As a wedding consultant, you must always respect and defer to the celebrant's wishes. In places of worship, celebrants are known as being very territorial, and rightly so. Some ceremony venues do not even permit a wedding consultant to be present, as they handle all ceremony planning internally. It is not your place to tell a celebrant how the wedding ceremony should run. Instead, listen very carefully and become familiar with the rules and policies of each ceremony site. Over time, you will gain the trust and respect of these valuable leaders.

One way you can gain the admiration of celebrants of different cultures is to learn and remember their titles. Table 13.1 offers an alphabetical listing of various religions, the common place of worship, the associated leader, and the sacred text.

While Table 13.1 offers some general guidelines, keep in mind that significant variations exist within each category. For example, there are three types of Judaism: Orthodox, Conservative, and Reform. Furthermore, as discussed in Chapter 2, over 1,000 different denominations comprise Christianity, further categorized into 15 groupings (Robinson, 2005). To lump all these various groups together and suggest they all follow the same guidelines for weddings would be inappropriate. Give yourself time. After a few years of working with a

TABLE 13.1 Religions Around the World

Religion	Place of Worship	Title of Leader	Sacred Text
Baha'i Faith	House of Worship	Lay Leader	Most Holy Book
Buddhism	Temple	Priest	The Tripitaka
Christianity	Church, Cathedral, Temple or Mission	Pastor, Priest, Minister, Reverend	The Bible
Confucianism	Temple, Shrine, Seowan	N/A	Lun Yu
Hinduism	Temple	Priest	The Vedas
Islam	Mosque	Imam	Qur'an and Hadith
Jainism	Temple	Priest, Pandit	Siddhanta, Pakrit
Judaism	Synagogue	Rabbi	Torah, Talmud, Likrat Shabbat
Shamanism and Tribal Religions	In Nature	Shaman	Oral Tradition
Sikhism	Gurdwaras	Granthi	Guru Granth Sahib
Taoism	Temple	N/A	Tao-te-Ching

Source: Adapted from Robinson (2005).

ellen and pierre's interfaith and interracial wedding

The Couple: Ellen is Caucasian and practices Conservative Judaism, while Pierre is affiliated with the African American-based National Baptist Convention. The couple met in graduate school and dated for nine years before becoming engaged. Prior to proposing, Pierre spoke with both sets of parents to affirm their support of the union and to ask for their blessings.

Co-celebrants: A Reform Jewish rabbi and a Christian Methodist Episcopal (CME) minister joined in the co-celebration. The two officiants entered together and alternated in delivering readings, priestly blessings, and the drashah (charge to the couple) in Hebrew and English. The rabbi wore a traditional Jewish prayer shawl known as a tallit, while the minister wore a clergy collar and a shawl of African kente cloth.

Jewish Elements: As is required for kidushin (Jewish marriage ceremonies), Ellen and Pierre did not wed on the Sabbath, waiting until after sundown on Saturday. Regardless of religious affiliation, each male guest was requested to wear a kippah or yarmulke, a skullcap worn in a Jewish house of worship or consecrated area to show respect for the Lord. The ceremony and reception were held in a hotel, which is common in interfaith marriages, and also facilitated the logistics for many out of town guests. While a secular setting, a sacred area was established by installing a four-poled floral chuppah, a canopy representing the Jewish home. As marriage is the union of communities, the bride and groom were individually escorted down the aisle by their parents and joined standing under the chuppah by the officiants, wedding party, and families. During the ceremony, the ketubah was read—a marriage proclamation signed in a private ceremony by Ellen and Pierre prior to the service—as well as verses from the Jewish Prayer Book, Likrat Shabbat, and Song of Songs. Following recitation of the Seven Wedding Blessings, the couple drank from a kiddush cup during the wine ceremony. At the conclusion of the service, Pierre participated

(Continues)

in breaking the glass. This custom originally symbolized the destruction of the temple and the fragility of life; however, in contemporary times it has come to represent the idea that no vessel can contain the amount of joy experienced in the coming together of two to make one. At the reception, following a heartfelt toast by Pierre's Best Man, Ellen's uncle recited traditional Hebrew blessings over the wine and bread. Following the meal, all joined in dancing to the hora, an Israeli circular folk dance.

African American Elements: Several African American elements were present in Ellen and Pierre's ceremony. The groom's brother read the poem "We Unaccustomed to Courage" by Maya Angelou, which reflects upon how love leads to freedom and life. In addition, a passage from *The Prophet* by Kahil Gibran was delivered by the officiants, as was a discussion of the tradition of the broom. Historically, African American slaves were forbidden to marry; jumping the broom became the ritual by which marriage was pursued. The broom was used as a symbol of family, creation of a new home, removal of evil from a joyous event, and acceptance of new obligations. Entering the reception, Ellen and Pierre jumped the broom to remember the struggles of their shared past and to pay homage to their ancestors for their legacy.

The Program: Ellen and Pierre designed a wedding program that presented not only the chronology of the ceremony, but a detailed explanation of the many religious and cultural elements interwoven throughout the service. In this way, family and friends were better able to appreciate the festivities and to share a more thorough understanding of Ellen and Pierre's respective and cherished traditions.

Case submitted by Ellen and Pierre Rodgers

PHOTO 13-2 *Nontraditional venues are often chosen for wedding ceremonies*

variety of clients, you will become familiar with the primary places of worship and the associated leaders in your area. Though not always the case, many religious leaders are open to learning about other religions and will even join in a co-celebration, also sometimes referred to as a concelebration, which means that the religious service has two leaders, as illustrated in Culture Corner, Case 13.1.

For some cross-cultural weddings, having co-celebrants may not be desirable or feasible, but it may still be the case that a couple with different religious backgrounds wishes to have both faiths represented. Couples facing this situation might consider having two separate ceremonies, as shown in Culture Corner, Case 13.2. If your clients do not wish to have a religious ceremony, they can turn to a marriage commissioner, justice of the peace, or judge to act as the celebrant.

readings and vows

Most weddings include readings and a formal exchange of vows. Readings are generally selected by the couple or the celebrant and, for religious ceremonies, are typically taken from the sacred text of the faith.

allyce and hassan's wedding: two faiths and two ceremonies

The Couple: Allyce was born in Canada and raised in America in the Presbyterian faith. Hassan was born and raised in Iran and educated in London and the United States. Hassan's parents are devout Muslims, while Hassan has a more Westernized approach to the Islam faith. Allyce and Hassan met in college and, when they decided to marry, knew that while their parents would be supportive, both sets would want the ceremony to be specific to their religion. They decided to have two ceremonies to please their parents.

The Muslim Ceremony: The Muslim ceremony was very Westernized in that the men and women were seated in the same room and many of the traditions were bypassed. It was also held in a rented beach-front property rather than a mosque. Had the ceremony taken place in Iran, where the majority of Hassan's family lives, it would have been much more traditional. The Muslim celebrant is known as an Imam and he read from the Qur'an, which is the sacred text. The readings were in Arabic, but the Imam then explained the meaning to the guests not familiar with the language or the Muslim faith. Allyce and Hassan also signed a nikahnama, which is the Muslim marriage contract. Allyce took a ceremonial Persian (Farsi) name, which was Parvanèh (meaning butterfly). After the ceremony, photographs were taken with Allyce wearing a shawl that covered her arms and back. These images were taken specifically so they could be sent to Hassan's family in Iran, where being covered is an important sign of respect. Allyce also wore many gold bracelets that were sent to her as gifts from Hassan's relatives in Iran. Gold jewelry is very commonly given to Iranian brides.

The Presbyterian Ceremony: Shortly after the Muslim ceremony was complete, the wedding party and guests went to a Presbyterian church, where the second ceremony took place. Here, a reverend acted as the celebrant. Rather than a reading from the Bible, the Christian sacred text, the couple chose as their first reading Max Erhmann's famous poem "Desiderata", which details how to live a peaceful life. This was followed by a homily, which is a talk given by the celebrant and then the exchange of vows. The couple also lit a unity candle, which is common in many Christian wedding ceremonies.

The Reception: The wedding party and guests returned to the beach property, where they enjoyed both seafood and traditional Persian food including javaher polow (jeweled rice: made with chicken and different colored foods like orange peel, barberries, carrot strips, almonds and pistachios, all layered with rice to look like jewels on the plate), dolmeh barg mow (stuffed vine leaves), kabab hosseini (skewers of meat, onions, peppers, and tomatoes), and Persian pastries.

Case submitted by Page Karami-Adgani

These sacred texts are summarized in Table 13.1. Many of these texts have readings that are commonly chosen for weddings. For example, in the Christian faith, the Old Testament reading Genesis 2:18–24, which speaks of the creation of woman from Adam's rib so that he would not be alone, is a classic wedding reading. Also frequently selected is the New Testament reading, 1 Corinthians 12:31–13:8a which details the importance of love. Other common Bible readings are John 15:1–17 and Matthew 22:35–40, both of which speak of love.

Many couples select readings that are not found in religious texts, but are spiritual and meaningful to them nonetheless. Prose and poetry about love or nature written by famous authors such as Maya Angelou, Charlotte Brontë, Emily Brontë, Elizabeth Barrett Browning, e. e. cummings, Robert Frost, Langston Hughes, Shakespeare, Walt Whitman, and William Butler Yeats provide endless options for wedding readings.

Readings offer couples the opportunity to include more individuals in the wedding party. While the couple may want to limit the number of attendants, they can readily involve two to four more friends or family members by having them read during the ceremony. Advise your clients to select readers carefully, as many people are not comfortable speaking publicly. Readings should be selected and distributed to the appropriate individuals at least one month in advance of the wedding so there will be plenty of time for review. Furthermore, each reader should practice out loud at least once, preferably twice, during the wedding rehearsal to become familiar with the acoustics of the venue and so they will be comfortable with being "on stage."

Readings are also an excellent way to blend diverse cultures. For example, at one wedding where the bride's family was from Japan and the groom's family was American, the same readings were delivered first in Japanese and then in English. This approach allowed for a common experience and understanding among all the guests, which was particularly important because although the wedding was held in the United States, over 30 guests flew in from Japan to attend, most of whom were not fluent in English. The dual reading format also broadened this couple's ability to involve many friends from both countries.

The exchange of wedding vows brings the commitment of the couple to the forefront, as this is when they publicly declare their love. Standard wedding vows are led by the celebrant, who asks the bride and the groom independently if each wishes to take the other as a spouse and will vow to love, cherish, honor, comfort, and be true in times of good and bad, sickness and health, and forsaking all others for as long as each shall live. The terminology differs slightly based on religious denomination, and the traditional term "obey" has been removed from most versions. For nondenominational vows and civil ceremonies, similar phrasing is used, but the vows are read by the couple rather than recited by the celebrant.

TABLE 13.2 Steps for Writing Vows

1. *Talk to your celebrant.* Before you get started, make sure that there are no restrictions as to what the vows can include. Some places of worship will not allow couples to write their own vows, so you do not want to start the process until you have approval.
2. *Begin separately.* You should each set some time aside to write down ideas. Begin with the phrase: "I love (insert name) because..." or "I want to marry (insert name) because..." Do not overanalyze or edit at this point. Just create a list of words and phrases. At the completion of the brainstorming list, write a rough paragraph compiling the ideas.
3. *Compare notes.* Pick a time where you can get together in a setting that is comfortable, relaxing, and private. Perhaps bring a picnic to a local park. If you are working from home, turn off the television and your cell phones. Each of you should take turns reading your ideas. This is a good time to start getting used to reading the vows out loud. See what you have in common. This should be a fun and spontaneous time, so encourage each other.
4. *Do not force the same wording.* Many couples want to recite the same exact vows, but this is not essential. There may be a distinctive or important characteristic that you love about your spouse-to-be that you really want to include in the vows (e.g., eye color, career type), but this same characteristic does not apply to you. Allow the uniqueness of each individual to be expressed in the vows if you so choose.
5. *Create a draft.* Work together to create a draft. Tag team with the writing so that this is a truly shared effort.
6. *Wait a week.* Set the project aside for a week and then pick it back up. Each of you should read the vows out loud. If you still love what you wrote, you are ready to go. If you find there are a couple of awkward phrases, fine tune at this point. Share the final draft with your celebrant for approval.
7. *Finalize and beautify.* Your vows are a keepsake, so prepare at least two copies. The copy used for the ceremony should be beautiful but also functional. Use a large font size (at least 16-point) for readability. Consider laminating this copy so that the guests hear your voices rather than the rustle of paper. You should be able to fit this copy of the vows on a half sheet of paper, so that it is not overwhelming in size and is easy to hold. Even if you decide to memorize your vows, make this copy and keep it close by during the ceremony, just in case. For the second copy, you may want to enlist a calligrapher or have your stationery specialist use a beautiful font on elegant paper that can be framed and kept as a constant reminder of your pledge to one another.

As weddings become more individualized, couples are increasingly opting to write their own vows. If your clients elect this route, encourage them to start the process early so it can be a fun and creative endeavor rather than an event wrought with stress. The vows should not go on forever, so encourage your clients to limit them to a maximum of six lines. Table 13.2 includes steps for writing vows that you can share with your clients.

✎ the exchange of rings and special artifacts

The exchange of rings is one of many symbolic acts that occur during weddings where specific artifacts are needed. The movement to a double ring ceremony was discussed in Chapter 4, where the marketing endeavors that influenced this tradition are highlighted. The style of the ring is often embedded with history, as exemplified with the Irish Claddagh ring, introduced in Chapter 2.

In some cultures, the exchange of rings is just one of many artifacts used during the ceremony. Cultures and faiths around the globe have beautiful and unique ceremonial traditions, and entire texts have been devoted to the subject (e.g., Spangenberg, 2001). Five groups that use particularly unique representations during the ceremony are those celebrating Jewish, Hindu, Greek Orthodox, Korean, and Mexican weddings.

Many Jewish wedding artifacts are detailed in the Culture Corner, Case 13.1. Images in this chapter illustrate the yarmulke, chuppah, tallit, and

Photograph by www.Photos4Life.com

PHOTO 13-3 *The exchange of rings is highly symbolic*

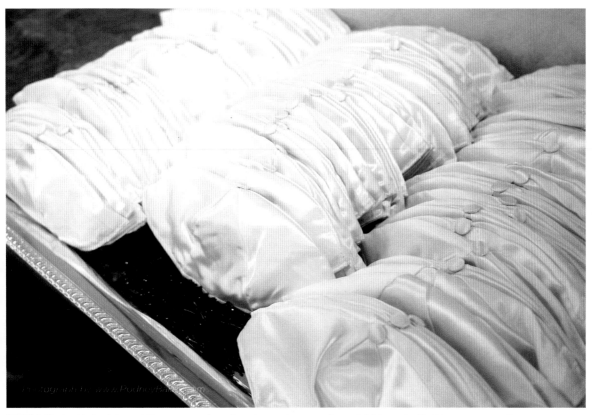

PHOTO 13-4 *At Jewish wedding ceremonies, all male guests regardless of faith are invited to wear yarmulkes*

breaking of the glass. Images of a ketubah and the Likrat Shabbat can be found in Chapters 18 and 27, respectively.

Beyond Indian bridal attire, which is discussed in Chapter 12, the Hindu mandap, floral garlands, and the pouring of rice are three additional artifacts illustrated in this chapter that are common to many Indian weddings. A Hindu wedding can last several days and may even include ceremonial rides on a horse or elephant.

During Greek Orthodox ceremonies, the couple has special sponsors, known as the koumbaro and the koumbara, who assist with three primary artifacts of religious significance. First, the sponsors assist in the exchange of rings, which takes place three times as a symbol of strength. The sponsors are also involved with the interchange of wedding crowns known as stephana, which are held together with a white ribbon to symbolize the unity of the couple. Finally, the sponsors accompany the couple as they walk around a table or altar three times, representing their journey.

In addition to Korean wedding attire, discussed in Chapter 12, two particularly important ceremonial traditions with associated artifacts

PHOTO 13-8 *The pouring of rice is one of many Hindu wedding traditions*

are the sharing of drink and the presentation of wild geese. The sharing of rice wine and exchanges of kowtow, which include bowing, kneeling, and touching foreheads to the ground, suggest commitment, harmony, and respect (Hong, 2003). The presentation of either live or wooden wild geese symbolizes fertility and fidelity, as wild geese have many goslings and mate for life (Hong, 2003).

Two important Mexican traditions include the arras and the lazo. A set of wedding arras is comprised of 13 gold or silver coins presented to the couple in a small chest that represent Jesus Christ and his 12 apostles and symbolize wealth and strength. The lazo (lasso) is a cord, rope, or oversized string of rosary beads placed around the shoulders of the couple and symbolizes the love that binds the couple together.

PHOTO 13-5 *(see p. 224) A Jewish tallit unites the couple*

PHOTO 13-6 *(see p. 225) The chuppah is a symbol of the Jewish home while the breaking of the glass is a much anticipated moment*

PHOTO 13-7 *(see p. 226) Mandaps provide a beautiful focal point for Hindu weddings, and elaborate garlands are worn by the bride and groom*

The Marriage Celebration of

Laura Lynn Cogar

and

Edward Andrew Hayes

August Sixteenth

Two Thousand and Eight

Brookside Gardens

Celebrant

Dr. Mary Hares

Parents

Jimmy and Marita Cogar

and

Connor Hayes and Tina Myress

Bridal Party

Maid of Honor	Best Man
Janet Cogar	Sean Hayes

Bridesmaids	Groomsmen
Lori McCaslin	Carl Gianotti
Carol Hayes	Rick Less
Rosemarie Myress	Andre Cogar

Flower Girl	Ring Bearer
Brooke McCaslin	Luke Prest

Prelude	Evergreen
Processional	Unforgettable
First Reading	Friendship
	Read by Susan Iacasse
Solo	All I Ask of You
	Soloist: Bree D'Amico
Second Reading	Nature
	Read by Janice Hayes
Sign of Peace	What a Wonderful World
Reflection	Meaning of Marriage
	Dr. Mary Hares

Exchange of Wedding Vows

Presentation of the Rings

Exchange of Rings

Declaration of Marriage

Recessional	From this Moment On

Thank you for sharing this joyous day with us!

FIGURE 13.1 *(top) Sample Ceremony Program*

PHOTO 13-9 *(opposite) Unique ceremony moments are often introduced in the ceremony program*

the ceremony program

The ceremony program, discussed further in Chapter 18, ties all the pieces of the wedding ceremony together. Figure 13.1 offers a generic example of a program to illustrate the main information that is included: full names of the couple, date, venue, parents, bridal party, an overview of the order of service, and a note of appreciation. In general, programs should be kept short so that the ceremony will speak for itself. However, it can be very helpful to provide information on unique practices that will take place in the ceremony, in particular if many of the guests do not share the cultural or religious background from which these practices originate. Culture Corner, Case 13.1 presented earlier in this chapter offers an excellent rationale for including a program to increase the guests' appreciation of blended traditions.

guidelines and policies

Bear in mind that many ceremonies have guidelines and policies that can affect the experience of all involved. For example, when you work with your first Catholic or Greek Orthodox couple, you may be surprised at the length of the ceremonies common to these faiths. If standing is required throughout, lightheadedness abounds, and situations like the one found in Consultant in Action, Case 13.3 become more frequent. Encourage the bridal party in any wedding to stand with one foot slightly in front of the other. This helps prevent the knees from locking and decreases the swoon-factor significantly. Every wedding consultant has a fainting story, as illustrated in Case 13.3, but you want to do what you can to minimize these occurrences.

Some faiths have policies regarding when couples can marry. For example, traditionally, the Jewish faith does not permit weddings on the Sabbath or holidays or during two extended periods, one following Passover and the other preceding the fast day on the ninth of Av (a day of mourning to commemorate the many tragedies in Jewish history) in the summer. A local rabbi is your best guide when determining these restrictions. In some faiths, policies also exist regarding those who can be present during the ceremony. For instance, when a marriage ceremony called a sealing ordinance takes place in a temple of The Church of Jesus Christ of Latter-day Saints (LDS or Mormon), only those who hold a valid temple recommend—a document certifying that the holder is in good standing with the faith—can attend the ceremony. Thus, without this document even immediate family members cannot be present. This policy can cause confusion and hurt feelings for those not familiar with LDS doctrines and practices. However, many in the Mormon faith are sensitive to these feelings and will go to great lengths to make nonmember friends and relatives who cannot attend the ceremony feel welcome and involved, as illustrated in Culture Corner, Case 13.4.

the disappearing altar boy

The formal Catholic wedding of Laura and Mark is progressing nicely as the storybook couple and their 20 attendants (10 on each side) gather around the altar and are listening to the priest as he gives a homily pertaining to the couple's future as husband and wife. The church is crowded and quite warm during the late summer wedding. Just when you think the ceremony is under control, you see a 10-year-old altar boy quietly slump to the ground behind the priest. Because the wedding party is so big and there are several altar boys, no one at the altar or in the congregation appears to have seen the boy fall.

What do you do?

Case submitted by Diane Haworth

the wedding of katie and steve: the temple sealing ordinance

The Couple: Katie and Steve belong to The Church of Jesus Christ
of Latter-day Saints (LDS or Mormon) and wanted to have a temple
marriage. While the couple and Steve's parents had temple recommends,
Katie's mother does not practice the LDS faith. She respects the faith
and was in full support of the couple's desire for a temple sealing. In
order to prepare nonmember guests, the invitations announced that
the marriage would be solemnized in the Mesa Arizona Temple and
indicated that guests were cordially invited to attend the ring ceremony
and reception. The time of the sealing ordinance is purposefully not
provided on the invitation, as this information could create confusion.

The Temple Sealing Ordinance: The marriage sealing is a very sacred and
solemn experience. The temple is only used for specific ordinances and
is different from the meeting houses that are used for weekly services.
While any visitor can enter a meeting house, to enter the temple
requires a valid temple recommend, which is the card that indicates
good standing with the church. Katie was escorted to the bridal room
and Steve to a changing room, where each exchanged their street clothes
for modest white garments, as required when receiving an ordinance.
Katie was able to wear her modest white wedding gown but not a veil,
while Steve changed into white clothing specifically for the sealing.
They then received counsel from a representative of the temple
presidency prior to being ushered into the sealing room. Only the
closest of friends and immediate family were present at the ordinance,
as sealing rooms generally hold less than 20 people. Many friends with
valid temple recommends did not attend in respect for the sanctity of
the ordinance. The LDS sealing means that the bride and groom are
sealed both during mortal life and after death. In keeping with the rules
of the temple, there is no exchange of rings, no wedding party is
allowed, and no photographs or video can be taken. Katie and Steve
kneeled across from each other at an altar in the center of the room and
held hands. Rather than an exchange of vows, the marriage ordinance is

recited to them by an officiator who holds the proper priesthood authority. The wording is the same for every Mormon temple wedding and acts to seal the marriage for eternity.

The Greeting: As is common for many Mormon weddings, close friends and family members were waiting outside of the temple to greet and congratulate the newlyweds. After exiting the sealing room and before leaving the temple, Steve changed into his tuxedo and Katie put on her bridal veil. Photographs were taken once the couple was outside of the temple.

The Ring Ceremony: Similar to many Mormon couples who have large groups of friends and family, Katie and Steve had a ring ceremony that all guests could attend. This was held at their reception site and included a wedding party with bridesmaids and groomsmen. Like other Christian ceremonies, Katie's father walked her down the aisle, there were readings, music, speeches, and a friend from their church led them through the exchange of rings.

Policies may also be in place regarding second marriages. For example, in the Catholic faith, if either the bride or the groom has been divorced, the previous marriage must officially be annulled by a Catholic tribunal in order for the ceremony to take place in a Catholic church. The annulment process is extremely involved, usually taking over a year to complete and including a written petition, witnesses, and formal hearing. The outcome is that, in the eyes of the Roman Catholic Church, the marriage is voided as if it never took place. A couple following the Mormon faith must undergo a similar process if they wish their marriage to be unsealed.

Some couples are forbidden by law to marry, or cannot marry due to extenuating circumstances. However, many couples without the ability to legally marry still desire to have their relationship publicly recognized. As discussed in Chapter 5, same-sex couples are unable to legally marry in many countries, giving rise to commitment ceremonies where they symbolically form a union. Others may want to marry but cannot form a legal union because it would cause them to lose certain benefits that they cannot do without. For example, some individuals waiting for an organ transplant require such extensive and ongoing medical intervention that they are unable to work, and their treatment is covered by government programs. However, should a person in this situation marry, the medical benefits might be lost and the new spouse

TABLE 13.3   Tips for Couples Including Pets in Wedding Ceremonies

1. *Call ahead.* Find out if the venues will accept pets. Also, if you are having a destination wedding, locate hotels that are pet-friendly.
2. *Consider your guests.* Determine if anyone who will be interacting directly with the pet has an allergy. Also, some wedding party members may get nervous around animals and should be notified in advance.
3. *Resist kitty and puppy love.* Because kittens and puppies are unpredictable, they are particularly difficult to include in ceremonies.
4. *Test the temperament.* Many pets are uncomfortable around strangers or act differently in new surroundings. Only well-behaved animals should be included in wedding ceremonies. The pet should know who is in charge and be able to respond to commands as needed. Include your pets in the wedding rehearsal to help them become familiar with their surroundings and duties.
5. *Use fashion sense.* Pick attire that your pet will tolerate and test the chosen garments on several occasions. Avoid wires and floral varieties that are toxic to animals, such as lilies, daffodils, and hydrangeas.
6. *Avoid chowhounds.* Your pet can get sick if they are not trained to avoid human food and drink.
7. *Get them ready.* Your pet should be pampered and exercised before the wedding and be taken for bathroom breaks throughout the day.
8. *Employ bribery.* Bring your pets' favorite treats and spoil them with affection so that they will be content during the ceremony and while being photographed.

Source: Adapted from Moore (2006).

could quickly face financial ruin. Commitment ceremonies present an option for couples facing legal stumbling blocks to marriage.

Many ceremony venues are also likely to have restrictions regarding the inclusion of pets in the bridal party, so you will want to be familiar with the sites that do allow animals. Pet expert and award-winning writer Arden Moore offers tips for couples who wish to include a pet in their wedding ceremony, summarized in Table 13.3.

As a consultant, you must remember that there is no right or wrong way for a couple to pledge their commitment. If you strongly support one faith or approach to marriage and do not feel comfortable with other practices, simply choose your target market and specialize in that area. If, on the other hand, you wish to support a broad range of clients, then you must be open to diverse outlooks and belief systems.

REFERENCES

Hong, N. Y. (2003). Korean wedding dress from the Chosun Dynasty (1392–1910) to the present. In H. B. Foster and D. C. Johnson (eds.), *Wedding Dress across Cultures* (pp. 53–65). New York: Berg.

Moore, A. (2006). Wedding tails: Couples share an important day with their pets. Palm Springs Life: 2006 Weddings, available at http://www.palmspringslife.com

Robinson, B. A. (2005). Religions of the world. Ontario Consultants on Religious Tolerance, available at http://www.religioustolerance.org/worldrel.htm

Spangenberg, L. M. (2001). *Timeless Traditions: A Couple's Guide to Wedding Customs around the World*. New York: Universe Publishing.

Consultant Checklist and Reminders for Ceremonies

☐ Always defer to the celebrant's wishes, as this leader is the guiding force behind the ceremony.

☐ Respect the fact that many celebrants are territorial.

☐ Share the seven steps to writing vows with couples who wish to take this route.

☐ Provide programs, to guide guests through ceremonial traditions with which they may be unfamiliar.

☐ Become familiar with ceremony guidelines and policies associated with places of worship in your area.

review questions

1. Name two religions that are common in your area, as well as the associated leader's title and the name of the sacred text.

2. What are the seven steps for writing vows?

3. Name three artifacts that are commonly used in ceremonies where you reside.

4. What information is usually represented in a ceremony program?

terminology

- Annulment

- Artifacts

- Celebrant

- Ceremony program

- Co-celebration or concelebration

- Sacred texts

- Vows

floral décor 14

Flowers and related decorative elements underscore the mood and tone of a wedding. They also represent a significant expense, generally taking up 7 percent or more of the budget. Because flowers are such a prominent feature of the ceremony and reception, thoughtful care should be taken when making decisions. Four considerations when selecting floral décor include (1) the recipients and locations that require flowers; (2) selecting flowers; (3) centerpieces and other decorative elements; and (4) installation and removal.

PHOTO 14-1 *(opposite) Wreathes made with artfully arranged foliage can make a strong statement.*

recipients and locations

Marianne Raub of Helen Olivia, featured in Vendor Spotlight, Case 14.1, has an organized system of determining the "who" of personal flowers. When working with clients, she helps them determine designs for all of the following recipients and asks the number that will be needed for each category:

- Bridal bouquet
- Toss bouquet
- Other bridal flowers (e.g., hair, dress)
- Number of bridesmaids, including maid of honor
- Number of flower girls (petals/basket)
- Number of mothers (corsages/nosegays)
- Number of grandmothers (corsages/nosegays)
- Other women needing personal flowers
- Groom's boutonniere
- Number of groomsmen, including best man
- Number of ushers
- Ring bearer (boutonniere and pillow)
- Number of fathers
- Number of grandfathers
- Other men needing personal flowers

When considering the "other" category, this may include the officiant, readers, soloists, guestbook attendant, and, in some cases, all of the guests if flowers are used for favors. For example, the company Speaking Roses (2006) custom embosses flowers with personalized messages or photographs, offering a unique type of monogrammed favor.

Randy Christian of Green Mansions Florist, featured in Vendor Spotlight, Case 14.2, has an equally efficient way to determine the floral décor needs for the ceremony and reception:

Ceremony

- Entrance flowers and greenery, decorative wreaths, and bows
- Freestanding arrangements
- Altar arrangements
- Pew/chair décor
- Aisle runner
- Ceremony special elements (e.g., chuppah, arch, gazebo)
- Other ceremony flowers (e.g., unity candle décor, kneeling bench décor)

Reception

- Number of centerpieces for reception tables
- Tent décor

marianne raub

helen olivia

How did you become interested in floral design? I grew up around flowers because my father was a gardener. Prior to starting this business, I was a professional ballet dancer for companies in the Midwest and New York for 13 years. Because of living in New York and my background in dance, I had a good sense for design. When I retired from ballet, I took courses at Parsons School of Design, then worked as an apprentice and a designer before we opened our shop.

How did you come up with your business name? My husband, Craig Noah, and I co-own the business, and Helen Olivia represents the first names of our grandmothers. He handles the management side and I focus on design.

What makes your designs unique? I bring a very contemporary edge to designs. I am always looking at books and then find new twists on ideas to make them my own and give them personality. We specialize in nontraditional centerpieces with flowers that people are not used to seeing and unique groupings. Also, I know how to set the stage, so to speak. When the couple and their guests walk into the ceremony and the reception, they should feel like they are at a special event.

What trends are you seeing in bridal bouquets? Bouquets are currently very natural looking and hand-tied. You rarely see cascades or holders. While most brides still want all white, it is becoming more common to have a 60–40 match for the bride (60 percent white and 40 percent color) and the opposite 40–60 for the bridesmaids. Also, mini calla lilies are currently very popular.

What advice would you give wedding consultants regarding floral décor? Consultants need to be very educated about the seasonality and costs of different floral varieties. You don't want to pump up a client about a specific flower or arrangement only for them to be disappointed when they discover that they can't execute the plan because of availability or price.

Web site: www.helenolivia.com

randy christian

green mansions florist

What has changed in the floral industry in the past 20 years? The entire complexion of the business has changed, some great things and some challenges. On the positive end, we can obtain just about any flower year-round because of global relationships with growers and wholesalers. On the negative side is the "Wal-mart effect," where stores that buy in bulk can sell certain flowers at a minimal cost. This has hurt the reputation of some flowers, namely, roses and alstroemeria, which are now commonly seen as grocery store flowers. It is a shame for roses in particular, because they can take a beating and still look fabulous, but more and more brides are saying that they do not want any roses in their bridal bouquets.

What other trends are you seeing in bridal bouquets? A huge trend on the West Coast is "bling bouquets," where sequins, glitter, and jewels up to 3 inches wide are mixed in as if they were flowers. In the past two years I have also seen a significant movement toward incorporating bold colors in bridal bouquets. Many brides do not want any white at all. Orchids are huge, phalaenopsis in particular and cymbidium to an extent.

What about boutonnieres? It used to be primarily roses or stephanotis. Now some grooms are moving away from flowers altogether, and are using mixed foliage with a variety of textures and sometimes seashells or berries mixed in. If the bride insists that she wants him to wear a flower, I suggest a lisianthus boutonniere that we have perfected. It is light and flat. We pin it on and the groom forgets about it—they love it.

Tell us about your fish centerpieces. I had a couple that was really into snorkeling and the groom had a wonderful aquarium, so I suggested that we have fish swimming in their centerpieces and they loved the idea. We use large, clear vases and have the floral design on top and the fish swimming below. Now I have an indoor pond up front and our fish go out, strut their stuff, and then come back home.

Web site: www.greenmansionsflorist.com

- Sweetheart table or head table
- Buffet table arrangements
- Cake flowers, cake table, cake knife décor
- Ice sculpture décor, punch bowl décor
- Toasting glasses décor
- Escort card table
- Bar and cocktail area
- Ladies restroom
- Banisters
- Other flowers needed (e.g., pool floats, guest rooms, cars)

The entrance to the ceremony site is the first chance to make an impression and tie in the theme of the wedding. Prior to this point, most guests have only seen stationery elements such as save-the-date cards and the invitation, so the entrance sets the stage for the rest of the day. When considering the placement of flowers and greenery at the entrance location, it is important to keep in mind that garlands can gently and gracefully welcome guests without enormous expense. Doorway treatments with a hint of color, such as swags, wreaths or garlands made of leaves, berries, pine, herbs, or artfully arranged twigs and ribbons can have a big impact with minimal investment. Similarly, topiaries are ornamental trees trimmed in unique shapes that are fresh and have an ethereal feel with the addition of tulle or bows.

Trees and large potted plants can be rented for weddings, offering another cost-effective means to make a statement. Floral wreaths can beautifully mark the entrance as well but can be cost prohibitive as a single wreath can include hundreds of flowers. However, the portability of a wreath allows it to be used at the ceremony, reception, and brunch the day after the wedding, and then it can be dried and kept as a beautiful memento that can be used for years. If investing in floral wreaths, keep in mind that they do not have to be round, as square, heart-shaped, and vertical wreaths offer distinctive options.

With an outdoor wedding, flowers can create a focal point for the ceremony if one is not apparent. Outside weddings need fewer flowers beyond the focal point and should not be fussy or overly arranged as you will want them to complement the natural outdoor elements. Outdoor ceremonies also allow for floral décor along an aisle runner and for real petals to be dropped by the flower girl. For indoor ceremonies, these items are generally prohibited because of their ability to stain carpeted or wood floors. Even for outdoor ceremonies, it is best to select pale petals for the flower girl, as dark petals can stain the bride's dress. Dark silk petals are equally problematic because the dyes used can leave marks.

Both indoor and outdoor weddings may have a canopy, arch, or other structure that the couple stands under during the ceremony. As you

learned in Chapter 13, in Jewish weddings this is known as a chuppah, and for Indian weddings it is called a mandap. Structures such as these are often beautifully accented with flowers.

In addition, arrangements are placed close to the couple as they add elegance to the ceremony photographs. Floral accents such as pomanders, which are small balls of flowers, are frequently used to mark the rows or pews.

selecting flowers

The bridal bouquet is an excellent place to start when selecting flowers, for it is the most photographed floral element and often informs the choices for the wedding party and other floral décor. When selecting flowers for a wedding, five things to keep in mind are the season, color, scent, shape, and size.

First, the season will dictate what floral elements are available. Couples on a budget who have creative flair can purchase the majority of their floral décor at a local farmers market. These outdoor bazaars are seasonal but will have the best of what is blooming in the local area at that time of year. Floral designers will use local materials as well, but also work closely with international distributors from locations such as Colombia, Ecuador, Holland, and Thailand to ensure that they have a broad range of flowers available throughout the calendar year.

Some flowers that are popular for weddings have an extremely short season, with the classic example being lily of the valley, which has a three- to four-week season that falls in May. The small stems are priced as high as $15 each, with even very small bouquets starting at $400. Lily of the valley stems are so expensive that many florists will not even carry them. Obtaining flowers with a short season or during their off-season can be cost prohibitive, so you will want to work closely with florists in your area to gain a sense of seasonality. In cases where a desired flower is simply not available, many florists will offer silk accents or arrangements.

The Flowers & Plants Association (2006) offers an excellent overview of the seasonable availability of specific flowers, but keep in mind that this requires the ability to ship the flowers from the location where they

PHOTO 14-2 *(see p. 244) Wreaths can be used in multiple locations throughout the wedding day.*

PHOTO 14-3 *(see p. 245) At outdoor ceremonies, flower petals can enhance the aisle.*

PHOTO 14-4 *(see p. 246) Floral accents are used to accent and mark rows at a ceremony.*

PHOTO 14-5 *(see p. 247) Special seating is often indicated with elaborate floral décor.*

TABLE 14.1   Seasonal Flower Availability Sampler

Spring: cherry blossom, daffodil, gardenia, hyacinth, lilac, lily of the valley, tulips

Summer: agapanthus, alliums, goldenrod, hydrangea, peony, phlox, sweet pea

Fall: aster, celosia, dahlia, gladiolus, hypericum, sunflowers, yarrow, zinnia

Winter: amaryllis, hellebore, hollyberry, narcissus, protea, kangaroo paw

All Year: bird of paradise, calla, chrysanthemum, delphinium, freesia, gerbera, iris, lily, phalaenopsis orchid, rose, snapdragon, statice, stephanotis

---

Source: Flowers & Plants Association (2006).

happen to be in season. For example, many winter flowers are exotics that are only available in tropical climates. Refer to Table 14.1 for a sample of their recommendations by season. Although many flowers will be available off-season, the cost will be significantly higher.

A second consideration when selecting flowers for a wedding is color. In terms of bridal bouquets, approximately 70 percent of brides select all white, which is a fresh, elegant look. As important as the flowers are, traditionalists argue that guests should look at the bride first, not her flowers, and dark flowers against a white gown will dominate the view. For the 30 percent of brides who mix color into the bouquet, the complementary colors tend to stay on the light side such as pink, pale yellow, peach, and lilac. Bold and dark bouquets, which are becoming more popular, can make a very dramatic statement. Randy Christian suggests that elaborate, beaded gowns, such as those worn by many brides from India, should be balanced by simple floral designs, while a simple gown can be complemented by a more dramatic floral statement. He suggests, however, that a tailored gown works best with a tailored bouquet.

With bridesmaids' bouquets, mixing in bright colors is more common. A trend for bridesmaids is that in lieu of a bouquet, they will carry a purse, fan, or muff accented with real or silk flowers. Generally, the chosen ornament will be a gift from the bride, which the bridesmaids carry during the wedding and then have for later use.

The scent of the floral décor is a third consideration. This is most relevant when selecting centerpieces, as a heavy floral scent can interfere with the reception meal. Magnolia blossoms, gardenias, and stargazer lilies are three examples of beautiful varieties that should be kept out of the immediate vicinity of food. Gardenias also brown and bruise easily and so are better used in wreaths than in centerpieces where they will be regularly breathed upon or touched.

A fourth consideration is shape. For bridal bouquets, the three primary shapes are hand-tied, round, and cascade. The hand-tied bouquet is

PHOTO 14-6 *Traditional bridal bouquets are white, while bridesmaids bouquets are more likely to include bright colors.*

natural looking, as if the flowers were just picked from a garden. Hand-tied bouquets can either be tailored, such as a grouping of six calla lilies with an elegant ribbon, or a mixed arrangement, such as peonies, dendrobium orchids, and freesia stems. Some hand-tied bouquets are held with a single ribbon, while others have the stems wired or taped and then tied to finish the look. A nosegay is a small hand-tied bouquet that is popular for flower girls, junior bridesmaids, mothers, and others receiving smaller sprays. Tussie-Mussie is a Victorian-inspired nosegay that is small, compact, and often in a cone-shaped holder.

Round and cascade bouquets have a more arranged appearance and are generally mounted on a bouquet holder with a handle. A classic round bouquet, whose popularity was revived after Jessica Simpson carried it in her wedding, is made up of hundreds of delicate steph-anotis blossoms with each stem hand wrapped and tied. Often a pearl pin is placed in the center of each flower for a touch of elegance and then the arrangement is brought together in what looks like a large, round ball. Roses are also commonly used to make beautiful round bouquets. Both hand-tied and round bouquets can be collared, which means that the arrangement literally has a collar of greenery creating a border. A cascade bouquet, also referred to as a teardrop or water-fall shape, tends to be the largest and heaviest, incorporating long stems that give the bouquet length and drape.

A final concern when selecting floral décor is size. In terms of bridal bouquets, the adage used to be the bigger, the better. However, a large bouquet can overwhelm the bride, making her look like she is all flowers, and simultaneously is too heavy to carry for extended periods. Now the tendency is to have more compact bouquets. In terms of boutonnieres, the consensus is that smaller is better. Most floral designers will encourage clients to match the boutonnieres with some aspect of the bridal bouquet. Single roses and mini calla lilies are popular options that can be easily coordinated.

centerpieces and other decorative elements

Most couples are fairly traditional in their choice of bouquets, bouton-nieres and ceremony decor. However, centerpieces and other decora-tive elements used for the reception allow contemporary statements to be made. When entering the reception site, one of the first things that guests will see is the escort card table. This table is a key focal point that can set the tone for the rest of the reception and is often lavishly decorated. A beach theme wedding, for example, can include an escort table where the cards are set in sand and surrounded by exotic flowers and conch shells.

Centerpieces are limited only by a couple's budget and their floral designer's creative capacity. Some couples still select classic designs such as candelabras entwined with flowers, while others employ the imagination of the designer to tie elaborate floral décor into their theme. While there can be a distinction in the formality of the floral décor for the ceremony and reception, the difference should not be so radical that an imbalance results.

A current trend in centerpieces is to use large, clear glass vases in modern shapes. On the top of the design, flowers are placed in a removable plastic riser. Beneath this tray, the sky is the limit, and options such as bright fruits, vegetables or berries, colored glass or lights, buckeyes, live grasses growing in a soil base, pinecones, and live fish represent just a few design ideas. Centerpiece size should be dictated by table size and should not be so large that the centerpiece inhibits conversation. Marianne Raub explains that once a centerpiece design is selected, most florists will schedule an appointment for a sample showing so that clients can see their selections come together and make changes as necessary.

Very large arrangements, such as those using bamboo or rented palm trees for a tropical theme should be prominently displayed, as should

PHOTO 14-7 (top) Centerpieces are as bountiful as the budget will allow. **PHOTO 14-8** (bottom) A dramatic statement can be made by alternating high and low designs.

PHOTO 14-9 (opposite) A current trend is to use large, clear vases in modern shapes.

PHOTO 14-10 (top) Fresh fruit adds interest to clear vases.

PHOTO 14-11 (bottom) Large arrangements should be prominently displayed.

PHOTO 14-12 (opposite) A floral chuppah takes an hour or longer to install.

expensive arrangements, so that the couple feels they are worth the investment. Some flowers, such as carnations and alstroemeria, are often avoided for weddings because they are perceived as being "grocery store flowers." However, these less expensive varieties can lead to spectacular wreaths and arrangements that otherwise would not be affordable. Furthermore, the use of greenery, unique twigs, and bold ribbon can inexpensively finish the statement.

installation and removal

Prior to meeting with the floral designer, it is a good idea to inform your clients of charges for packing, delivery, installation, and removal. Depending on the size of the order, the complexity of the designs, and the distance traveled, these fees can be significant. Basic installation charges will vary by area, but anticipate a minimum charge of $150. Installation charges are based primarily on time, and many large arrangements cannot be transported and must be built on site. A floral chuppah, for example, is raised and decorated at the venue, which usually takes a minimum of an hour. Decorated tents, where each pole is intertwined with greenery and flowers, can take several hours to install. Furthermore, if the ceremony and the reception are at the same site, the floral designer will have to wait through the ceremony to do the changeover, which could increase the charge. However, this charge will probably be no different than the travel charge that will apply if the ceremony and reception are in separate locations.

At most venues, nails and tape will be prohibited, so hanging designs must be installed with ribbons, clips, decorative ropes, and ties. When the designer has finished the install, you should walk through to make sure that all the areas are clean and neat and that no trash or extra materials were inadvertently left behind. It is your job to make sure that the "curb appeal" is maintained.

The floral designer will also handle removal, and it is common for ceremony arrangements to be transported to the reception site. When bringing floral décor into a house of worship, it is important to know the policies, as some facilities require the arrangements to stay as a donation, others insist that they be removed, and others do not allow floral décor at all. If the flowers are required to stay, many couples will make more modest selections as they will only get to enjoy these arrangements during the ceremony. Because venue policies vary considerably, it is important to familiarize yourself with the regulations before your clients make their floral décor selections.

REFERENCES

Flowers & Plants Association. (2006). Available at http://www.flowers.org.uk/index.htm

Speaking Roses. (2006). Available at http://www.speakingroses.com/

Consultant Checklist and Reminders for Floral Décor

- ☐ Assist your clients by asking them to make a list of all individuals who will be receiving personal flowers prior to meeting with the floral designer.

- ☐ Be aware that seasonality dictates availability and price of floral décor.

- ☐ Remember that local farmers markets can be an excellent avenue for flowers when working with clients on a budget.

- ☐ Recognize that flowers set the stage and create a focal point for the ceremony.

- ☐ Keep in mind that dark petals, both live and silk, can stain wood floors, carpets, and clothing.

- ☐ Make sure that your clients budget in packing, delivery, installation, and removal as part of floral décor costs.

- ☐ Know the floral décor rules of the ceremony and reception venues in terms of permission, installation, and removal.

review questions

1. Name three floral varieties that are unique
   to each of the four seasons.

2. Name two floral varieties that are known
   for their heavy scents.

3. What are the three primary shapes of bridal
   bouquets?

4. What are three things that should be kept
   in mind with regard to floral installation
   and removal?

terminology

- Cascade bouquet

- Collared bouquet

- Hand-tied bouquet

- Nosegay

- Pomander

- Round bouquet

- Topiary

- Tussie-Mussie

photography 15

All the guests have returned home, the cake is eaten, the flowers have died, and the dress has aged to yellow. What remains are the memories, many of which have been captured digitally or on film. Photography comprises 10 percent of the average wedding budget. However, its enduring results justify why many couples invest 15 percent or more. Consultants typically advise clients to get the best photographer they can afford because their photographs can continually bring them back to their wedding day.

PHOTO 15-1 *(opposite) Photography evokes memories of the wedding day.*

C hanges in technology have revolutionized wedding photography. This chapter will highlight (1) the movement from film to digital photography; (2) the two primary styles of photography; and (3) album design and trends in photography.

the movement from film to digital photography

While some wedding photographers still use film, the vast majority have moved to digital because of the benefits it offers their clients. First, digital improvements over the past several years allow color, saturation, and sharpness to be superior to what film can achieve. Second, digital allows for online proofing, which means that the couple and their friends and family can look through the proofs regardless of where they reside. Third, digital allows for almost instantaneous feedback. Rodney Bailey, who is the exclusive photographer for this book and is featured in Vendor Spotlight, Case 15.1, explains that when he is hired for two-day coverage such as the wedding day and a brunch the following day, he can pull together a set of images from the wedding and set them to music for a slide show that can be presented during the brunch. Finally, digital images can be safely stored in multiple locations so there is no fear of losing original work.

Digital media is mistakenly thought to be less expensive to execute than film. Top photographers run five or more high-end computers with enormous amounts of storage in each to handle the flow of processing. They also constantly update their cameras to have access to the latest technology. Rodney explains that digital processing takes three times the effort of film processing, owing to the number of images captured as well as the creativity that goes into modern album design. When helping your clients compare prices, ensure that the photographer's packages include photo shoot time, production time, album design, reprint costs, and options regarding access to digital negatives.

styles of photography

Two primary styles of photography are traditional and photojournalistic. Consider your parents' or grandparents' wedding album. You probably see a fair amount of black and white, but more significantly, all the pictures are carefully posed. Using the traditional style, photographers will even stop the reception to stage a moment. For example, the bride and groom might pretend to cut the cake to get a good pose. Then they move on to the next staged moment. Wedding albums used to include nothing but groups lined up and the couple

rodney bailey

wedding photojournalism by rodney bailey

How did you select photography as a career? I fell in love with photography at a very young age. At the age of 12, I worked all summer mowing lawns in my neighborhood to save up enough money for a camera. I began on the path of documenting weddings at age 16 when I took pictures, just playing around, at a friend's wedding. They had hired a professional photographer but ended up liking my images much more. So at that point, I contacted a local photographer for an apprenticeship; he saw talent in me and allowed me to do 50 weddings on my own in the first year. I developed my photojournalistic style early on and started my business from there.

What is the most unique wedding you have ever photographed? Probably the most interesting and memorable wedding that I documented took place in Rome, where the couple received a papal blessing. After Rome, I documented their honeymoon in Paris.

What do you like about the photojournalistic style? Most of my clientele and their wedding guests don't even realize I'm there taking pictures. One of the best things about this approach is that the bride and groom really get to enjoy their wedding day, and I'm there to document it in a witness form. I love the photojournalistic style because to me the real emotion comes through when someone doesn't realize that they are being photographed. If a moment is captured and not directed, it feels and looks more natural because it is more natural.

What distinguishes you from other photographers? I recently had a 13-hour wedding, and I ended up with about 4,500 images. I find that most clients are just overwhelmed, even with 500 images, with the process of saying, "How are we going to select 60 images or 90 images for our wedding album?" So I take it a step further. And that's one of those things that definitely sets me apart from a lot of the other

(Continues)

photographers. I actually design the album myself and provide my clients an album proposal that walks them through the images I think look best. I'm going for artistry and storytelling, and spend about 10 hours in the layout and design process. I spoke to three or four thousand photographers at a conference in New York and polled them by asking if they would ever consider doing a proposal for their clients. Ninety-nine percent of them said "No," so this is absolutely what makes my services unique. I want my clients to LOVE their wedding images and have their album be reflective of their wedding day.

Beyond weddings, what are your other specialties? Probably 20 percent of our business comes from corporate and commercial work, which brings in everything from Vogue and Disney calling us to working with clients like Oprah and *O Magazine*. I did a great shoot with Oprah and 5,000 women that included an online aspect where all the event participants could download the photographs from that day's seminars and activities. It was great to meet her. It was probably one of the highlights of my career because she is just an amazing woman in every aspect. I also do quite a bit of work with the Library of Congress and enjoy the political aspect as well.

Web site: www.RodneyBailey.com

TABLE 15.1   Comparing Two Wedding Photography Styles

Traditional Style	Photojournalistic Style
• Posed	• Candid
• Staged	• Natural
• Directed	• Spontaneous
• Front and center	• All angles
• Hands-on	• Hands-off
• Significant communication	• Little communication
• Traditional mount album	• Flush mount album

stiffly positioned for staged shots. The emotion that can be associated with traditional staged moments is highlighted in Consultant in Action, Case 15.2.

Only within the last decade has the photojournalistic style evolved within the context of weddings. This style means that the photographer is documenting real moments, almost like telling a story. It is very candid, fluid, spontaneous, and versatile. Photos are taken from a variety of directions, with pictures from angled positions more likely than those taken front and center. When hiring a photojournalist for their wedding, most couples will still request a few staged photographs, but the vast majority of the images will be real moments that are captured. The distinctions between traditional photography and photojournalism are highlighted in Table 15.1.

Most photographers, regardless of style, will work with at least one assistant and generally have more than one if there are more than 500 guests at the wedding. With an assistant, one photographer can capture images of the bride as she is getting ready while the other can be with the groom. Furthermore, at many ceremony sites, one can be on the floor, while the other can get the overhead perspective from the balcony. Importantly, some ceremony sites do not allow photography, and even those that do generally have strict policies regarding photographer location and flash. Experienced wedding photographers will use available light rather than flash and remain unobtrusive by using a telephoto lens and gathering images from the back of the ceremony site.

SELECTING THE RIGHT PHOTOGRAPHER

Not all couples will prefer the photojournalistic style, and many photographers remain partial to the traditional style. As a wedding consultant, you should introduce both styles to your clients and allow them to select the one that speaks to them. The number of images that a photographer will take at a wedding can vary significantly based on personal style and approach, so this is an important consideration when comparing photographers. Recommend to your clients

picture perfect

Your clients, a lovely Asian bride and groom, want to have a very traditional American wedding complete with an elegant evening poolside reception. The bride is a fan of American movies and knows exactly how she wants her special day to appear in her wedding photos.

On the wedding day, the ceremony goes beautifully. The newlyweds arrive at the hotel reception site and enter the pool area to find stylish floral decorations balanced with a sea of floating, flickering candles that create a truly magical setting. The food and music are fabulous and the guests are happy. Everything is perfect.

At 9:30 P.M., the couple approaches the cake table for one of the bride's most anticipated pictures, the cake cutting. The photographer is standing close by, prepared to capture images of this activity. Suddenly, three excited children rush past the couple, fighting to be the first in line for a piece of cake. In the scuffle, the three-tier wedding cake is knocked off the table and falls into the pool.

The room falls silent as the stunned crowd comprehends what has happened. The devastated bride begins to sob uncontrollably. Hearing the commotion, the chef rushes in to assure the couple that he has elegant individual desserts he can serve; however, the bride continues to sob, knowing that she will not have one of her most important wedding photos. The bewildered groom tries to comfort her.

What do you do?

Case submitted by Diane Haworth

PHOTO 15-4 *No detail is too small for the photographer.*

that they meet with a minimum of two photographers to take a look at sample albums and get to know them in person. The personality of the photographer can be as important as the skill set, and each couple should feel that they can get along with the photographer. Furthermore, each couple has a sense of what they want their wedding album to look like, and there is no single correct interpretation.

It is also important that the wedding consultant and the photographer get along well, in particular for a traditional photo shoot. The consultant will be the main point of contact with the photographer and can indicate what pictures are requested as well as gather those who will be featured in the images. This allows the couple to enjoy their day without worrying about herding the bridal party, family members, and others for key photos. The photographer should also understand the cultural needs of your clients. When, where, and how wedding photographs are taken can vary significantly by culture, as illustrated in Culture Corner, Case 15.3.

PHOTO 15-2 *(see p. 267) The cake is one of the most photographed elements of the wedding day.*

PHOTO 15-3 *(see p. 268) The photojournalist style captures the wedding as it unfolds.*

wedding photography in china

For most Chinese couples, the wedding photography is taken three to six months before the actual wedding day. The couple will visit photography studios and look through albums and costumes to decide which studio suits their needs. Once they have decided on a studio, they will select a photography package that will include hair and makeup for the photo shoot, the photos, album, and then separate hair and makeup for the actual wedding day. The package does not include photos taken on the wedding day, just staged photos taken well in advance. The couple returns to the studio on the appointed day for the photography session. This is an all-day wedding shoot. This session can last as long as 12 hours and can involve as many as 15 changes of clothing and backdrops. For example, a bridal couple will be photographed wearing traditional Chinese silk wedding attire, Western wedding attire, a mix of cocktail outfits, and romantic costumes inspired by the media, such as Cinderella and her prince standing in front of a castle backdrop. Each change of clothing is provided by the photography studio and is worn only for the day. The resulting wedding images are a stylized mix of what the couple looks like and what they fantasize they will look like as a married couple. Photography studios are generally selected for the costumes they have rather than for the skill of the photographer. For the actual wedding day, a videographer may be hired to record the day's events or the couple will just rely on the photographic skills of their guests.

Case submitted by Yao and David Wosicki

album design and trends in photography

The albums that result from the two styles of photography are also vastly different. With a traditional album, the photographs are bound and bordered. Clients can split the page apart and pull the photograph out of the page. The onset of digital photography and the photojournalistic style allowed for the origination of the flush mount album. Flush mount albums allow a picture or a group of pictures to be the page, just like photographs in a book or magazine. Top-quality flush mount album companies offer up to a 200-year guarantee and coat the pages to protect the photographic paper from liquid spills, fingerprints, fading, and peeling.

Keep in mind that with any album, your clients will definitely get what they pay for, with the album leaders offering noticeably superior quality. For example, only the highest quality flush mount album companies have patented binding systems that allow the center seam to be flat, offering a beautiful panoramic spread without a bulky midpoint.

The flush mounted album has also increased the options for album size. Traditionally, couples would have one album made and then get a handful of individual photos reprinted for family and friends. Now, the couple's entire album can be readily duplicated in a smaller size. Rodney explains that for the couple, 11 x 14 and 11 x 11 sizes are the most common, and some will go as large as 15 x 15. Commonly selected scaled down versions are 8 x 8, 6 x 6, and even a 3 x 3 mini-album.

Most couples will want a mixture of color and black and white photos in their albums. The flush mounted style allows for a seamless integration of color and black and white. Black and white or sepia photos, which include brown and gray tones, are classic, elegant, and timeless. The lack of bright colors allows the viewer to focus on specific details; for example, rather than noticing the pinks and yellows in a bouquet, the eye is drawn to the shape of the petals and the curve of a ribbon. Also, black and white is forgiving in that inconsistent makeup or an inadvertent wine stain on a white tuxedo is less likely to stand out. From an historical perspective, black and white allow for consistent documentation.

Counsel your clients to inquire about the average processing time for wedding albums. The time needed between the wedding and delivery of the final album is influenced by factors such as (1) the photographer's style and post-wedding process for creating and designing an album; (2) the client's turnaround time, which includes the review of

PHOTO 15-5 *A lack of bright colors allows the viewer to focus on specific details.*

proofs, final image selection and/or feedback regarding album layout; and (3) the album company's production time.

Beyond changes in technique and album design, three additional trends in photography are engagement photo shoots, photo guest books, and photo-video hybrids. Top photographers will schedule engagement photo shoots two or three times a year. Spring and fall are common, and the photographer will often select a beautiful outdoor location and can meet with a dozen or so clients over a period of a few hours rather than making individual appointments with each couple. Engagement photos can be used for newspaper announcements, save-the-date notices, and holiday greeting cards. A more recent trend is to flush mount engagement photos to create a personalized guest book. Therefore, instead of having a generic guest book, clients can have their photos go across the top of each page and then lines for signatures are provided underneath. A final trend is the photo-video hybrid. Videography offers the ability to capture audio, which is particularly important for couples who would like to have specific moments such as the exchange of vows or the voice of a soloist captured. Digital photography and related software products allow for the creative placement of images in a slide show that is set to music. As the video capabilities of digital cameras continue to evolve, more couples may opt to hire a photo-video hybrid specialist.

Consultant Checklist and Reminders for Photography

☐ Introduce your clients to both traditional and photojournalistic styles of photography, including sample albums, to determine which best suits their personalities.

☐ Be aware of the dates available for engagement photographs for photographers who schedule them two or three times a year.

☐ Help your clients make a list of the "must have" photos that they wish to be taken.

☐ Be familiar with the rules for photography at area places of worship.

☐ Ensure that the photographer will have an assistant for the wedding day.

☐ Ask the photographer to tell you the average number of images s/he takes at weddings.

☐ Determine if the photographer will be shooting all color or if a percentage of black and white is available.

☐ When comparing packages, ensure that the photographer's options include photo shoot time, design and production time, album options, reprint costs, and the option to purchase the digital negatives.

review questions

1. Explain three advantages of digital over film photography.

2. Name three distinctions between traditional photography and the photojournalistic style.

3. What are two purposes of engagement photos?

4. Explain two advancements in album design.

terminology

- Available light
- Flush mount album
- Photojournalistic style
- Photo-video hybrid
- Sepia
- Traditional photographic style
- Videography

PHOTO 16-1 *String instruments are commonly chosen for the prelude.*

music
and entertainment

If music be the food of love, play on.

—William Shakespeare, *Twelfth Night*

Play on indeed. A wedding, like life's other special moments, is enhanced by special music interspersed throughout the celebration. From the seating of the first guest to the newlyweds' getaway, music fills the day. As a wedding planner, clients will rely on your expertise to guide them in selecting the soundtrack to their wedding day. Music should always enhance and never overshadow the point of the wedding—the commitment of the couple. When selecting music and other entertainment, each stage of the wedding day should be considered: the ceremony, the cocktail hour, and the reception.

❧ ceremony music

Unless the bride and groom are music aficionados, they will often turn to their wedding consultant for recommendations of music to be played during the ceremony. It is your job to assist the couple in selecting music to punctuate significant moments during the ceremony, from the bride's entrance to the recessional. Most wedding ceremonies can be divided into five main parts: prelude, processional, the ceremony itself, recessional, and postlude, (Pirtle, 2006).

PRELUDE

Just as the prelude of a book foreshadows events to come in a novel, the musical prelude for a wedding ceremony sets the mood for the service to follow. The type of music selected should reflect the personalities of the bride and groom, the formality of the wedding ceremony, and the setting. On one hand, if a wedding is to be held on the beach in Maui, the prelude music might include ukuleles, steel drums, or slack key guitars. On the other hand, if the wedding ceremony is held at a venue such as St. Patrick's Cathedral in New York, which is the largest gothic-style Catholic cathedral in the United States and seats 2,200 (St. Patrick's Cathedral, 2006), a classical string quartet and trumpet player would be appropriate. You should plan for 30 to 45 minutes of prelude music before moving into the processional music. Some options for live music during the prelude, with clarification as necessary, are presented in Table 16.1.

TABLE 16.1   Options for Live Music During the Prelude

- Chamber music ensemble (a small orchestra with strings, wind instruments, and percussion)
- Children's choir
- Classical guitar
- Church choir
- Church organ
- Flute and keyboard
- Guitar, cello, and flute
- Gospel choir
- Harp
- Harp and flute
- Piano
- Solo violin
- String quartet (two violins, viola, and cello)
- String trio (violin, viola, and cello)
- Vocalist
- Wind trio or quartet (assorted wind instruments such as clarinet, oboe, flute, trumpet, French horn, or bassoon)

PROCESSIONAL

For the wedding processional, which is when the wedding party walks down the aisle, it is wise to consider the length of the aisle and the number of members in the wedding party before selecting the music. You might also time the trip down the aisle if you are working at an unfamiliar venue. Sometimes the processional is simply one song; most often, it is two or more songs played to differentiate between the arrival of the wedding party members and the arrival of the bride. The processional music, if done well, will build anticipation as the wedding party enters and continue to build suspense until the bride's dramatic appearance.

Wagner's Bridal Chorus from *Lohengrin* (better known as Here Comes the Bride) is the most traditional choice for the processional. However, because of Wagner's anti-Semitic writings, he remains a controversial figure and his music is seldom chosen for Jewish ceremonies (Eylon, 2006). Other popular options are Stanley's "Trumpet Voluntary," Bach's "Jesu, Joy of Man's Desiring," and Pachelbel's "Canon in D." In addition to the classics, some couples prefer a nontraditional twist on

PHOTO 16-2 *Processional music can incorporate cultural traditions.*

their processional music and incorporate Broadway show tunes, classic jazz, or contemporary pop songs into their wedding day. The decision rests with the bride and groom, and anything goes. However, if the wedding is to take place in a house of worship, be sure to clear any secular music choices with the officiant well in advance of the wedding day, as nonreligious works may be prohibited.

CEREMONY

During the ceremony itself, there may be musical interludes for such moments as group prayers and responses, lighting the unity candle, taking communion, or making special offerings. These moments are made for incorporating a special hymn or other piece of music. The ceremony also commonly includes a performance by a soloist or even a full choir. If your clients will be utilizing musical interludes, be sure that the music is chosen well in advance and coordinated with the needs of the officiant. Many couples choose a close friend who is musically talented to act as their soloist. It is important that this person be given an opportunity to practice during the rehearsal to become familiar with the acoustics of the facility and the style of the accom-

PHOTO 16-3 *Special musical selections are often used during the ceremony.*

japanese dance at a shinto wedding

During a Shinto wedding ceremony, before the bride and groom exchange sips of sake, known as San San Ku Do or three sets of three sips, there may be a dance performed by ladies to the accompaniment of traditional Japanese wooden flutes. The ladies or shrine maidens wear white kimonos with red skirts called hakama. The dancing ladies are symbols of virginity. The dance will last 10 to 15 minutes and will have five parts: (1) acknowledging the meeting of the boy and girl; (2) honoring the love of the couple; (3) keeping the love alive; (4) exchanging or sharing the sake; and (5) honoring the couple's ancestors. If the wedding is held at one of the most traditional Shinto shrines, such as Izumo Taisha in Japan's Shimane prefecture, the bride and groom will join the shrine maidens in dance. As the couple dances, crossing each other, it is to signify sharing a bed with each other. They will dance forming the shape of the number eight, which is a lucky number in Japan, representing eternal prosperity of the family.

Case submitted by: Takeuchi Yayoi, Kubo Sanae, Iwamura Michiyo, Asai Toshiko, Soga Yoshiko, and Suzuki Fusako

Photograph by www.RodneyBailey.com

PHOTO 16-4 *Recessional music is celebratory and highly personalized.*

panist. In some cultures, the ceremony music will be accompanied by entertainment, as illustrated in Culture Corner, Case 16.1.

RECESSIONAL

Once the couple has been pronounced husband and wife, the music should turn festive and celebratory. The recessional music occurs as the wedding party exits the ceremony venue, setting the mood for the party to follow. Popular recessional music includes Beethoven's "Ode to Joy," Handel's "Water Music," and Mendelssohn's "Wedding March." Contemporary song choices might include selections from diverse artists such as Garth Brooks, Destiny's Child, Billy Joel, Shania Twain, U2, and Stevie Wonder. Most importantly, the music your bride and groom select should be joyful and meaningful to them.

For the recessional, consider a creative sound to enhance the exit from the ceremony site. Perhaps your clients want to hire a bagpiper or bell choir to play at the door of the church. If the venue is a hotel, maybe they will hire a blue grass band to set the tone, or perhaps a marching band will play the fight song from the groom's alma mater. The options are vast when it comes to recessional music. The main point is to keep it celebratory, uplifting, and highly personalized.

POSTLUDE

As they say, it ain't over 'til it's over, and the ceremony is not over until the guests exit. This is why planning for a postlude, which is continuous music that plays as guests exit the ceremony space, is important, in particular if there is a large guest list. You should allow for about 10 minutes worth of postlude music, which allows guests to exit quickly and smartly to the sound of upbeat music rather than the shuffling of feet.

Keep in mind that for many weddings, the ceremony and the reception are in the same venue, such as a hotel, museum, or resort. For weddings where there is not an obvious change of scenery, the postlude music becomes particularly important as a means to transition between the ceremony and reception. Music will also help encourage movement. For example, in a resort setting the ceremony may be located in a ballroom area, and then the cocktail hour is held on a patio while the ballroom is quickly turned for the reception.

Photograph by www.RodneyBailey.com

PHOTO 16-5 *A string trio works especially well during cocktails.*

TABLE 16.2 Examples of Cocktail Hour Music

- Louis Armstrong
- The Beatles
- Jim Brickman
- Michael Buble
- Mariah Carey
- Ray Charles
- Patsy Cline
- Harry Connick, Jr.
- Vince Gill
- Norah Jones
- Yo-Yo Ma
- Michael McDonald
- Tim McGraw
- Sarah McLachlan
- Van Morrison
- Rod Stewart
- Vivaldi
- George Winston

❧ cocktail hour music and entertainment

With the wedding ceremony behind them, the music for a couple's cocktail hour should be light and breezy so as not to interfere with the guests' conversation. As there are limited opportunities for guests to converse during the wedding ceremony, the cocktail hour becomes the perfect setting for them to meet and mingle. Nat King Cole, Billie Holiday, and Frank Sinatra are just a few icons whose pleasing sounds are represented in compiled albums such as *The Original Great American Songbook*. Whether your client's music is live or prerecorded, playing the classics, light jazz, or big band during cocktails will start the reception on the right note. A sample of artists whose music works especially well during cocktails can be found in Table 16.2.

If there is a piano available at the reception venue, put it to good use and hire a pianist to play during cocktails. Make sure the piano is tuned and in good working order prior to the wedding day. Other live music for the cocktail hour might include a jazz trio, a violin and a flute, or even a banjo and a guitar. When hiring musical talent, be sure to check with the local music schools for up-and-coming talent at discounted prices. Also, managers of reception venues are excellent sources for finding a specific type of musician or specialty music such as a German polka band or a salsa band.

When advising your client on musical options for cocktails and the reception, keep the space limitations in mind. You don't want a single acoustic guitar to be lost in a large space; conversely, you don't want

PHOTO 16-6 *Many venues come equipped with pianos.*

to overwhelm your guests with too many musicians playing in tight quarters. In addition, be certain to familiarize yourself with any noise restrictions imposed by the venue. Amplified music may be forbidden if your venue is in a residential area. There may also be a limit on the number of musicians allowed or the duration of the music. If the venue is located in a quiet neighborhood, the last dance may have to conclude by 11:00 P.M. or earlier. Check with the venue for specifications and discuss them with your client. Make sure these restrictions are noted in the music contract.

reception music and entertainment

Once cocktails have ended and the guests are invited to sit down for the reception, the music and entertainment take on a new direction. For the dinner itself, the music will be similar to the cocktail hour so as to encourage conversation. Once dinner is complete, there are specific moments that need to be highlighted through the music and the dancing. These special moments include the couple's first dance; the father/bride dance and the mother/groom dance; the cake cutting ceremony; music for the bouquet and garter toss, if included; music for the leave-taking of the couple, if prior to the end of the reception; and the last dance of the night. Beyond these specific breaks, the rest of the reception is often devoted to the pleasure of dancing.

Some couples will have a strong opinion regarding whether they want their music to be performed live. If they are uncertain, they will ask your advice on hiring a DJ versus hiring a wedding band. As a wedding consultant, you should be able to objectively present both sides for them to consider. The pros and cons of this important decision are listed in Table 16.3. Also, it is important that you stay up on the latest artists. If your clients say that they want a band that has a sound

TABLE 16.3 Pros and Cons of Live versus Prerecorded Music

Prerecorded Music (DJ): Pros
- Less expensive than a band
- Immediate access to a wide variety of music
- Short or no breaks
- Can act as emcee
- If space is tight, a DJ takes up almost no room
- Can take the pulse of the room and adjust music selections to keep the party going
- Can play the latest, contemporary music that cover bands may not play
- Because a DJ is just one person, there is less that can go wrong
- Setup time and special equipment are minimal

Prerecorded Music (DJ): Cons
- Personality may be abrasive or inappropriate
- May try to take over the organization of the reception
- Pre-recorded music cannot be easily adjusted to fit the timing of a moment
- Typically seen as less sophisticated and innovative than a live band

Live Music (Band): Pros
- There is great variety in bands in terms of size and style
- Live performance motivates guests to dance
- Lead singer can act as emcee
- Can readily adjust tone and speed of music
- An excellent band is a memorable part of the wedding
- Can establish a time period through dress, style, and equipment (e.g., Big Band)

Live Music (Band): Cons
- Usually more expensive than a DJ
- More complex contracts and personalities
- Lots of mouths to feed
- More that can go wrong with equipment
- Their repertoire will be more restricted than that of a DJ
- Setup time and equipment may be extensive
- Will require breaks; movement to recorded music during breaks will change tone

Source: Adapted from Seto (2006).

www.RodneyBailey.com

JULY 23, 2005

Kara & David

BOSSA NOVA WEDDING MIX

PHOTO 16-7 *(top) Many couples select live music for the reception.*

PHOTO 16-8 *(bottom) Couples can share their appreciation of music with their guests.*

similar to Kelly Clarkson, Green Day, Toby Keith, Beyonce Knowles, Rihanna, or Shakira and you have no idea who these artists are, it will be hard to help them find the right talent. One way to stay up to date is by following artists who are on top of the charts. Web sites such as Billboard.com constantly update their listings and include biographies that will help you learn about the newest and hottest talent.

OTHER RECEPTION ENTERTAINMENT

Other reception entertainment is generally accompanied by music. The most common form of entertainment aside from the music itself is dance, and specific dances are anticipated moments of many weddings. Examples of common cultural dances are presented in Culture Corner, Case 16.2.

When considering these dances, the comfort of the couple should be kept in mind. Lababidi (2004) explains the love-hate relationship that persists with the Egyptian belly-dancing tradition at weddings (pp. 54–55):

> Egyptians are deeply conflicted about the respectability of the art form.... The fact that weddings are hardly complete without

Photograph by www.RodneyBailey.com

PHOTO 16-9 *Dance is the most common form of entertainment at receptions.*

dancing across cultures

- Belly-dancer (Egypt): Shimmering dance often accompanied by drums

- Chinese Wedding Dance (China): The guests surround the bride in a circle and keep the groom from getting to her. He must try to get into the circle to be with the bride. After several attempts, he will slip an envelope of cash to the bride's family and finally be allowed to join the bride in the center.

- Highland Fling (Scotland and Ireland): Spontaneous and often danced to bagpipes

- Hora (Jewish): Circle around bride and groom and lift them in chairs, often accompanied by the song Hava Nagila (Let us rejoice and be glad)

- Irish Step Dance (Ireland): Can vary from simple jigs to intricate choreography; brought to the limelight in the past decade with the popularity of touring Riverdance companies

- Kaslamantiano (Greece): Circle dance around the couple

- Money Dance (Cyprus, Philippines, United States, and others): Money pinned or taped to the newlyweds' clothing in exchange for a dance with the bride or groom

- Polka (Czech Republic, Slovakia, Germany, Poland, and others): Typically associated with fast-paced accordion music

Source: Adapted from Spangenberg (2001).

a belly-dancer is revealing, given the function of marriage as sanctifying the union between a man and a woman who is supposed to be a virgin.... The bride must fret: How can I possibly compete with this woman invulnerable to taboo? Having spent a lifetime shrewdly protecting her virtue and a small fortune on the appearance of her dress, she is being upstaged at her own wedding by a woman who seems to care for neither.

The garter toss, common in American culture, can also push the limits of decorum, and many couples forego this tradition. Other dances are controversial for completely different reasons. Whether to have a money dance, for example, can be a source of significant conflict for a couple raised with different cultural traditions. One person might see it as an anticipated and fun way to dance with an abundance of guests in a short period of time, whereas the other may view it as greedy and tacky. Making decisions regarding whether to incorporate specific dances or other forms of entertainment should be done at least a month before the wedding, as differences in opinion regarding related traditions can cause the couple stress.

tips for hiring entertainment

Whether your clients ultimately hire a soloist, a pianist, a string trio, a band, a DJ, or all of the above, your communication with the entertainment will be a key to the success of the wedding day. You should confirm, confirm, confirm and know the cell phone numbers of the entertainers themselves, so you will not be caught in a situation like the one presented in Consultant in Action, Case 16.3.

Beyond making sure the entertainment actually shows, be certain to have your clients prepare a list of songs they wish to hear and, just as important, a list of songs they do not wish to hear. This is particularly important for the reception. If your bride and groom want a "Macarena"-free reception, it must be stipulated in writing and presented to the entertainment liaison in advance. Also, the entertainment will need to receive a list of the wedding party for introductions, including the names and the correct pronunciations. Any additional special instructions should be spelled out in the contract and highlighted again prior to the wedding. Examples of this would be stipulations such as "No garter toss" or "No father-daughter dance" or "Announce the cutting of the cake at 10:00 P.M." With entertainment, like the other wedding elements, nothing should be left to chance.

When hiring entertainment, prices are often negotiable based on the time of year, day of the week, and time of day. David Fletcher of Washington's Best Musicians (2006) explains that there are five secrets to hiring entertainment at the best prices.

the case of the missing musicians

You have coordinated the hiring of a string quartet to play throughout
Courtney and Mario's wedding ceremony, being held in a large
Presbyterian church. The wedding is to start at 4:00 P.M. At 3:15 P.M.,
there is not a musician in sight. You make repeated phone calls to
the quartet's agency only to be told, "They're on their way." At 3:30
P.M. the guests start to arrive. The ushers begin to seat the guests to
the accompaniment of silence. Time marches on and it is 3:45 P.M.
The wedding is supposed to start in 15 minutes, but still there is not a
musician to be found and the agency does not know why they have not
arrived.

What do you do?

1. *Negotiate.* It is often better to state how much you can afford to pay rather than asking the entertainer how much he or she will charge. However, appreciate the fact that the person is an artist, and don't offend an entertainer with an unreasonable offer.
2. *Consider the "proximity to the event" discount.* In other words, if your clients are willing to wait until two to three weeks prior to their wedding, they might be rewarded with paying less for musical talent that is not yet booked. While this tactic is implemented frequently in the corporate planning world, it may be more difficult to convince a stressed-out couple that there are merits to waiting.
3. *See who is already at the venue.* If your event is in the evening, see if there is a band or DJ already playing earlier in the day. You can save a significant amount by hiring them through the rest of the evening.
4. *Eliminate the liaison.* Talk directly to the person who provides the service. Online searches will provide an abundance of information when trying to find the immediate point of contact for a specific talent.
5. *Establish personal contact.* Become familiar with the best DJs and bands in your area. Learn the names of key personnel and remember them.

REFERENCES

Eylon, L. (2006). The controversy over Richard Wagner. The American-Israeli Cooperative Enterprise, available at http://www.jewishvirtuallibrary.org/jsource/anti-semitism/Wagner.html

Fletcher, D. (2006). Washington's Best Musicians (personal interview), company information available at http://www.washbest.com/

Lababidi, Y. (2004). The belly dancer at the wedding. *Arena Magazine* 72: 54–55.

Pirtle, J. (2006, Spring). *Music for Every Moment. Martha Stewart Weddings.* New York: Martha Stewart Living Omnimedia.

Seto, L. (2006). Party pros: Finding a band or DJ, available at http://www.theknot.com/ch_article.html?Object=A60428121934

Spangenberg, L. M. (2001). *Timeless Traditions: A Couple's Guide to Wedding Customs around the World.* New York: Universe Publishing.

St. Patrick's Cathedral. (2006). Archdiocese of New York: About St. Patrick's Cathedral, available at http://www.ny-archdiocese.org/pastoral/cathedral_about.html

PHOTO 16-10 *(opposite) When hiring specialized entertainment, be certain to get approval from the venue.*

Consultant Checklist and Reminders for Music and Entertainment Options

- ☐ Recognize that each stage of the wedding day will require music: ceremony, cocktail hour, and reception.

- ☐ Be aware that there are five main parts of the wedding ceremony: prelude, processional, the ceremony, recessional, and postlude.

- ☐ Make sure the music selections are consistent with the overall tone of the wedding.

- ☐ Plan for 30 to 45 minutes of prelude music.

- ☐ For the processional, consider the length of the aisle and the number of members in the wedding party before deciding on music.

- ☐ Provide for a music change or dramatic pause before the bride makes her entrance.

- ☐ During the ceremony, highlight special moments through interlude music or vocal performances.

- ☐ Get approval on all secular music choices if the ceremony is at a house of worship.

- ☐ Be prepared to discuss the pros and cons of prerecorded versus live music with your clients.

- ☐ Familiarize yourself with all restrictions for the reception venue.

- ☐ Be prepared with a boom box and a CD of ceremony music and reception music just in case the entertainment is missing in action.

review questions

1. What are the three stages of the wedding day that require music?

2. Name the five parts of a wedding ceremony, as pertaining to music.

3. Name four different options for live music.

4. Brainstorm three creative ways for your clients to exit the ceremony.

5. What are the pros and cons of hiring a DJ for a wedding reception?

6. What are the pros and cons of hiring a band for a wedding reception?

7. Name three things you can do to help get the best price for entertainment.

terminology

• Chamber music

• Postlude

• Prelude

• Processional

• Recessional

• String trio or quartet

• Secular music

• Wind trio or quartet

PHOTO 17-1 *Tent poles can be glamorously hidden with an abundance of fabric.*

rentals and site layout

Rentals allow couples to set the stage for their wedding in a way that would not be cost effective if they had to purchase all of the items. Rentals such as tents, lighting, tables, chairs, linens, tableware, equipment, and other specialty items serve dual purposes. First, each rental will have a specific function. Second, rentals add to the theme and mood of the wedding, varying from traditional sophistication to funky modernity. This chapter offers the essentials that consultants need to know about wedding rentals and layout, including (1) tents; (2) tables, chairs, linens, and tableware; (3) lighting; (4) other outdoor considerations; and (5) bringing it together with the site layout.

ᴄ tents

For outdoor ceremonies and receptions, tents are a common rental item because the weather is seldom perfect. Rain is not the only worry; cold, heat, humidity, wind, and bugs can also lead to uncomfortable guests. This section will cover three aspects of tents: (1) styles and accessories; (2) size and setup; and (3) cost.

TENT STYLES AND ACCESSORIES

The two primary styles of tents are pole tents and frame tents, and many subcategories fall under these two broad groupings. Davis Richardson of Sugarplum Tent Company (2006) offers the following information that will allow you to distinguish between different styles of tents. He explains that pole tents are held up by exterior and interior poles and then anchored in the ground by staking. Modern pole tents are referred to as tension tents, since high-tension winches or ratchets are used to create the taut appearance. Pole tents are the classic choice for weddings, allowing for dramatic, high peaks and a sweeping, billowy look. However, the interior poles can be unattractive and obtrusive, so they are often wrapped with fabric or greenery and decorated with flowers.

Frame tents, in contrast, eliminate the need for interior poles because they are supported with aluminum piping that frames the top and sides of the structure. Frame tents become necessary when the installation is on concrete, asphalt, or any surface where poles cannot be anchored. While the frame tent is more self-supporting, it typically still must be staked down. Installation of frame tents is more time consuming; thus rentals are more expensive. Furthermore, the mass of aluminum supporting the top of the tent can be unattractive, so fabric liners are often used to make the interior aesthetically pleasing.

Picking the style of tent is the first of many decisions that must be made for tent rentals. Other considerations include flooring, sidewalls, entrance canopies, lighting, liners, electricity, heating or air conditioning units, and staging. If the ground is wet, uneven, and/or gravelly, flooring will keep guests from stumbling or getting covered with mud. Flooring can be wood, plastic, carpeting, or an all-weather artificial turf. If your clients are planning on having dancing, they will want to minimally select a dance floor. Sidewalls and entrance canopies offer an elegant touch and extra protection from the elements. Sidewalls, canopies, and the ceiling can be clear, allowing for an open look that can be complemented with lighting and decorative liners. Electricity is essential for lighting as well as generators used to heat or cool the tent. Finally, staging and steps are often used for the head table and musicians. Taken together, it should become clear that selecting a tent is not done to save money on a ceremony or reception site, because the tent and additional rentals are often much more costly than renting

PHOTO 17-2 *This frame tent makes a wooded event possible.*

TABLE 17.1 Guidelines for Selecting the Correct Tent

Number of Guests	Tent Size If Seated at Tables	Tent Size If Standing or Buffet
50	20 × 40	20 × 30
100	30 × 50	30 × 30
150	40 × 60	40 × 40
200	40 × 80	40 × 60
250	60 × 70	40 × 80
300	60 × 80	60 × 60

Source: Rodriguez (2004).

a ballroom or other venue. Instead, tents offer a unique opportunity to truly tailor an event space.

TENT SIZE AND SETUP

Table 17.1 gives basic guidelines for selecting a tent size. Keep in mind that actual dimensions can vary, but in general tent sizes start at 10 feet × 10 feet, with both length and width increasing in 10-foot increments. The guidelines in this table do not include the dance floor, which averages an additional 600 square feet. So, for example, if you were planning a wedding for 100 seated guests, this would suggest selecting a 30 × 50 tent, which gives you 1,500 square feet. However, if your client wants to include a dance floor, this would suggest a minimum of 2,100 square feet; thus you would consult with your tent vendor to determine the closest size available. Looking at the chart, you might be wise to select a 40 × 60, giving you 2,400 square feet. Bear in mind that it is better to have too much room than not enough, as you do not want guests to feel crowded.

When discussing price with the tent vendor, make sure that the proposal includes tent rental cost as well as the amount of time needed to set it up and the number of workers who will be dedicated to the job. Advise your clients that it is also a sound investment to pay for a technician who will stay for the entirety of the event to manage the tent as needed. If the sidewalls need to be raised or the heat level needs to be adjusted, a technician can efficiently and professionally handle the task. Reputable tent companies may cost a bit more, but they are well worth it, for the last thing your clients want is a tent that is unsafe. Couples will sometimes wait until the last minute to decide if they want a tent or similar covering, as illustrated in Consultant in Action, Case 17.1.

TENT COSTS

As stated earlier, tent costs go way beyond the tent. Jerry O'Connell, president of the eastern region of the national tent company HDO Productions, offers the general guidelines summarized in Table 17.2. He emphasizes that the pricing of tents varies considerably by region and the actual placement for the tent. For example, he explains that tent pricing in Manhattan, New York, will be significantly higher than in Birmingham, Alabama. Furthermore, he states that if the company installs a tent on an asphalt rooftop, it will cost much more than a tent

TABLE 17.2 General Guidelines for Pricing Tents

Item	Price Range
High-peak tension tent for 130 guests	$2,500–$3,000
Side walls (white or clear)	$300–$700
Liner (white / off-white, higher price for color)	$3,000–$4,000
Heating and fuel	$400–$1,600
Air conditioning	$5,000–$10,000
Catering tent	$1,500–$2,000
Staging for eight-piece band	$600–$800
Flooring (varies based on material)	$4,500–$10,000
Dance floor (16 × 20)	$550–$700

Sources: O'Connell (2006); Groer (2006).

april showers

Your clients have a $40,000 budget that they have already surpassed. Two days before the wedding, you check the forecast and there is a 90 percent chance of rain on the wedding day. The ceremony and reception are at the same site, but the 200 guests will have to walk 100 feet between the two rooms using an uncovered walkway. You contact a rental company and get a quote of $1,500 to tent the walkway. You then call the groom, who is handling the budget, and talk with him about this option. He is hesitant and says that he will be really upset if they spend the money and then don't actually need the walkway. He asks you to make the decision.

What do you do?

placed in an open, grassy field. Therefore, the information provided should be used primarily as guidance for the relative expense of tent-related items. For instance, liners are much more expensive than side-walls, and air conditioning far outpaces heating. Check with the rental company to ensure that the quoted price reflects the delivered product, which means that it includes all installation charges.

When planning a meeting with a tent company, Groer (2006) states that you must be prepared to answer many questions pertaining to issues such as number of guests and associated tables, surface (grass, asphalt, etc.), whether the ground is level, interior and exterior conditions, drainage, type of meal service (buffet, plated, etc.), number of bars and service stations needed, type of music, and desired dance floor size. In other words, it is helpful to have drafted the site layout prior to meeting with the tent representative.

tables, chairs, linens, and tableware

When starting with a tent, your clients will also need to rent tables, chairs, linens, and tableware. At many indoor venues, some of these items need to be rented, or upgrades may be available for a price. Although some venues will require that you use their equipment, others will be flexible and allow rentals to be brought in for the wedding. It is important to know what they have available in advance so that you can gauge how the couple feels about the options and offer alternatives. For example, when visiting a reception venue, you may notice that the chairs all have mauve cushions, yet your clients' colors are navy and gold. Knowing this information, you can discuss the possibility of renting chair covers or alternative cushions with your clients.

Tables are the most straightforward choice and are available in a multitude of sizes. Common guest tables are 5-foot rounds, which seat 8 or 10, and 6-foot rounds, which seat 10 to 12, while an 8-foot oblong table can seat 8 to 10. Sweetheart tables have become more common for the bride and groom who want to be seated by themselves. Should they choose to sit with the wedding party, the trend is for couples to select a round head table rather than oblong. Square tables that seat two guests per side are another increasingly popular alternative. Tables of various sizes are also needed for items such as the escort cards, gifts, favors, and the cake, as well as wait stations for the catering staff. For escort cards, gifts, and favors, 6-foot or 8-foot oblong tables are commonly chosen, while the cake can be placed on a 4-foot round.

Chairs are also relatively finite in terms of variety, with folding chairs offering a budget-friendly option. These chairs come in a variety of colors, with material options of wood, metal, or plastic influencing the

PHOTO 17-3 *(opposite) Chiavari chairs and custom ceiling liners can transform a venue.*

price, as well as the presence of padding. For upscale weddings, Chiavari chairs are a popular selection. Chiavari chairs are formal, elegant, and enhanced by accompanying cushions which can be covered in a wide array of fabrics to match the table linens. As a point of comparison, a padded wooden folding chair averages around $3 to rent, while a Chiavari chair with cushion will run about $9 per chair in rental fees.

When bringing tables and chairs into a venue, it is extremely important to know the regulations. Some historic buildings will not allow tables to be rolled on the flooring, and each table and chair leg must have rubber or felt-tipped bottoms. Policies such as these mean the room has to be laid with pads and each item must be carefully prepared and placed; accordingly, staffing costs will go up significantly.

Selecting linens and tableware can be a time-consuming endeavor, as seemingly endless options pertaining to color, style, and material are available. Advise your clients to have their theme, color scheme, and floral décor in mind when selecting items like china, glassware, flatware, and linens. Of these, linens are traditionally the most overlooked; couples often do not think past the traditional white tablecloth. On the contrary, linens offer one of the least expensive ways to make a

PHOTO 17-4 *Colored linens and beaded chargers add drama to a table setting.*

huge impression, and most reception venues allow clients to bring in rented linens. Top rental companies offer hundreds of styles and cuts from which to choose, available in fabrics such as damask, lace, organza, satin, silk, taffeta, toile, twill, and velvet. Linens are available in an endless array of colors and styles such as embroidered, floral, fringed, iridescent, pin-tucked, and striped. A current trend is layering linens to create a dramatic and memorable effect. If the linens are bold and patterned, it is a good idea to go with simple floral décor to create a balance so that the elements will not "fight." Keep in mind that you will need linens for areas such as the cake table and escort table, which may also require table skirts. Longer linens that do not require skirts are a current trend. The linens should be long enough to cover the legs of all tables, which are often rough looking from use.

When selecting linens, once your clients have narrowed down their options, you can work with the company specialist, who will often send you samples. You can then schedule an appointment with the reception venue to set three tables with three different sets of linens and decide which looks best. This is a good time to work with the floral designer so you have a sample of the centerpiece on hand.

When placing the order, if the budget will allow, have your clients order a few extra napkins and an extra table cloth. Spills are common, so it is helpful to have spares just in case. When the linens are delivered, always double-check the order. Make sure you received the correct pattern and correct number, as your clients will be accountable for any missing pieces. This same advice applies to any rental item. Generally, the rental or catering staff will set the tables for you, because table-ware shouldn't just be thrown on randomly. The correct placement of plates, glasses, flatware, and the intricate folds that are common to napkins for formal weddings can be time-consuming endeavors.

At the end of the reception, you need to re-count the rentals. If a linen order was for 12 tablecloths and 100 napkins, you are responsible for getting those exact numbers back to the rental company. Invariably, someone throws a napkin away, and your client will be charged. If it costs $3 to rent a napkin, it will cost $6 or more to replace that linen. Specialty table linens are much more expensive, with rental fees averaging $30 and higher and replacement fees at least double that amount.

lighting

Lighting is used to establish the mood of a setting, and innovative lighting can bring a ceremony or reception venue to life. Just as a coat of paint and new carpeting can transform a house, professional lighting can take a bland venue and make it look like a glamorous Hollywood movie set. Fred Elting of Frost Lighting, featured in Vendor Spotlight, Case 17.2, explains that there are three areas of concern with

fred elting

frost lighting

What separates you from other lighting companies? We're a decorative lighting company versus more of a production event lighting company that goes in and puts up stage lighting. We primarily work on weddings, social events, and corporate events and have offices in New York, Chicago, Florida, and Washington DC.

How did you get involved with specialty lighting? My mother is a florist and a wedding planner. I started doing lighting for her when I was 14 years old and have been doing it ever since. Currently, I set up lighting at approximately 100 weddings a year.

What is your biggest concern with lighting? Honestly, my biggest concern is what people are going to see when they walk into the room. Because that is the impression they are going to get, and their impression is going to be from my lighting. I want guests to walk in and say, "Wow, it's so cool; the lighting is so cool."

What is your favorite type of tent lighting? I love a clear top tent where you can see through the ceiling. It's a fun tent to light and they're great with trees. I love doing landscape lighting. With the clear top tent, you have to have more lights outside than inside. So we light up all the trees around the tent and if the branches go up and over the tent, we light up those branches and that will create a glow inside the tent and it's fabulous.

Web site: www.frostlighting.com.

lighting: (1) centerpiece lighting; (2) dance floor and wall lighting; and (3) tent lighting.

CENTERPIECE LIGHTING

Fred Elting explains that in a ballroom, where existing lights are in place, the first lighting consideration pertains to the centerpieces, which can include pin spotting or a wash of light. Pin spotting is a tightly focused beam of light directed on the table centerpieces, which allows the centerpieces to "pop," as the light does not spill over onto the rest of the table. Pin spots can even be placed underneath a table to shoot up through a clear glass centerpiece for a unique effect.

The wash of light came about as a response to the fact that centerpieces started getting larger and taller. For large arrangements, the pin spotting would allow for one hot spot on the arrangement but couldn't capture the whole piece. A wash of light is a wider beam that will light up the whole table. This light is particularly effective when the linens are spectacular, as the wash will pick up any shimmer or play in the tablecloth. Fred explains that LED (light-emitting diode) lights are the latest trend because they offer an even wash of light with very little electrical usage.

Photograph by www.RodneyBailey.com

PHOTO 17-5 *Pin spotting allows centerpieces to "pop."*

Regardless of the lighting style, white light should never be used because it does not look becoming on people. Lighting should make the room, the flowers, and the guests look great. In order to achieve this effect, lighting specialists choose from a range of pinks and ambers that are subtle and flattering.

DANCE FLOOR AND WALL LIGHTING

After the centerpieces, the next consideration is the dance floor. The dance floor is a large open space that takes up a significant portion of your room. Fred states that there are three possible steps in lighting a dance floor. The first and most common is a wash of light onto the dance floor, typically two pink and two lavender fixtures. These colors give a warm glow and look great on people. The dance floor becomes more appealing as opposed to having a big empty space.

The next step is a breakup of light over the dance floor achieved through the use of artistic tools known as gobos. Gobos are thin templates often made of metal that are placed at the end of a lighting fixture, with design options that allow for an endless number of pat-

PHOTO 17-6 *Monogrammed gobos and a wash of light customize the dance floor.*

terns. Gobos add interest, color, and texture to a dance floor, walls, or ceiling. Outlines of leaves, snowflakes, stars, and sunbursts, as well as a multitude of geometric patterns, are common.

A third option for lighting the dance floor is computerized intelligent lighting. This allows for moving patterns that are controlled by a technician who can constantly change the look to set the tone of the reception. For example, a father-daughter dance might include amber and pink with subtle gobos moving slowly over the dance floor, but when the music gets faster and more exciting for general dancing, the colors change to contemporary, cool spectrum colors such as lavenders and blues, and the pace is kicked up. Behind the stage might be a black backdrop with computer-generated fiber optics that are controlled on a computer and change colors and pulse. Intricate patterns such as leopards and lions looking down on the crowd can also be employed. As Fred notes, top lighting companies work with designers and decorators; combined, the imaginative team can do just about anything with lighting.

Wall lighting is not necessary in most hotels because the chandeliers already in place can be controlled to create ambient lighting, or glow. However, in cases where a client wants to add color to what is in place, up lighting can transform a space with minimal investment. Up lighting is an excellent choice for spaces such as a community center or hall that doesn't have attractive ambient lighting in place.

TENT LIGHTING

Tent lighting is more complex and significantly more expensive than ballroom lighting because the specialist is dealing with an empty structure and has to bring everything in, including power. Fred offers the comparison that ballroom lighting can be set up in seven hours for around $5,000, while it takes an average of two days and $15,000 to install tent lighting for a wedding. The cost of lighting presents another reason why clients on a budget should think twice before selecting a tent for their wedding. The first step is a wash of light onto the ceiling to create the ambient glow. This is followed by the installation of chandeliers for illumination, which are often covered with crystal beading to make them elegant or greenery and flowers for a garden effect. A sea of paper lanterns can also be used for illumination. Lighting companies also commonly work with fabric and can take a structure such as a picnic pavilion and transform it into a ballroom with draping fabric and custom lighting. A tent ceiling can also be draped with swags of miniature lights for a graceful look.

Because lighting companies use a great deal of equipment, be certain to ask them how they install their fixtures. The bottom line is that the lighting should blend into the architecture of the space rather than stand out as an eyesore. Keep in mind that specialty lighting can also be used outside and around a tent or venue to brighten up the surrounding area.

Photograph by www.RodneyBailey.com

PHOTO 17-7 *Paper lanterns are a colorful and decorative lighting option.*

✆ outdoor considerations

Beyond weather, two significant considerations when planning outdoor weddings are bathrooms and bugs. In terms of bathrooms, if the wedding is in someone's backyard rather than at a rented space that already has restroom facilities, it is in the best interest of the home-owners to rent bathrooms. Even if the house is large, having hundreds of people traipsing through to use their facilities can put an enormous amount of pressure on the sewer system. Homeowners have had their plumbing systems literally wiped out by having a tent wedding on the property and not investing in washrooms. Bathroom rental from well-known companies such as Porta-Potty can be as simple as a holding tank or as luxuriously equipped as their Executive Restroom Trailers which have lighting, music, carpeting, air conditioning, heating, flush, and running water with the sinks. Make sure to get at least one rental washroom for every 100 guests and carefully position them away from the main activities.

A second outdoor consideration is bugs, which in warm climates can move beyond a nuisance to extreme discomfort and leave-taking.

PHOTO 17-8 *(opposite) Specialty lighting can tie in the theme of a wedding.*

Imagine an outdoor, Southern wedding in July: mosquitoes, flies, wasps, ticks, gnats, yellow jackets, and no-see-ums, just to name a few. They swarm around the food and bite the guests. They smell sugar and go crazy. They are drawn to the light for evening weddings. Citronella candles help but have a pungent smell, so they should be kept out of the immediate vicinity of the tent to avoid interfering with the meal. Machines that zap bugs can be rented, but they have an irritating sound. Tent entryways, on the other hand, are very helpful because they control the flow of people and other outside elements. You could also spray the surrounding area, but you have to be careful because children will often run in grassy areas and the chemicals then present a safety issue. A final option is to have the wait staff walk around with trays of wipes or bottles of bug repellant. A supply should also be available in the restroom facilities.

site layout

Your site layout does not need to be a masterpiece that any architect would envy; instead, it is a straightforward drawing that offers a concise overview of placement and spacing. If there are no online site

PHOTO 17-9 *Good site layout will enhance the flow of a reception.*

maps available of the venues, start with a blank page for both the ceremony and reception sites and fill in the applicable essentials covered in Table 17.3.

Site layout is straightforward when weddings are held in established venues that offer few options for variation. As the planning space becomes more open and the number of rentals increases, the site layout becomes more complex. For example, outdoor weddings and receptions held in tents require more attention to detail and increase the number of decisions that must be made. Figure 17.1 offers an example of a blank site layout of The Atrium at Meadowlark Gardens (2006), where over 120 weddings are hosted every year, as explained by facilities manager Wayne Hager and events coordinator Bernadette Thompson. Figure 17.2 illustrates the same venue, detailing the specific information for a wedding reception.

TABLE 17.3 Site Layout Essentials for Weddings

Ceremony
- Parking
- Room dimensions
- Entrances and exits, with special marks for accessible paths and ramps and indications of controls (e.g., metal detector, security check)
- Restroom facilities
- Number of rows, with marks for reserved areas, and indications if the areas are separated for the bride's guests versus the groom's guests
- Waiting area for bride, groom, and wedding party prior to ceremony
- Indicators for the location for floral décor and other special ceremony elements
- Space to be used for central focus (e.g., altar, arch, chuppah, or other visually accessible area)
- Fire lanes and other emergency information

Reception
- Parking
- Room dimensions
- Entrances and exits, with special marks for accessible paths and ramps and indications of controls (e.g., metal detector, security check)
- Restroom facilities
- Cocktail hour area, if separate from reception space
- Number of guest tables with marks for reserved tables
- Head table and/or sweetheart table
- Service stations for wait staff
- Tables and areas associated with seating stationery, gifts, the cake, and favors
- Kitchen and/or food-related areas
- Bar area
- Music and dance area
- Areas for the placement of specialized lighting
- Indicators for the location for specialized floral décor and other special reception elements
- Fire lanes and other emergency information

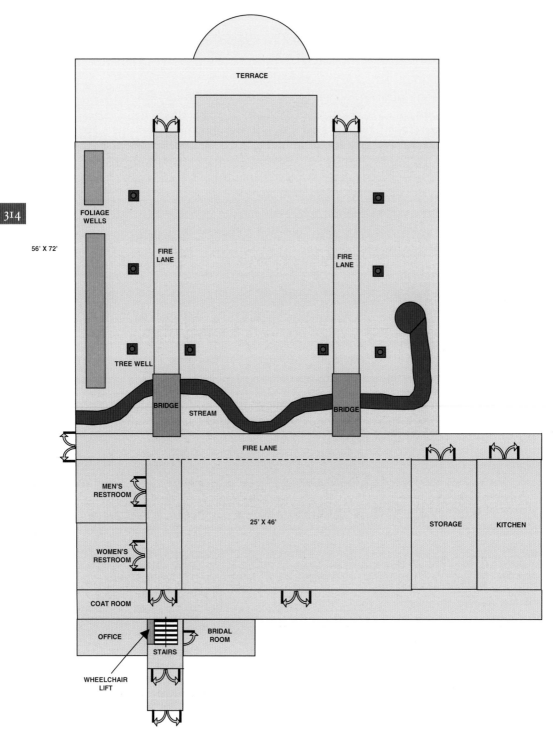

FIGURE 17.1 *Blank site layout of a reception space*
Source: The Atrium at Meadowlark Gardens (2006).

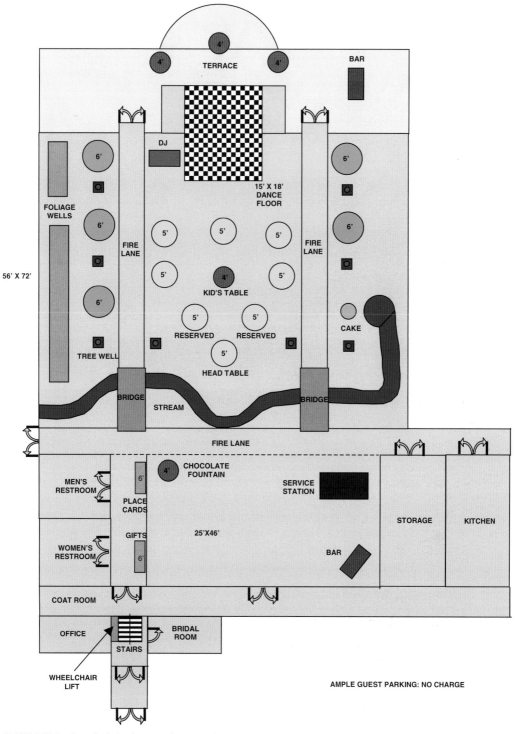

FIGURE 17.2 *Detailed site layout of a reception space*
Source: The Atrium at Meadowlark Gardens (2006).

PHOTO 17-10 *Open planning space requires careful site layout.*

As discussed earlier, tables come in different shapes and sizes, so you must understand the floor plan and the square footage of a room to determine how many tables will fit and how to space them. Be sure to leave at least 48 inches, and preferably 54, between tables so there is adequate space for movement, allowing guests not to feel cramped and the wait staff to easily move around while carrying large trays. Understanding the spacing of the venues for each wedding you plan will help you maximize the safety and comfort level of the guests and staff.

REFERENCES

The Atrium at Meadowlark Gardens. (2006). Site layout (Web site and personal communication), available at http://www.nvpra.org

Groer, A. (2006, April 27). Celebration cover charge. *The Washington Post*, H1; H5.

O'Connell, J. (2006). Tent pricing (Web site and personal communication). HDO Productions, available at http://www.hdotents.com

Richardson, D. (2006). Tent styles and accessories (Web site and personal communication). Sugarplum Tent Company, available at http://www.sugarplumtents.com

Rodriguez, V. (2004). *Celebrate! The Washington Post Guide to Successful Celebrations*. Washington, DC: The Washington Post.

Consultant Checklist and Reminders for Rentals and Site Layout

☐ Prior to meeting with a tent rental company, familiarize yourself with the different types of tents and accessories and prepare a draft of the desired site layout.

☐ Have too much room rather than not enough in a tent.

☐ Note that the cost of a tent and the necessary associated rentals is often significantly higher than renting a ballroom or other venue.

☐ Impress guests with creative linen selections.

☐ When placing the linen order, add a few extra napkins and an extra table cloth in case of spills.

☐ Count rentals upon delivery and before pickup to make sure there are no missing items.

☐ Use lighting to transform a space from bland to glamorous.

☐ Recognize that bathrooms and bugs are two significant considerations with outdoor weddings.

☐ Understand that site layout offers a concise overview of placement and spacing.

review questions

1. Distinguish between pole (tension) tents and frame tents.

2. If you have 150 guests for a buffet reception and no dance floor, what size tent should be selected?

3. Name at least four types of fabric that are used for linens.

4. Distinguish between pin spotting and a wash of light as related to centerpieces.

5. What are gobos, and how are they used?

6. What are three ways to handle bugs for outdoor weddings?

7. What information should be included in a site layout for a ceremony?

8. What information should be included in a site layout for a reception?

terminology

- Ambient lighting
- Chiavari chairs
- Frame tents
- Gobos
- Pin spotting
- Pole (tension) tents
- Site layout
- Up lighting
- Wash of light

PHOTO 18-1 *Programs guide guests through the ceremony.*

stationery elements and etiquette

Stationery elements are present throughout the wedding process and play ongoing roles in setting and carrying out the theme of a wedding. Stationery elements also bookend a wedding, in that they are generally the first thing the guests see, with save-the-date cards and invitations, as well as the last, with thank-you cards.

a s a consultant, it is important to remember the spelling of stationery, which ends with an "ery" and not an "ary," as it is often mistakenly spelled. This chapter provides an overview of the different components and purposes of stationery, including common rules of etiquette. While only taking up 3 percent of an average wedding budget, the wardrobe of stationery elements is quite broad including: save-the-date notices, invitations, calligraphy, ceremony programs, seating stationery, menus, personalized paper products, wedding announcements, and thank-you notes.

save-the-date notices

Save-the-date notices, which are usually sent out 6 to 18 months before the wedding, have become an increasingly popular trend in the past five years. As discussed in Chapter 8, they are particularly important for destination weddings or those taking place over a holiday weekend. The use of refrigerator magnets is quite popular, since they can act as a constant reminder but cards or postcards are also commonly selected. Save-the-date notices generally indicate the name of the bride and groom, the date, and the location. The time of day may be included, as well as the wedding Web site should the couple have one. Often the phrase, "Invitation to follow," is included so that the recipient knows that this is not the actual invitation. Save-the-date notices are usually informal and fun, but should still tie into the overall theme of the wedding.

Advise your clients that all potential guests should receive save-the-date notices. Some clients may want to save by just sending them to out-of-town guests, but the schedules of local friends and relatives are just as busy. Furthermore, people know each other in these groups. If one friend comments on how clever the notice was, another might think, "I didn't get it. I must not be invited to the wedding." So it is important to be consistent.

invitations

Invitations involve a significant number of decisions. This section covers the parts of the invitation, printing style, paper, font, wording, ordering, and delivery. The decisions that are made for the invitations are commonly carried over to other stationery elements.

PARTS OF THE INVITATION

The most formal invitations include the following: outer envelope, inner envelope, invitation card, reception card, and response card. Invitations may also include additional information such as a directions card or a card with lodging options. Lynne Sandler from Lettering by Lynne, featured in Vendor Spotlight, Case 18.1, explains that the dual envelopes originated from the time when mail was delivered by horse and carriage. Unpaved, muddy roads and the open elements would cause the outer envelope to become stained. The outer envelope was discarded upon arrival, and the invitation was then presented to the homeowner with the clean inner envelope. Now outer and inner envelopes are used for different wording purposes, which will be discussed in the wording section of this chapter. The outer

lynne sandler

lettering by lynne

How did you get interested in stationery? I started out as a calligrapher in 1978 so that I could address the envelopes for my daughter's Bat Mitzvah because it was coming up that year. I took another class and then before I knew it, I was designing invitations as well. Then I began addressing envelopes for friends and designing some of their invitations. One thing led to another, and I slowly developed a small part-time business. I ordered two invitation albums—now I have close to 100 of them and a full-time business.

What are the benefits of working with an invitation specialist? We deal directly with the invitation companies, can locate any invitation, and can troubleshoot any problems that may arise, thus relieving the couple of that stress. We know the invitation etiquette in terms of the appropriate wording and the language that should be used. I have come across all different types of families and cultures and can help with unique situations. The invitation specialist will also help clients understand the paper styles, colors, and ink options.

How have invitations changed in the past 20 years? It used to be you always wanted ivory or ecru with black ink. Today anything goes. I am also seeing more cultures and blended cultures. I've done invitations for Hindu, Chinese, Korean, Jewish, African American, Arabic, German, Spanish, and Mexican weddings, and each culture has its own methods. For example, one custom common to many Hispanic weddings is that it is not appropriate to mail the invitations—they are hand delivered to all the guests. Many cross-cultural couples will select an invitation that opens, allowing the wording to be printed in both languages, for instance, English on one side and Chinese on the other.

How do you help clients in terms of etiquette? I tell my clients, number one, this is your wedding. And although I know all the rules of etiquette and

(Continues)

can tell them what is correct, I also reassure them that the etiquette police won't come after them if they want to do something different.

How far in advance should invitations be ordered? Four months on average, but it can be done in less. I've had clients who came in seven months in advance, and they get everything ordered and addressed ready to go out. The only danger with doing it too early is that occasionally things change. For example, last year I had a bride who was having a destination wedding and a hurricane came through and the venue had to cancel. She was able to find another place but had to have her invitations redone.

Web site: letteringbylynne.com

envelope is gummed so that it can be sealed. The inner envelope is never sealed.

The invitation card gives the specifics of the event, which will be discussed thoroughly in the wording section of this chapter. A reception card is needed primarily when the ceremony and reception are held at different venues; if they are at the same location, the words "Reception to follow" are often included on the invitation itself.

The response card, also called the reply card, has an interesting background in that traditionally this was never included; instead, the recipient of the invitation would write a formal letter of acceptance to the event. The response card emerged as a time-saving device in light of a more hurried pace of life. Furthermore, some response cards will include a listing of entrée options so that each guest can select his or her reception meal. The response card must include an addressed, stamped envelope for return purposes.

Some clients will ask you if it is appropriate to include a registry card in the invitation. This card offers the details regarding the stores where the couple has registered for gifts. While becoming more commonplace, etiquette suggests that it is highly inappropriate for couples to include this information in a wedding invitation, as it implies to the invited guests that they are required to purchase a gift and, moreover, that the gift must come from a certain place. Guests who wish to honor the couple with a gift should not feel constrained to a predetermined listing. For those who prefer to select something from the couple's registry, this store information can be readily requested and obtained through word-of-mouth or e-mail.

PRINTING STYLE

For wedding invitations, four primary printing styles are used: engraving, letterpress, thermography, and flat. Engraving is a traditional printing style that is very formal and expensive. Typically, brides that request engraved invitations are encouraged to do so by their mothers, who recall this classic style. With an engraved invitation, when you run your hand over the wording, you will feel a texture that is slightly raised and when you turn the invitation over, there is an impression. A metal plate with the wording etched in is made specifically for the invitation. The paper, which is usually all cotton and watermarked, is pressed into the inked plate, and the impression is made.

A second style, which was also historically common, is letterpress. Letterpress is a process that is essentially the opposite of engraving, where the letters are raised and then pressed into a soft paper, leaving an indent on the front of the invitation. When you run your hand over it, you can feel the ridges. Letterpress is a classy and very expensive style of printing, in part because few companies now offer this technique.

Thermography, in contrast to the first two styles, is inexpensive and accordingly is also the most commonly chosen printing style. Similar to engraving, thermography is raised printing that can be felt, but if you turn the invitation over there is no impression. The invitation is printed through a regular printing press, allowing for a very fast process. While the ink is still wet, it is sprayed with a powder, and then it moves to another phase that has heat. The heat allows the powder and ink to chemically react, which results in the raised ink. Some companies do not thoroughly brush off the remaining powder, and a gritty residue may remain.

Flat printing is also inexpensive and is chosen when the couple wants to include design elements that do not lend themselves to a raised style. Contemporary invitations with photographs, graphic designs, or large images are not well suited for raised printing.

Invitations may also include an embossed image, which is a raised image that does not include ink and is used for monograms or thematic images such as cultural symbols, flowers, shells, stars, leaves, or snowflakes. These types of images may also be printed using the styles mentioned above.

INVITATION PAPER

The paper selected is determined in part by the printing style but is largely a matter of personal choice and budget. The cost of invitations is determined not only by the printing style, but also by the quality of the paper. Paper that is 100 percent cotton or linen rag will be significantly more expensive than a synthetic blend of paper. Bond weight of paper is another indication of quality, and 32 or 40 pound paper is a good letter quality (Stewart, 1999). As a point of comparison, typical computer paper is 20 pound. Handmade paper and/or features such as ribbons, gold leaf edging, vellum overlays, dried flowers, and envelope liners add significantly to the cost. When selecting paper, color is another consideration. In the United States, ecru-colored stock, which is a soft ivory shade, is the traditional choice, while in Europe white is more frequently chosen. For contemporary invitations, a full spectrum of colors is available, and a couple can readily find invitations to match the theme and tone of their wedding.

FONT

The range of fonts has grown significantly, and whether a classic or contemporary font is chosen will be based on the style of the invitation itself. Options to consider include: (1) cursive or printed style; (2) all uppercase letters versus a mixture of uppercase and lower case; (3) the inclusion of monograms or other large specialty fonts; and (4) ink color. The traditional ink color for the font is black, but colored inks have become very common. For example, a fall wedding might include a rust or olive green ink on an invitation with a leaf motif.

WORDING

Wording begins with the envelopes. The outer envelope is the most formal, with full names and titles used. For the addresses, there should be no street or state abbreviations. For example, use Road rather than Rd. and Colorado rather than CO. The outer envelope should be addressed to the primary recipient or recipients, while the inner envelope can include additional invitees using formal or informal names. For instance, the outer envelope might be addressed to Mr. Gregory Aabas, while the inner envelope states Greg and Guest. Similarly, an outer envelope might state Commander Robert Ariza and Doctor Linda Tighe-Ariza, while the inner states Rob, Lynne, Cindy and Joey, which includes the names of the guests' children. However, the most formal invitations would use the full titles on both the inner and outer envelopes.

The wording of the invitation itself can get quite complicated when considering changing family dynamics. Geller (1999) explains that the decorum of the traditional wedding invitations, which suggest uniformity and a patriarchal society, is challenged in an age where individualism and egalitarianism are widespread; when stable, nuclear families are giving way to divorce; when second marriages and blended families are commonplace; and when cross-cultural unions are prevalent. For example, some brides have two sets of parents or even three, so it is not feasible to list all of their names on the invitation. In general, there are six parts to the invitation wording with associated lines: host; request; bride and groom; date and time; location; and special instructions (Stewart, 1999).

The wording of the response card should mimic the formality of the invitation wording. Three elements found in most response cards include a space for guest name(s); an indication of attendance; and the date by which a response is desired. If the guests are able to choose an entrée or if other decisions are to be made, information regarding their selection options is also included.

Following are three examples of how the invitation might be worded, each accompanied by a response card that reflects the invitation's tone. Figure 18.1 is the most traditional and formal, with the parents of the bride acting as hosts. Furthermore, the R.S.V.P. in the request line means that the guests are to send a personal reply; therefore, no response card will be included. A formal invitation without the R.S.V.P. line would include a response card with wording such as that found in Figure 18.2, where the guests would write a formal reply and the assumption is that they will know the information to be included. The open response card can also be used for less formal weddings, as it

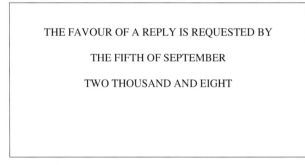

MR. AND MRS. PETER OLMSTED	Host Line
REQUEST THE HONOUR OF YOUR PRESENCE	Request Line
AT THE MARRIAGE OF THEIR DAUGHTER	
SHANNON MARIE	Bride and Groom
TO	
MR. DONALD MICHAEL WOOD	
SATURDAY, THE EIGHTEENTH OF OCTOBER	Date and Time
TWO THOUSAND AND EIGHT	
AT TWO O'CLOCK	
INTERNATIONAL CATHEDRAL	Location
OKLAHOMA CITY, OKLAHOMA	
R.S.V.P. BLACK TIE	Special Instructions

FIGURE 18.1 *Invitation wording for traditional, black tie wedding*

THE FAVOUR OF A REPLY IS REQUESTED BY

THE FIFTH OF SEPTEMBER

TWO THOUSAND AND EIGHT

FIGURE 18.2 *Formal response card*

allows guests to write creative notes that are often saved by the couple in a memory album.

Figure 18.3 offers an option of wording for a couple with blended families and therefore too many hosts to list on the invitation. The wording also gives one example of how couples can inform their guests that children will not be invited to the wedding. The associated response card, seen in Figure 18.4, has directed wording, offering a line for the names, where the uppercase "M" can be used to indicate

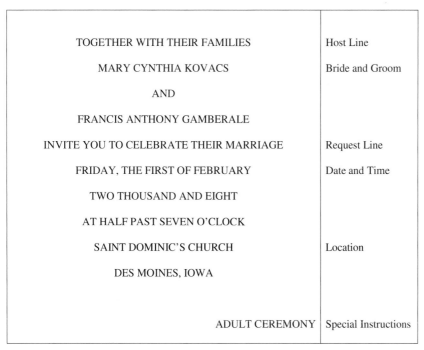

TOGETHER WITH THEIR FAMILIES	Host Line
MARY CYNTHIA KOVACS	Bride and Groom
AND	
FRANCIS ANTHONY GAMBERALE	
INVITE YOU TO CELEBRATE THEIR MARRIAGE	Request Line
FRIDAY, THE FIRST OF FEBRUARY	Date and Time
TWO THOUSAND AND EIGHT	
AT HALF PAST SEVEN O'CLOCK	
SAINT DOMINIC'S CHURCH	Location
DES MOINES, IOWA	
ADULT CEREMONY	Special Instructions

FIGURE 18.3 *Invitation wording for blended family with adult-only ceremony*

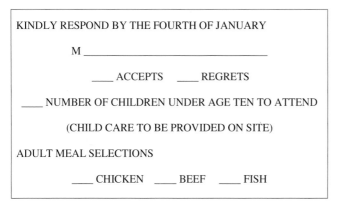

KINDLY RESPOND BY THE FOURTH OF JANUARY

M _____

____ ACCEPTS   ____ REGRETS

____ NUMBER OF CHILDREN UNDER AGE TEN TO ATTEND

(CHILD CARE TO BE PROVIDED ON SITE)

ADULT MEAL SELECTIONS

____ CHICKEN   ____ BEEF   ____ FISH

FIGURE 18.4 *Directed response card*

Mr., Mrs., or Ms. Guests are to check whether or not they will attend in the space provided, indicate the number of children they will bring, and select the desired meal for each guest. The fact that child care will be provided on site reinforces the adult nature of this wedding.

Figure 18.5 illustrates how a casual invitation can be worded, where the bride and groom are acting as hosts and the reception is held in the same location as the wedding, so no reception card would be included. Notice that in this example the numbers are not spelled out and the lettering includes lower case. The response card, seen in

Camie and Jake	Bride and Groom
Would Love to Sea You	Request Line
At Their Casual, Beach Front Wedding	
Saturday, June 21, 2008	Date and Time
12:00 Noon	
Wild Dunes Resort	Location
Isle of Palms, South Carolina	
Lunch and an Afternoon at the Beach to Follow	Special Instructions

FIGURE 18.5 *Invitation for a casual wedding with reception at same location*

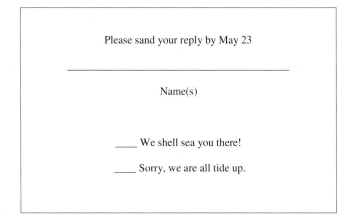

Please sand your reply by May 23

_____

Name(s)

_____ We shell sea you there!

_____ Sorry, we are all tide up.

FIGURE 18.6 *Informal response card that ties into wedding theme*

Figure 18.6, is similarly casual and consistent with the beach theme. Note that, as seen in this example, most invitation specialists are now suggesting that couples use "Name(s)" rather than the uppercase "M" because it avoids the problem of what to do for doctors, attorneys, religious leaders, those with military ranks, and others with titles that do not begin with an "M."

The wording of the reception card is the most straightforward and includes the location and time of the reception. If there are going to be a significant number of out-of-town guests, it is also advisable to include a directions card. Also, if it is an adult ceremony and/or reception, this is generally repeated on the reception card. Couples who feel very strongly about not having children at their wedding should indicate this in two or three different places. Ambiguity may arise as to what age represents the cutoff: some couples do not want young children, such as those under the age of 5, whereas others do not want guests under the age of 18. Often word of mouth and e-mail communication are used to clarify any questions that arise.

ORDERING INVITATIONS

Suggest to your clients that they start working with a stationery specialist four to six months before their wedding. As pointed out by Lynne Sandler, stationery companies can work within a shorter time frame, but the creative options become limited the closer couples get to their wedding date. It is also important to allow plenty of time to go through the proofing process. Some invitations take multiple proofs before the desired look is achieved. Remind your clients that once they have approved the proof, they accept full responsibility for the information, spelling, print style, font, punctuation, layout, and color separation.

When ordering invitations, the couple should count the number needed based on households rather than individual people. A common mistake is to order the number of invitations based on the number of guests, but if they are inviting 100 people, they typically will not need 100 invitations. They probably need between 50 and 75 depending on how many singles, couples, and children will be invited. At the same time, encourage your clients to make sure they do not under order, for it is much more expensive to reorder invitations than it is to have 10 or so extra invitations printed. Once a company has the initial order off the press, the order is done, and if it comes back, it is a brand-new job. Remind your clients that the first 25 of any stationery item will be the most expensive and the price drops significantly after that. Furthermore, most high-end companies will not accept invitation orders of less than 50. For example, 50 high-quality invitations will cost $12 or more each but when ordering 100 of the same design, the price can drop to $10 apiece. Less expensive invitations follow the same pattern and can drop from $6 each for orders of 25 to $2 each for orders of 100.

DELIVERY

Encourage your clients to have the invitations weighed for postage purposes. Many invitations weigh more than one ounce with all of the inserts, and the last thing a couple wants is for their invitations to arrive with postage due. Even if the mailing weighs less than one ounce, additional postage will still be necessary if the envelope is bulky or the invitation is oddly shaped; for example, square invitations require additional postage. You should also advise your clients to have the invitations hand canceled, again because the number of inserts can cause bulk and can be mangled going through the postage meter. For etiquette purposes, the hand cancellation is also a more elegant look. Suggest to your clients that, before sending out the full mailing, they mail one invitation to themselves as a test run. They should include all parts of the invitation. This test will allow them to see how long the invitation takes to reach them and determine if it arrives in good shape.

The post office carries an array of floral and "Love" stamps that are popular for mailing invitations. In addition, your clients can order custom-designed postage stamps through Web sites such as Photo-Stamps.com. The stamp might be the couple's engagement photo or an image that ties into the theme of the wedding. For example, if the couple is having a beach theme, the stamp might include a photo of an ocean, shells, or palm trees.

Couples should also consider to whom they want the response card to be returned. Traditionally it was returned to the parents of the bride, but today it is just as likely to be returned to the bride. Two recent trends do not involve a surface mail return, as guests can respond through 1–800 numbers managed by companies that track RSVPs or through Web site addresses.

Invitations should be mailed anywhere from 6 to 10 weeks before the wedding. Some couples will mail to their "A" list 10 weeks out, then their "B" list, and sometimes even a "C" list, based on rejections from the earlier groups. A tiered guest list has significant etiquette implications, as peer groups talk and people can quickly become aware that they are not in the top group, which can cause hurt feelings.

☙ calligraphy

A calligrapher's hand printing is a very elegant and personal way to create stationery elements. Guests have been known to talk for years about invitations they received that were hand lettered by a calligrapher. A calligrapher can be hired to letter any stationery element but is most commonly brought on to address the envelopes. If a calligraphy specialist is hired for the invitation, menu, or other item that can be used for all guests, this person will hand design a template that will then be typeset and printed. Because envelopes are unique to each guest, the time investment and cost are significant, with the charge for each set of inner and outer envelopes ranging from $5 to $7. This beautiful touch is therefore usually reserved for weddings with above-average budgets.

Because hiring a calligrapher can be cost prohibitive, couples generally explore other options for addressing their envelopes. Handwriting is considered to be more personal, and some couples even have gatherings where friends or family members with elegant handwriting will help them with this task. Etiquette dictates that black ink should be used when addressing envelopes by hand. Be certain to have your clients order plenty of extra envelopes if they plan to use hand addressing, as this process is subject to error.

Because of the wasted envelopes and time associated with handwriting, couples are increasingly turning to computerized addressing. Most stationery vendors can assist with this task, and calligraphy fonts now exist that are nearly as beautiful as hand calligraphy. The address should be printed directly on the envelope and labels should be avoided.

ceremony programs

Approximately 70 percent of couples use programs to guide guests through their ceremony. Programs come in all different shapes and sizes and are often designed and printed by the couple to save on costs. The purpose of the program is to introduce the guests to the wedding party and set forth the organization of the ceremony. If held in a house of worship, it is important to determine if there are any restrictions regarding program wording.

Generally, all members of the wedding party will be listed, and information regarding readings, prayers, responses, music, and vows will be included. Some programs will give details regarding special ceremony elements. For example, if the couple will be jumping the broom, an African American tradition, a paragraph regarding the history of this tradition might be included. Many couples will also include a dedication or message of thanks in their program. A sample ceremony program can be found in Chapter 13 with the discussion of ceremony specifics.

For the most part, guests do not want to read *War and Peace* during the wedding ceremony, so advise your clients that they do not have to go overboard. Too much reading will draw guests' attention away from the ceremony itself. If the couple is cross-cultural and there are guests present who speak different languages, it is a very welcoming touch to have the program printed in both languages, side by side.

For more casual weddings, the program is also a place where the personality of various members of the wedding party can be shared. For example, one sports-loving couple wrote the following dedication in their program:

> Todd Jamis and Lorna Cantillon introduced us to each other. Five traumatized dog sitters later and with enough good luck to see the Steelers win a Super Bowl, we stand before you today. We share fond memories with each person here and many have

The Marriage Ceremony of

Catherine Yung-Ching Sun

to

Benjamin Dalrymple Wood

...rday, the Twenty-Fourth of September
Two Thousand and Five
Meridian House
...ashington, District of Columbia

PHOTO 18-2   *Programs allow couples to share cultural traditions.*

traveled a great distance to be with us. Good fortune and good friends brought us together and it is a true gift to share this day with each of you.

This same program gave fun little pieces of information about members of the wedding party. For example, under the name of the maid of honor it stated: "An avid Broncos fan and rock climber, Jules is a pediatrician and long-time friend of the bride." This type of program humanizes the wedding party and gives people something to talk about when they interact during the reception.

Program design is frequently initiated late in the planning process, as the ceremony is often finalized only a few weeks before the wedding. However, if your clients are creating their own programs, advise them not to wait until the last minute as they do not want to be tying raffia or ribbons on programs the night before the wedding.

Beyond the program, other specialized ceremony elements require stationery. For example, pew cards can be used when reserving special seats for honored guests or if the immediate family needs more than the first two rows. Many stationery professionals also can design a

PHOTO 18-3 *Tying program ribbons should not be done at the last minute.*

PHOTO 18-4 *Many stationery professionals can design a personalized ketubah, which is the Jewish marriage contract.*

personalized ketubah, which is the Jewish marriage contract introduced in Chapter 13. Furthermore, couples who write their own vows often like to have them printed and framed. Finally, guest books are often specially designed and can be used for the ceremony and/or the reception.

ᑌ seating stationery

If a couple wishes to designate where guests will sit at the wedding reception, seating stationery should be used. For example, if cocktails are over at 6:45 P.M. and dinner is going to be served at 7:00 P.M., then that leaves only 15 minutes to navigate what might be several hundred people into the dining area. Seating stationery can include a seating chart, escort cards, place cards, and table markers.

A seating chart gives an alphabetized listing of guests. Next to each name, the table where each is seated is indicated. Seating charts are large and can be mounted on foam board or placed in a rented frame, but can cause congestion if the number of guests is more than 100.

Photograph by www.RodneyBailey.com

PHOTO 18-5 *Escort cards guide guests to their tables.*

Escort cards are a different seating option, and list the person's name and table number on an individual card.

Table markers tell guests when they have reached the right place. If using numbers, options such as #1, ONE, or Table 1 can be selected. Advise your clients to avoid using Roman numerals because in a muted ballroom, numbers such as XI, XII, and XIII look too similar and cause confusion for both guests and staff. Keep table markers simple and make the font big and bold for easy location. Table markers are often placed in stands or frames that can be rented from your stationery specialist, catering company, or floral designer if incorporated in the centerpiece.

A place card will also be used if the guests have not only a specific table, but also a designated seat. When reaching that level of detail, remind your clients that they will need to allow plenty of time to work on the site layout, which is discussed in Chapter 17.

Seating stationery allows for design touches that tie into the theme of the wedding. For example, a winter theme might have escort cards

PHOTO 18-6 *Seating stationery can tie in the wedding theme.*

Photograph by www.RodneyBailey.com

PHOTO 18-7 *Decorative ribbon secures escort cards.*

embossed with a snowflake, while a Parisian theme might use tourist sites such as the Eiffel Tower and the Louvre to designate tables. A couple that loves to hike may use the names of rivers, mountains, or trees to differentiate the tables.

menus

Formal receptions often include menu cards, which are used to indicate the names of the dishes to be served and may also designate the primary ingredients. Menus heighten guests' expectations, create a sense of culinary anticipation, and can promote understanding of cultural traditions.

In terms of design, menus often include the monogram of the newlywed couple and can also include creative terminology. For example, instead of using the expression "First Course" this meal stage can be called "Romance" or another term related to the couple's theme. Similar to signature drinks, caterers will work with couples to create specialty entrées with clever, enticing names. Menu cards can be printed on cardstock or, alternatively, a fine parchment paper that is

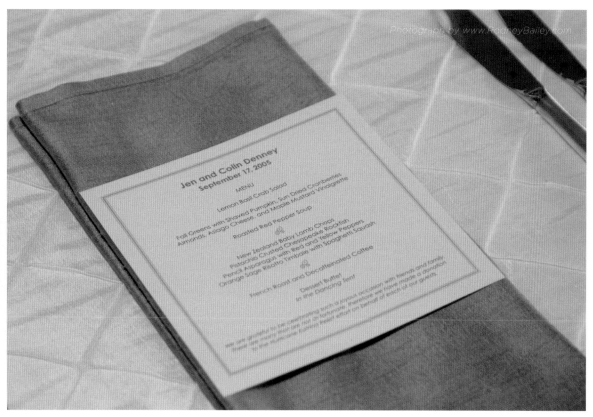

Jen and Colin Denney
September 17, 2005

MENU

Lemon Basil Crab Salad

Fall Greens with Shaved Pumpkin, Sun Dried Cranberries,
Almonds, Asiago Cheese, and Maple Mustard Vinaigrette

Roasted Red Pepper Soup

New Zealand Baby Lamb Chops
Pistachio Crusted Chesapeake Rockfish
Pencil Asparagus with Red and Yellow Peppers
Orange Sage Risotto Timbale with Spaghetti Squash

French Roast and Decaffeinated Coffee

Dessert Buffet
in the Dancing Tent

PHOTO 18-8 *Menus create a sense of culinary anticipation.*

rolled and then tied. They are often tucked inside each guest's napkin, placed on a charger plate, or leaned up against the water glass. Your clients should order menus with plenty of time to spare, so as to avoid situations like the one presented in Consultant in Action, Case 18.2.

personalized paper products

Personalized paper products such as napkins, boxes, bags, or matches can further develop a wedding theme. Napkins are the most commonly chosen and come in a multitude of colors and styles. They are generally placed on the cake table and in the bar area. Often the napkins just include a monogram or the newlyweds' names and the wedding date, but they can also include a touch of humor. For example, one couple had the phrase, "Eat, drink and remarry" printed on the napkins, as it was the second marriage for both bride and groom.

Personalized boxes and bags are often purchased for use with favors and are typically filled with mints, chocolates, or some other treat. Matches have become less common, in particular because most

the stationery was stolen!

Your client had the menu for a 200-person sit-down meal printed on top-of-the-line stationery so that each guest would have an elegant, personal menu. Your stationery vendor had to special order the menus because of the high quality of the paper, and it took a month for the order to be processed. You pick up the menus from the stationery vendor one week before the wedding. Tucking them safely in the trunk of your car, you then drive around town to complete a number of other tasks in preparation for your client's wedding. Upon completing one of your errands, you return to your car and discover that it has been broken into and the menus have been stolen.

What do you do?

PHOTO 18-9 (top) Menus can be delicately balanced on a first course plate.

PHOTO 18-10 (bottom) Favor boxes offer an excellent opportunity for a personalized touch.

reception venues now prohibit smoking; however, when the favor is a candle, personalized match books can add a nice touch.

wedding announcements

Many couples elect to have small weddings for personal reasons, based on budget constraints or because they held a destination wedding where many friends and family member were not invited or could not attend. In cases such as these, a wedding announcement is a courtesy notice sent to those not invited, informing them that the wedding took place. The announcement simply states the names of the bride and groom, the date of the wedding, and the location where it was held.

Announcements are only sent to those who were not in attendance at the wedding because it would be redundant to send these notices to those who were present. They are usually mailed within a week after the wedding. Announcements should never go out until after the wedding, on the off chance that it does not take place.

thank-you notes

Thank-you notes are a type of social stationery and are also known as informals. Informals can match the invitation or they can be generic, which allows them to be used for other purposes. As stated earlier, small stationery orders cost significantly more than larger orders. For instance, 50 informals might cost $100, while 100 are priced at $130.

Informals commonly include the monogram of the couple. If the bride is taking the last name of the groom, her first initial is on the left, the initial of the shared last name is in a larger font in the middle, and the groom's first initial is on the right. If she is not taking his name, it is common to have her initials or full name printed on the left followed by a large ampersand and then the groom's initials or full name.

Some couples will include a wedding photograph in their thank-you notes. Every guest might receive the same picture, or the photos can be personalized, which is common with weddings where an instant camera is left at each reception table. This allows the couple to share moments that were documented by their guests.

Thank-you messages should never be preprinted or generic; each note should be specific to both the guest and the gift. For large weddings, consultants often assist with gift documentation and thank-you note writing so that the information is correct and the notes go out in a timely fashion. Advise your clients to keep each card with the associated gift, so as to avoid the situation found in Consultant in Action, Case 18.3.

identity theft

Your clients' wedding reception for 250 guests is being held at a local aquarium. The reception space has two floors. The lower level is being used for receiving guests, cocktails, and the gift table, while the upper level is for the plated dinner, dancing, and cake cutting. After the main meal, the groom asks you to locate Grandma Pearl for upcoming family photos. You look everywhere to find Grandma Pearl and finally go down to the lower level, thinking she might have stepped out for some fresh air. You find Grandma Pearl at the gift table, where she has just carefully removed every card from every gift on the gift table. She informs you that thank-you notes are very important to her, and she wanted to make sure that the cards did not get lost in the wedding mayhem. This is her special surprise for the couple.

What do you do?

Case submitted by Patricia Borosky

In terms of etiquette, informals should be sent out within one month after the wedding. However, a late thank-you note is better than no thank-you note, so inform your clients that they should not use tardiness as an excuse for bypassing this important task. Separate shower and wedding gifts from the same person should be acknowledged in different notes; furthermore, monogrammed informals indicating a changed last name should never be sent out until after the wedding.

REFERENCES

Geller, J. (1999). The contemporary wedding invitation: A social document in crisis. *Salmagundi*, 121/122: 175–187.

Stewart, M. (1999). *The Best of Martha Stewart Living: Weddings*. New York: Carlson Potter Publishers.

Consultant Checklist and Reminders for Stationery Elements

- ☐ Remember that stationery ends with "ery."
- ☐ Note that printing style and paper quality will dictate the cost of stationery.
- ☐ While the wording of stationery elements is etiquette driven, reassure your clients that they should select wording that fits their personalities.
- ☐ Remind the couple that does not wish to have children at their ceremony or reception to make this clear in their invitations and response cards.
- ☐ When ordering invitations, base it on the number of households rather than the number of individuals.
- ☐ Order enough invitations to prevent the need for a reorder.
- ☐ When mailing invitations, be aware of increased postage for bulky or square-shaped envelopes and have them hand canceled.

review questions

1. Name the five parts of most formal invitations.

2. Name and explain the distinctions between the four styles of printing.

3. What are the six lines typical to invitation wording?

4. Name one rule of etiquette for each of the following stationery elements: save-the-date notices, envelopes, response cards, announcements, and thank-you notes.

terminology

- Bond weight
- Calligraphy
- Ecru
- Embossed
- Engraving
- Informals
- Letterpress
- Save-the-date notices
- Thermography
- Tiered guest list
- Vellum

PHOTO 19-1   *You will need to have a clear understanding of the transportation requirements of your clients.*

transportation 19

So you think you have coordinated the perfect wedding? Your client selected gorgeous flowers designed by the best florist in town and gourmet food from an elite caterer. The reception looked like something straight out of the pages of *Grace Ormonde Wedding Style* magazine. You begin to congratulate yourself on a job well done when you discover there is a backup at the door, and it is taking guests 45 minutes to retrieve their cars from valet parking.

Coordinating transportation logistics may make you feel like a glorified dispatcher, but, at the end of the wedding, getting the guests home in a timely fashion becomes one of the most important details. While they may not remember seamless transportation, they are sure to recall the wedding where they had a seemingly endless wait in the cold because the transportation was disorganized. Arranging transportation for your client's wedding involves five main areas: (1) getting started; (2) transportation to the ceremony venue; (3) transportation from the ceremony to the reception; (4) transportation from the reception to the final destination; and (5) transportation costs and final details.

getting started

When you meet with your clients to discuss their transportation needs, a good place to start is to have them consider the number of people who will need transportation at various times throughout the wedding festivities. You will need to have a clear understanding of all transportation requirements from picking up guests at the airport to arranging a vintage Rolls-Royce to bring the newlyweds home after their honeymoon has ended.

Prepare a list of questions to ask your clients so that you can begin to understand their unique transportation needs. These questions will pertain to what, who, and when. First, what style or styles of vehicles will they want for their wedding day? Are they interested in a white stretch limo, Hummer, SUV, Lincoln town car, or vintage automobile? The number of choices is limited only by your client's imagination and their transportation budget.

Second, who needs to be transported? Have your clients spell out exactly who will need to be moved from point A to point B on the wedding day. It is important for you to know the exact number of people who require transportation so that you can recommend the appropriate vehicles. Have your clients prepare a list of the names of the wedding party and the guests needing transportation so that you will know exactly who needs to be picked up and from where. If the bride's grandmother is confined to a wheelchair, this will influence the type of transportation you send to pick her up. All of this information is useful in shaping your vehicle recommendations.

Third, when will individuals need to be transported? For destination weddings, the transportation needs can get out of control if not coordinated. Cross-check flight schedules to determine the various arrivals and departures so that the number of trips to the airport can be minimized. As introduced in Chapter 8, having a separate timeline specific to transportation can help make the wedding run smoothly.

transportation to the ceremony

After determining the number of people requiring transportation, the next step involves deciding how to transport the bride and her attendants to the ceremony. The bride will need wedding day transportation from the location where she is dressing to the wedding ceremony

PHOTO 19-2 *The bride receives special transportation on her wedding day.*

location. The bride takes this last ride as a single woman accompanied by her father, mother, or her bridesmaids. Since it is typically the father who escorts the bride down the aisle, it is wise to keep them together prior to the wedding ceremony.

For just the two of them, the transportation can be a classic car, a horse and buggy, or another intimate type of vehicle. If the wedding takes place on the family farm, the vehicle of choice might be an antique Ford truck or a hot air balloon. As long as you can match the vehicle style to the theme of the wedding, you will be well on your way to successfully conveying your bride and her father to one of the most important events of their lives.

If, however, the bride wishes to meet her father at the ceremony venue and ride with her attendants, you will need to find a comfortable vehicle to hold all of the women. A stretch limo holds 10 to 12 passengers, while a regular limo can accommodate 6 to 10 passengers comfortably. A town car can hold two to four passengers. Take a head count and then see which type of vehicle will best suit the size of the wedding party.

After planning the bride's transportation, you should discuss the arrangements for getting the groom to the ceremony. Perhaps you will hire another limo to pick up the groom and his family at their home or hotel. Maybe the groom wants to ride with his groomsmen to the ceremony in a stretch Hummer. Whatever the plan is for the groom, make sure that you are aware of all the arrangements and that you have a contact phone number even if the groom is simply riding with his brother in the family minivan. You will want to be aware of the groom's exact location throughout the wedding day.

You will next want to assist the rest of the bridal party, the families, and the guests with transportation. Again, the mode of transportation selected will be dictated by the style of the wedding and the number of people requiring assistance. Secure the transportation well in advance if your client's wedding is during prom or graduation season, when most limos and other luxury cars will be in high demand.

It is a thoughtful gesture on the part of the bride and groom to arrange for buses to shuttle guests to the wedding and bring them back to their lodging at the end of the reception. This will ensure the guests' safety and will cut down on late arrivals. Motor coaches can seat around 50 people, while executive coaches can accommodate up to 20 passengers (Rodriguez, 2004). Hiring a fleet of vehicles is another option. In addition to the standard types of vehicles, you can suggest a trolley, a double-decker bus, or a boat to make the trip more interesting and enjoyable for all passengers. If the time spent during transport is going to be substantial, advise your clients to hire a tour guide or local expert to entertain the guests with stories and anecdotes along the way.

If your client is planning to provide transportation for the guests, this information needs to be communicated well in advance so that the guests can take full advantage of the arrangement. Sending out a mailing with the invitations or to confirmed guests is an excellent way to coordinate this information. The information can also be posted on the couple's Web site. Tell the guests exactly where to find the transportation and when the vehicle will depart for the ceremony. You may want to pad this time by 10 to 15 minutes to accommodate stragglers.

transportation from the ceremony to the reception

After your clients are pronounced husband and wife, there will be an excited press of guests anxious to proceed to the reception. To

PHOTO 19-3 *(opposite) Wedding day transportation reflects the elegance of the wedding.*

facilitate this movement of people, it again makes sense to transport guests en masse, especially if the reception venue is located in a major city. Using the same transportation that brought them to the ceremony to drive them to the reception is the most economical option.

If you think, however, that the majority of the guests will drive their personal vehicles to the reception, then it might be more sensible to hire a valet service to assist with parking and retrieving the cars. Most valet services charge $20 to $25 per attendant per hour, plus gratuity. If the reception is in a crowded downtown district, then having a valet service will save the guests the time and aggravation of looking for an open parking space or the expense of putting the car in a pay lot. Figure on five to six valets per 100 guests. Give special consideration to the end of the evening when you will need additional staff to make sure all the guests get their cars quickly. You don't want to keep guests waiting for more than 5 to 10 minutes.

Guests who drive their own cars should be provided with clear directions to the reception with the starting point as the ceremony venue. Special attendants can hand out directions after the ceremony has ended. If directions are mailed far in advance, chances are the guests will forget them, so it is best to hand them out or, minimally, have extra copies available on the day of the wedding.

Another way your clients can take care of their guests is to prepay the parking fee if there is a charge at the venue. Have this fee built into the contract with the venue. If you are estimating 200 guests, then count on about 100 cars. If the hotel charges a flat fee of $15 per car, your client will pay $1,500 to the hotel to ensure their guests park at no charge. This is a gracious gesture that should be communicated to all guests so they don't end up accidentally paying for parking.

Once your clients are married, they will certainly want to depart for the reception in style. Their ride will be determined by how far the reception venue is from the ceremony. If it is just a few steps away, then perhaps they will walk hand in hand to the accompaniment of a string trio. If the reception site is a few blocks away, then perhaps a horse-drawn carriage will add just the right touch. However, if the reception is a good distance away, then the couple will want to be as comfortable and cozy as possible and perhaps a vintage car is the way to go.

Whatever type of transportation your clients select, make sure that you get all the details in writing, including arrival time (which you should pad by 15 minutes or so to be sure the transportation is on time), reception departure time, addresses of all locations, the size, color, and model of the car the client is renting, the name of the driver, cost, gratuity, special requests, and the duration of time that you have contracted the vehicle. If you want the driver to take the scenic route

PHOTO 19-4 *A newly married couple rides to the reception in style.*

on the way to the reception, make sure this information is included as well. Be as specific as possible and familiarize yourself with the limitations of each vehicle type. For example, if the couple yearns for a horse-drawn carriage, but the wedding is held in Seattle, it will be best to ensure that it is a covered carriage because Seattle is notorious for rain. You do not want your lack of awareness to result in a situation like the one presented in Consultant in Action, Case 19.1.

transportation from the reception to the final destination

As the reception winds down and the last dance has ended, the bride and groom, as well as their wedding party and guests, will be anxious to leave the reception and head off to their final destinations. For the newlyweds' exit, it is important that you ascertain from them exactly how they want to make their departure. Do they want to quietly steal away? Do they want to dash through an arch of sparklers into a waiting limo? Perhaps they want a Vespa scooter at the ready to whisk them to their hotel. Before you book the exit vehicle, you must understand

hotter than hades

Your clients are getting married in Chicago, Illinois, during the late spring. The groom has taken it upon himself to rent a vintage Packard to drive him and his new bride to their reception in grand style. Being the organized planner that you are, you get a copy of the contract plus all the contact information for the rental company and you confirm the logistics three days before the wedding. You also send the company a copy of the timeline and directions to and from the venues. You think that you have taken care of all the details. The wedding day arrives, and the Packard rolls into the church parking lot at the appointed time to wait for the bride and groom. You see the Packard and go over to speak to the driver. You notice that he is sweating profusely, as the typically mild Chicago spring has seen an unusual spike of temperatures into the 80s. You inquire about the car's air conditioning system only to be told by the driver that when the car was built, there were no cars with air conditioning. The bride and groom are just moments away from saying "I do" and will be jumping into the sweltering car at any moment.

What do you do?

their wishes and translate them into reality. Table 19.1 includes a list of creative modes of transportation that can be used for a memorable exit or at any other point during the wedding day.

For the guests and wedding party, it is important to ferry them back to where they started the day so that they can pick up their cars or fall into bed at their hotels. Leaving guests without a ride is very inconsiderate. As a wedding planner, you should encourage your clients to think about their obligations as hosts for the evening and

TABLE 19.1 Creative Modes of Transportation

- All terrain vehicles
- Antique fire engine
- Bicycle built for two
- Camel
- Canoe
- Chinese rickshaw
- Cross country skis
- Dog sled
- Duck boat
- Elephant
- Golf cart
- Horseback
- Ice cream truck
- Mini Cooper
- Monster truck
- Moped
- Motorcycle with sidecar
- Sailboat
- Sleigh
- Snowboard
- Snowmobile
- Subway
- Surfboard
- Vintage VW Beetle

Photograph by www.RodneyBailey.com

PHOTO 19-5 *Vintage automobiles allow for a memorable exit.*

TABLE 19.2 Sample Fee Structure for Common Forms of Wedding Transportation

Vehicle Type	Hourly Rate	Minimum Rental Time
Sedan 4 passengers	$68/hour	3 HR = $204
SUV 5 passengers	$78/hour	3 HR = $234
Limo 6 passengers	$90/hour	3 HR = $270
Limo 8 passengers	$105/hour	3 HR = $315
Limo 10 passengers	$125/hour	3 HR = $375
Limo Van 6 passengers	$75/hour	3 HR = $225
Limo Bus 18 passengers	$140/hour	3 HR + GT = $560
Van 14 passengers	$60/hour	3 HR + GT = $240
Van Terra 12 passengers	$80/hour	3 HR + GT = $320
Mini Bus 20 passengers	$85/hour	3 HR + GT = $340
Mini Bus 25 passengers	$90/hour	3 HR + GT = $360
Mini Bus 30 passengers	$95/hour	3 HR + GT = $380
Mini Bus 35 passengers	$100/hour	3 HR + GT = $400
Coach 55 passengers	$120/hour	4 HR + GT = $600
Tour Guide	$55/hour	4 HR = $220
Greeter on-site	$35/hour	4 HR = $140

Notes:
- The above-listed fees include fuel charge and gratuity.
- From mid-April through mid-June, there is a 6-hour minimum on all limos for Friday and Saturday evenings.
- There is a $12 early/late fee for trips from 11:00 P.M. to 6:00 A.M.
- GT = garage time (time needed to clean, refuel, and safety check each vehicle)
  Web site: www.restonlimo.com

the importance of taking care of their guests. These small considerations will be remembered for years to come. So whether you provide a bus, a van, or a line of yellow taxis, it is very important to get the guests safely home, especially those who have been drinking.

While transportation costs will vary from region to region, it is helpful to have a cost comparison. Most companies will require a 3- or 4-hour minimum for any form of transportation, so bear that in mind when comparing costs. Check with your transportation vendor to determine if the fee structure includes the fuel charge and gratuity. Furthermore, some high-maintenance vehicles will include a garage time (GT) fee for servicing after use. This fee usually pertains to large vehicles in which riders are eating and drinking. Table 19.2 includes a sample fee structure provided by Kristina Bouweiri of Reston Limo (2006). While these costs will vary based on the region where you reside, this table offers general guidelines.

The well-prepared wedding consultant has an eye for detail and an ear for trouble. Months prior to a wedding, you should check with local authorities on street closings, especially if your event is during a holiday weekend or in a large city where special events can snarl traffic for hours. For example, if your client's wedding reception will be held at a private club close to the United Nations headquarters in New York, call the city and speak to the department that issues permits to see if there will be a high-security event taking place. You should determine potential transportation difficulties with enough time to discuss options with your clients. In a post–September 11 world, street closings and heightened security have become a way of life. When you are planning for your client's transportation, remember to check with the city government or local law enforcement to make sure there is nothing that will interfere with the wedding.

REFERENCES

Reston Limousine. (2006). Transportation costs, available at http://www.restonlimo.com

Rodriguez, V. (2004). *Celebrate! The Washington Post Guide to Successful Celebrations*. Washington, DC: The Washington Post.

Consultant Checklist and Reminders for Hiring Transportation

☐ Know the couple's transportation preferences, determine who needs transport, and create a transportation timeline.

☐ Be aware of how the couple, bridal party, and guests will be transported to the ceremony site, from the ceremony to the reception, and to their final destination.

☐ Prepare a timeline that is specific to transportation.

☐ Make sure leave-taking from the ceremony and reception is efficient.

☐ Be aware of the restrictions and limitations of each vehicle type being considered.

☐ Determine if the transportation company's pricing structure includes the fuel charge, gratuity, and garage time.

☐ Confirm with transportation vendors and supply directions to each place a driver will be stopping.

☐ Get day-of phone numbers for the transportation company and drivers.

☐ Check with police and city government offices on street closings, parades, demonstrations, and other special events.

☐ Encourage your clients to pay for the venue parking fees for their guests.

☐ Secure transportation early if the wedding is during prom or graduation season.

review questions

1. What are the three main time periods during which transportation will be required on the wedding day?

2. Name five creative modes of transportation that can be used for weddings.

3. Name at least two good reasons to hire transportation for wedding guests.

4. What are the key points to get in writing when hiring transportation?

5. How can you find out about known street closings and expected traffic delays that will occur on the day of a wedding?

terminology

• Creative transportation

• Driver gratuity

• Fuel charge

• Garage time

• Valet service

wedding  20
day details

At last, the wedding day has arrived. Just as the bride and groom are making their final preparations, the wedding consultant should be too. While the bride is enjoying celebrity treatment and having her hair and makeup professionally done, the wedding planner is preparing for the long day ahead, reviewing last minute details and gathering supplies. This chapter focuses on wedding day details, including bridal preparations and consultant preparations.

PHOTO 20-1 *(opposite) Elegant hair and makeup give a bride confidence.*

⚲ bridal preparations

While the groom's preparation for marriage is typically efficient, bridal preparation is a process that often takes several hours. As the bride awakes on the morning of her wedding, she begins what can be an exhausting day of preparation, execution, and celebration. By hiring a wedding planner to manage the day for her, she can take a deep breath and focus on looking her best. It will be the consultant who manages the wedding day execution, leaving the bride relaxed and excited about the celebration.

While the groom often spends the morning of the wedding relaxing or playing golf, the bride will be off with bridesmaids in tow to have her hair styled and makeup applied. Having all of her bridesmaids with her starts the festive feeling of the day as the women laugh and have fun throughout the beautification process. Many hair and makeup professionals will even travel to the bride's dressing location to save the bride the stress of driving around town on her wedding day. Whether the bride is at her family's home, a hotel, or the bridal room in a house of worship, the hair and makeup professionals will come to the bride on her wedding day. However, this service comes at a cost.

On-site fees for styling the bride's hair usually start at $100 and can go up to $400 or more depending on the city and the popularity of the stylist. If the bride travels to the salon for her hair, the fees start at about $75 and go up from there. In addition, there will be a fee for each additional person styled (bridesmaids, mothers, grandmothers, etc.) which usually begins at $60. Lower fees apply for flower girls and junior bridesmaids and tend to run between $35 and $55. Trial hair styling for the bride typically starts at $65.

Makeup applications in the salon start around $75, and on-site fees range between $100 and $300. Each additional person receiving makeup will be charged somewhat less, depending on the makeup artist. The bride should also invest in a trial run for her makeup application. Many brides opt to save by doing their own hair and makeup or having a close friend or family member help them at no cost. However, because the bride will be constantly photographed throughout the day, professional makeup application is well worth the investment.

WEDDING HAIRSTYLES

The hairstylist begins with the bride's hair, regardless of how many bridesmaids are waiting. It is crucial to the day's timing that the bride is coiffed and ready to go first, as she is the focus of the wedding day. Giselle, who is the owner of Elegant Hair by Giselle featured in Vendor Spotlight, Case 20.1, explains that the latest trend for wedding hairstyles is simple elegance, such as a chignon for an up-do or large body

giselle

elegant hair by giselle

How did you become interested in hairstyling? My father came to the United States from Morocco in the 1960s as a hairdresser. We now have 15 hairstylists in my extended family, so this career runs in my family. I take great pride in the artistry of designing wedding hair and knowing that I helped someone look and feel beautiful.

What sets you apart from other stylists? I concentrate on one area and do it very well: up-dos and styles for weddings and special events. I do not color, perm, or do anything else but this. I was trained as an up-do specialist in New York and London and now offer classes in this special niche. I often use hairpieces and extensions to creatively expand the bride's options, since so many are looking to enhance fullness and length as part of the style.

What are the primary hair accessories for weddings? Brides are concentrating on decorative hairpins now. I have seen fewer tiaras and combs. Brides also often use one of my custom-made hair chignon pieces. They are light and comfortable and keep the hair in place for many hours without losing shape. The piece is placed under the bride's hair, so it is never seen.

Do you work with clients from different cultural backgrounds? Yes, and I find that women of different cultures have different textures to their hair as well as different preferences for what they will wear in their hair. For example, Indian hair tends to be thick, long, and heavy, while Asian hair tends to be silky, so it is harder to curl. Korean brides often wear traditional hats that need to be angled a certain way around their hairstyle.

What is the most complicated style you have designed? My most challenging style was an up-do for a client whose hair went down to her knees in length. I pulled it off by creating a unique technique, which to this day is a signature up-do of mine.

(Continues)

Any humorous anecdotes? I meet with clients in advance, so this really does help eliminate the unexpected. Although . . . I did have a bride who did not inform her newly wedded husband that there was a hairpiece used as part of her style to create fullness. Did she conveniently forget to warn him? Who knows, but when he was helping her take out the hairpins, that piece went flying out of his hand and across the room before he could understand what it was!

Web site: www.hairbygiselle.com

waves for those who want to wear their hair down. She notes that standard curls have worked their way out of state-of-the-art looks. As a consultant, you can share the following advice that Giselle thinks every bride should follow: "Let your hair dictate your sense of style along with your dress type before selecting your headpiece and veil. It should not work the other way around."

Prior to designing the hair on the actual wedding day, many brides have a mini trial run and then a main trial run. Giselle explains that the mini trial run, which can take place several months before the wedding, allows the stylist to become familiar with the bride's hair, personality, and special requests as well as going over some possibilities. The mini trial also allows the client and the stylist to discuss if the hair should be grown out, relaxed, colored, or cut before the wedding. The main trial run should happen one to two weeks before the wedding and should feel like the day of the wedding. At the main trial, the bride should bring her headpiece, veil, and hair jewelry, and her hair should be updated in terms of color and trim. Giselle explains that hair color regrowth can start to show after two weeks, so the main trial should not take place too far in advance of the wedding. By the end of these two trials, the bride feels very comfortable with the stylist, and a sense of rapport has been built. This process allows the style on the wedding day to be stress free. Advise your clients that the day of the wedding is not the time to decide between wearing their hair up and leaving it down.

WEDDING MAKEUP

When undergoing the transformation of hair and makeup, the preferred order is hair first followed by makeup. This order is preferred because often the hair will need to be wet to begin the styling process and in wetting the hair, there is a significant chance of ruining the makeup if it has already been applied. Moreover, heat is often used, which can cause the bride to sweat and the makeup to run. In addition, after the hair is styled, hair spray is applied to keep the look in place. Some of the spray might accidentally go on the face and ruin the makeup application.

Makeup artists know the importance of applying the correct amount of foundation so that the bride's skin will look natural yet flawless. The artist also knows the tricks of the trade, including how to keep shine off the bride's nose and how to keep her lipstick lasting throughout the day. The bride will be the center of attention all day long, and she will want to look her best, kiss after kiss and hug after hug. There is no better way to make this happen than to spend the money and hire a makeup specialist. Professional makeup artist Carola Myers, featured in Vendor Spotlight, Case 20.2, discusses some of the essentials of wedding day makeup.

carola myers

professional makeup artist

What is your training background? I started my training in Rio de Janeiro, Brazil; then I worked in New York and now in Washington, DC. I assisted one of Chanel's national makeup artists, which is how I learned the technique for perfecting the preparation of the face, which is a key element in wedding day makeup. When I started getting my own clients, I was primarily applying makeup on older women. When I was finished, they would say, "You must meet my daughter! I want you to do her makeup for her wedding day." That was my foot in the door. Now I have my own business and specialize in applying beautiful wedding day makeup for brides and their mothers.

What makes your approach special? I think it is my attitude. I enjoy listening and talking with my clients. I listen to what they want, and I try to achieve it with my makeup application. I like to bring out the personality in my clients. If I can build a rapport with my clients, they will open up and their inner beauty will come out.

What are the latest trends in makeup for weddings? Adding a little more sparkle on the eyes or the cheeks is a trend that I am seeing. Defined eyes, soft lips, and a bronze shimmer are also popular looks on brides this year. Sheer pinks and raspberry colors give a fresh and natural look. I am also seeing clean lines. A makeup artist's touch should be light handed. The goal is to see the beauty of the bride and not her makeup.

What are the primary tricks for keeping makeup fresh throughout a wedding day? I learned about layering in Brazil. It is a wonderful technique that will help the makeup last all day. Different pigments are used like a cream, then a liquid followed by a powder. When you layer the makeup, it stays fresh. Another trick is not to use foundation all over the face. Foundation should be used sparingly unless the bride specifically requests full makeup coverage. But be careful, if too much foundation is used, the bride can look harsh and like she is wearing a mask.

What is the most difficult aspect about your job? The most difficult situations happen when the mother of the bride wants one look while the bride wants another. The bride might want a light makeup application while her mother might want a more dramatic look, especially if dramatic makeup application is part of the cultural tradition like in India or Iran. This disagreement sometimes will erupt in a fight right in front of me. This is an excellent reason to schedule a trial, so that the mother and daughter can fight it out before the wedding.

What is one of the most unusual wedding situations you have encountered? Just recently, I was driving to meet a bride at an exclusive hotel in Washington, DC. When I pulled up, there were police cars and a bomb-sniffing team surrounding the front door of the hotel. Evidently, someone had phoned in a bomb threat. I arrived carrying my metal makeup box and a black bag. As I got out of the car, I was told that I could not enter the building. I attempted to tell them that I had a bride waiting for me and that I must pass, but to no avail. Then, because I was causing a fuss, they turned their attention to me and my metal makeup case. It was opened and searched. My bag was searched. I attempted to call the bride, but all the cell phone lines were down because of the hotel's proximity to the White House. An hour and a half later, the hotel manager came to my rescue at the request of the bride, and I was sprung from the SWAT team's clutches.

Web site: www.carolamyers.com

If your client is looking to cut corners on her wedding day, she might be inclined to skip the professional makeup application and simply do her own. After all, she's been doing her own makeup for many years, why should her wedding day be any different? You would be wise to steer your client to a professional for this important service. Proper makeup application is crucial for wedding photographs. Carola explains that communication from the consultant will make the makeup artist's job easier. She stresses that the makeup artist needs to know the timing of the day as well as the photographer's style and schedule. The makeup will differ if the wedding is held outdoors or if it will be photographed primarily in black and white. The number of guests will also influence makeup application. If the wedding is intimate, the bride will be seen close up; however, if it is a large wedding, the bride will be seen from a distance so her makeup will need to be more dramatic. The makeup artist needs to know this information well in advance so that the makeup can be applied for maximum benefit. Wedding hair and makeup application will also vary significantly by culture, as illustrated in Culture Corner, Case 20.3.

TIMING

For hair and makeup sessions, the bride and bridesmaids should be advised to wear button-front or zippered shirts, so they can easily change into their dresses without spoiling their hair and makeup. The process of putting hair into an up-do can take as long as an hour, depending on the length and type of hair. Makeup application takes between 30 and 45 minutes. If several bridesmaids are having hair and makeup done, the hairstylist and makeup artist will work with assistants. The bride should never feel like she is being rushed and should not leave the chair until she feels satisfied with her appearance. This expensive pampering should not go to waste, as illustrated in Consultant in Action, Case 20.4.

Additional beauty treatments such as teeth whitening, waxing, spray tanning, facials, Botox injections, ear piercing, hair relaxing, or highlighting should all be done well in advance of the wedding day to allow any adverse reactions to fade out of sight before the big day.

❧ the consultant's preparations

While the bride is receiving her last minute beauty treatments and relaxing, the consultant is busy finalizing the preparations for the wedding day. These preparations will include day-of details, risk assessment, security analysis, and the emergency kit.

DAY-OF DETAILS FOR THE CONSULTANT

As the wedding day dawns, it is crucial that you review all the details that were supposed to happen. For example, did the pin-tuck linens

wedding hair and makeup in china

A bride in China goes to the same photography studio where she and the groom had their formal wedding photos taken months before to have her hair and makeup done on the actual wedding day. She will arrive early in the morning, sometimes as early as 5:00 A.M., because these services are performed on a first-come, first-served basis. At 5:00 A.M., there could be 50 brides in line. The entire process of both hair and makeup takes 30 minutes or less per bride. There will be 10 or more stylists on hand, and they will give each bride the exact same look. With a population of 1.3 billion people in China, it is all about speed, not individuality. The cost for hair and makeup is 410 Renminbi (RMB) which is approximately $50 US. This may not seem very expensive, but in a country where the average wage is 150 RMB per week, this is indeed a luxurious expenditure.

Case submitted by Yao and David Wosicki

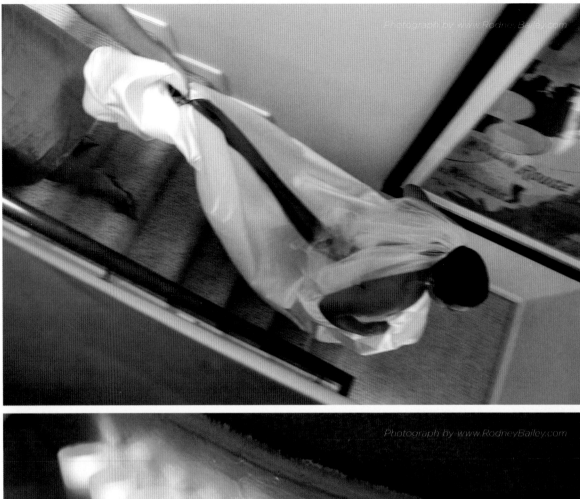

PHOTO 20-2 (top) The bride should never feel like she is being rushed on her wedding day.

PHOTO 20-3 (bottom) Last minute details are crucial to a wedding's success.

mirror, mirror on the wall . . .

Your client, Teresa, has gone to the best salon in Phoenix, Arizona, for her wedding day hairstyle and makeup application. You are to meet Teresa back at her hotel to check in and supervise the delivery of a catered brunch to her suite. You arrive at her suite, only to find Teresa in the bathroom rubbing off the makeup that she has just paid dearly to have applied. She thinks the makeup does not look like her, and she is clearly in distress as she starts to peel off her false eyelashes and remove the color from her cheeks. You stand at the bathroom door, watching a $250 makeup application literally start to go down the drain.

What do you do?

that were supposed to be delivered to the reception venue by 8:00 A.M. arrive? You will need to call the venue to ensure they were delivered. If they have not arrived, you have to call the linen company and track down the delivery. If the cake is supposed to arrive at 1:00 P.M., you will confirm that this happened at the appropriate time. Making phone calls to verify the wedding day details is a crucial component to a successful event.

Checking the weather and traffic conditions prior to the wedding is another smart use of your time on the wedding day. A quick check and you will know if the weather forecast has been revised from the previous evening's report. If you learn that a sudden cold spell has hit the area, you can call the rental company and get more outdoor heaters delivered to the reception venue. Before you leave your house, also make sure that you have all necessary contact information, timelines, and copies of all contracts and budgets. Make sure your mobile phone is charged. That way, if while heading to the ceremony, you learn that a major highway is backed up, you can call the transportation company and discuss an alternate route for the wedding party.

RISK ASSESSMENT

John Lennon famously said, "Life is what happens when you're busy making other plans." Before the day of the wedding, every planner should have a risk assessment in place for the wedding and a game plan for managing those risks should they come to fruition. A risk can take on many shapes and forms. It can be as obvious as rain at an outdoor wedding, or it can be less obvious, like habitually late relatives whose tardiness will cause the wedding to start late. The wise planner assesses the risks prior to the wedding and builds in a backup plan just in case "life" happens. Table 20.1 offers a list of common wedding

TABLE 20.1 Common Wedding Day Risks

- Accidents (cuts, burns, tripping, falling)
- Bugs at an outdoor event (mosquitoes, flies, gnats, bees, wasps)
- Electricity goes out (dark venue, food cannot be heated)
- Sickness (food poisoning, heatstroke, hangover, cold, flu, allergies)
- Streets around your venue are closed (water main breaks, car crash)
- Transportation (the coach bus breaks down on the highway, the best man missed his connecting flight, airports are shut down)
- Union goes on strike (no wait staff at the hotel)
- Vendor no-show (no ceremony music, no cake)
- Wardrobe malfunction (bride's veil gets caught in a car door and tears)
- Weather (high winds, rain, heat, snow, ice, humidity, cold, lightning)

PHOTO 20-4 (opposite) Checking weather conditions is a smart use of the consultant's time.

day risks, with examples of each. Keep in mind that every wedding is a unique entity. Think through what the most likely risks will be for each wedding and have a plan in mind should any of the risks become a reality. Remember, "hope" is not a backup plan.

SECURITY ANALYSIS

In a post–September 11 world, it has become commonplace to see some type of security at all events. From bag searches to metal detectors, security measures are the rule rather than the exception. It is not necessary for wedding planners to be security experts, but you should have an understanding of security issues and how they affect your events, your business, and your reputation. By understanding and managing security, you are protecting the assets, the venue, and the people present at the wedding.

The gifts are usually the largest assets at a wedding. The gift table may be overflowing with expensive items and envelopes of cash. You will need to ensure that the gifts are closely watched and monitored. There should also be a plan to deliver the gifts safely to the bride and groom after the reception has ended. Maybe the hotel valet will transport the gifts to the honeymoon suite. Perhaps the father of the groom will load the gifts into the family minivan. Make sure that there is a plan and that you are informed of what it is so that you can assist in its execution.

In addition to wedding presents, cash in an envelope is a common gift to newlyweds. Sometimes the envelopes will be placed in a decorated box or birdcage found on the gift table whereas at other weddings the guests will hand envelopes directly to the wedding consultant or an assistant. Regardless, each envelope should be accounted for and secured properly to ensure against theft. The last thing that you want is a phone call the day after a wedding asking you where the envelope from Uncle Danny was placed. As you are handed each envelope, introduce yourself to the guest so that you can quickly write down his or her name. This way you will have a master list in case a question arises.

The venue must also be protected from damage during the wedding. If young men at a wedding get bored and go to the restroom and place firecrackers down the toilet, there will be damage to the physical property and your clients could be held liable. If you are concerned about this type of behavior, suggest to your clients that they hire a security guard to patrol the reception looking for such incidents. If you have a large event with many people, you may need to hire several guards.

Finally, it is your responsibility to help ensure the safety of the guests at the event. If a couple's cocktail hour is to be held outdoors and you

PHOTO 20-5 (opposite) *Security analysis should be completed for all weddings.*

TABLE 20.2   Wedding Day Emergency Kit Essentials

• Baby wipes	• Lip ointment	• Smelling salts
• Band aids	• Nail clippers and file	• Snacks (crackers, protein bars)
• Bobby pins	• Nail polish and remover	• Stapler (miniature)
• Bottled water	• Panty hose	• Static removal spray
• Breath mints	• Pepto-Bismol	• Straight and safety pins in various sizes
• Brush, comb, and pick	• Powder (talc and face)	• Super glue
• Deodorant	• Q-tips and cotton balls	• Tape (duct, scotch, and double-sided)
• Drinking straws	• Rope (short and medium pieces)	• Tissues
• Feminine hygiene items	• Scissors	• Tylenol
• Hair spray	• Sewing kit	• Umbrella

see lightning in the distance, bring the guests indoors for their protection. If you see a puddle of water on the dance floor, it is your responsibility to get venue staff to clean it up so that a guest does not slip and fall. Keep an eye out for guests who appear to be intoxicated and make sure that they have a designated driver to escort them safely home. Your conscientiousness can save a life.

THE EMERGENCY KIT

A vital piece of equipment every wedding consultant should own is the wedding day emergency kit. This can be a duffel bag, a canvas bag, a rolling suitcase, or a large nylon zippered bag. The contents of the bag will vary based on the planner, the wedding, and the region; however, Table 20.2 lists the key items that should be in every wedding day emergency kit. As discussed in Chapter 16, a CD of wedding music and a boom box to play it are excellent additions to keep in your car just in case.

You will be surprised by how many items you will need from this emergency kit throughout the wedding day. The father of the bride will lose a button and come to you for a needle and thread. A bridesmaid will have a headache. The groom will want a breath mint. The pew arrangements might come undone after the florist has departed, so you will need to use a piece of rope and a safety pin to secure them back into place. Having a well-thought-out and comprehensive emergency kit will be worth its weight in gold to you and your clients. Start gathering supplies now before you really need them.

PHOTO 20-6   *(opposite) An emergency kit helps with wardrobe malfunctions.*

Consultant Checklist and Reminders for Wedding Day Details

- ☐ On the wedding day, advise the bride to have her hair done first.

- ☐ As a cost saver, urge the bride to travel to the salon rather than have the stylists come to her.

- ☐ As a general rule, do hair before makeup.

- ☐ Determine if the stylist is bringing an assistant.

- ☐ Have your client meet with the hairstylist for a mini trial run prior to picking out a veil.

- ☐ Remind your bride to bring her headpiece, veil, and hair jewelry to the main trial run.

- ☐ Have the bride and her bridesmaids wear button-front or zippered shirts to have their hair and makeup done.

- ☐ Check weather and traffic reports on the wedding day.

- ☐ Make follow-up calls on the wedding day to ensure that items were delivered according to your instructions.

- ☐ Complete a risk assessment and security analysis for each wedding.

- ☐ Prepare and bring your emergency kit.

review questions

1. Give two reasons why hair should be done before makeup.

2. Explain the difference between a mini trial run and a main trial run for wedding hairstyles.

3. Name one item that a bride must bring to her main trial run for hairstyling.

4. What paperwork will a planner need on the wedding day?

5. Name five examples of wedding day risks.

6. Name 10 items that should be found in a wedding day emergency kit.

terminology

- Backup plan
- Emergency kit
- Main trial run
- Mini trial run
- On-site fees
- Risk assessment
- Security analysis
- Up-do
- Wedding assets

Photograph by www.RodneyBailey.com

PHOTO 21-1 *The final phase of wedding planning includes wrap-up and evaluation.*

post-wedding 21 evaluation

Another successful wedding to your credit! The vendors came through, everyone had a fabulous time, and the newlyweds are off to Jamaica for their honeymoon. You may be ready for a well-earned vacation, but don't write off this wedding just yet. As you learned in Chapter 8, the final phase of wedding timelines includes wrap-up and evaluation, and some essential tasks still need to be completed, including satisfaction assessment and the completion of a final wedding summary. You may also be involved in some ad hoc services that take place after the wedding day. This chapter will introduce the basics of conducting a post-wedding evaluation and discuss the compilation of the wedding summary.

☙ conducting a post-wedding evaluation

Successful wedding consultants are always looking for ways to improve their services, and obtaining feedback from clients and vendors can be constructive and enlightening. Post-wedding evaluation is defined as a process of collecting information from clients and vendors in order to draw conclusions about services and make continuous improvements. When conducting an evaluation, there are eight things to keep in mind: (1) why evaluation is necessary; (2) when to evaluate; (3) what to evaluate; (4) quantitative and qualitative evaluation; (5) types of questionnaire items; (6) writing questionnaire items; (7) questionnaire format; and (8) the cover letter.

WHY EVALUATE?

Evaluation in the context of weddings should be conducted for four interrelated reasons. First, feedback will allow you to pinpoint areas of success and areas that need improvement. Second, the information provided will help determine the importance of and satisfaction with specific services, therefore helping you prioritize. For example, if your full-service package includes the provision that you will accompany the client on each vendor visit, but your clients consistently give you feedback that they do not feel this service is necessary, you can re-prioritize the options for this package. Third, constructive criticism and ideas for improvement will encourage you to make changes and stay fresh. Finally, implementing changes will lead to increased client satisfaction over time. Do not be afraid to get feedback, both positive and negative. No business is perfect, but your openness to the ideas of others will get you one step closer to perfect than your competition. Over time, the evaluation process will save you both time and money because you will better understand the needs of your customer base. Getz (2005) explains that evaluation needs to be a permanent part of any organization that deals with events because "nobody learns, and nothing progresses without open and honest evaluation" (p. 381).

WHEN TO EVALUATE

The timing of an event evaluation can be either formative or summative (Jordan, DeGraaf, and DeGraaf, 2006). The evaluation of weddings is generally summative in nature, which means that it takes place after service delivery is complete. For other types of events, formative evaluation also occurs, which means that information is collected during the actual implementation of the event. However, in the world of weddings, it would be inappropriate to the point of ludicrous to ask vendors or the couple to fill out a brief questionnaire on the wedding day. As the consultant, you should conduct an informal formative evaluation of every wedding, where you jot down notes of things that went awry as well as those that went particularly well. This information will go into the final wedding summary.

WHAT TO EVALUATE

A wedding evaluation should include items that assess three primary areas: product, process, and psychosocial elements. The product pertains to the tangible goods and services, while the process is specific to how the work was done (Jordan, DeGraaf, and DeGraaf, 2006). For example, a product-based questionnaire item might pertain to the degree of satisfaction with the variety of vendor options provided to the client, whereas a process item would relate to whether the consultant was consistently organized. Finally, the psychosocial relates to the human element and all of the emotions that are tied into weddings. For instance, you might ask whether your services allowed the couple to be less stressed on their wedding day.

QUANTITATIVE AND QUALITATIVE EVALUATION

Quantitative evaluation is concerned with numbers that can have real or implied meanings. For example, if on one hand you ask a client to give a budget breakdown, this will be based on actual expenditures. On the other hand, if you ask a client to rate how well you communicated during the wedding planning on a scale from 1 to 5, the numbers have an implied meaning, with 5 indicating the most positive rating. Quantitative information can be readily compiled. For example, if in a given year you have 15 wedding clients, you can collect data from each using the same questionnaire and then at the end of a year calculate averages based on the compiled responses.

In contrast, qualitative evaluation deals with words rather than numbers and generally is less structured. Every questionnaire should include at least two items that allow clients to express their thoughts and opinions openly. While you will not be able to formulate averages on qualitative data, over time you may start to see themes emerge that offer valuable guidance. For instance, if you include an item that asks your clients to comment on the quality of the reception venue and you find that for one particular venue, comments such as "It is too hot," "The ladies bathroom is cramped," and "The chairs felt unstable" crop up again and again, you may seriously want to reconsider whether you recommend that particular venue.

THREE TYPES OF QUESTIONNAIRE ITEMS

Questionnaires typically include three types of items: fixed-alternative, scale, and open-ended. Fixed-alternative items generally assess knowledge, meaning that there is technically a response that "is the case." Fixed-alternative items that you are familiar with are true-false and multiple choice. For wedding evaluation, common fixed-alternative items include yes-no items, questions where clients check off specific services used, and items requesting demographic information. Figure 21.1 includes a sample questionnaire. In this questionnaire, numbers 1, 2, and 7a are fixed-alternative items. Note that fixed-alternative items are usually written as questions.

Wakeside Weddings
Post-wedding Client Questionnaire

By completing this questionnaire, you are helping the consultants at Wakeside Weddings
to consistently improve their services

Your answers will remain confidential

Client's Name: _____

The Couple: _____

Wedding Date: _____

Consultant's Name: _____

1. How did you learn about Wakeside Weddings? *(please check all that apply)*

[ ] Word of mouth   [ ] Bridal showcase   [ ] Wakeside Weddings web site

[ ] Other (*please explain*) _____

2. What service package did you select?

[ ] Comprehensive package   [ ] Partial package   [ ] Day-of package

[ ] Ad-hoc services (*please explain*) _____

Please rate the quality of the services provided,
where 5 = Strongly Agree and 1 = Strongly Disagree

3. My wedding consultant was...	Strongly Agree	Agree	No Opinion	Disagree	Strongly Disagree
...helpful	5	4	3	2	1
...punctual	5	4	3	2	1
...organized	5	4	3	2	1
...professional	5	4	3	2	1
...knowledgeable	5	4	3	2	1
...conscious of my budget	5	4	3	2	1
...easy to contact when needed	5	4	3	2	1

4. Having a wedding consultant...	Strongly Agree	Agree	No Opinion	Disagree	Strongly Disagree
...saved me time	5	4	3	2	1
...saved me money	5	4	3	2	1
...made selecting vendors easier	5	4	3	2	1
...made my planning less stressful	5	4	3	2	1
...allowed me to fully enjoy my wedding	5	4	3	2	1

FIGURE 21.1 *Sample post-wedding questionnaire for clients*

5. What services did your consultant provide that were most helpful?

_____

_____

6. What services, if any, did your consultant provide that you felt were unnecessary?

_____

_____

7a. Based on your experience, would you recommend your consultant to a friend or family member?

[ ] Yes   [ ] No

7b. If no, please explain: _____

_____

Comments and Suggestions:

_____

_____

_____

THANK YOU FOR YOUR FEEDBACK!

Please return this questionnaire in the postage-paid envelope that has been provided.

FIGURE 21.1 *Continued*

Scale items are used to assess feelings and therefore allow for a range of responses. Many questions that you have for your clients deal with their emotions rather than fact, so there is no right or wrong answer. Such a question should allow for a more gray area; thus, it is more appropriate to use a scale item rather than a fixed alternative. For example, assume that you wanted to determine whether the client found that you were easy to contact when needed. This would be difficult to put into a yes-no format because it forces the client to make a choice when it could have been the case that sometimes you were accessible and at other times you were not. By allowing the client to answer on a scale that ranges from strongly agree to strongly disagree, the client has more response latitude. In Figure 21.1, the items contained in numbers 3 and 4 are examples of scale items. Note that scale items are usually written as statements.

Open-ended items are used to assess behaviors and impressions and must be presented in a way that encourages written feedback. Because open-ended questions take much longer to answer than fixed-alternative and scale items, you should limit the number to no more than four. If there are too many open-ended items, your clients will suffer from what is known as response fatigue. You have taken essay exams in the past and know how tiring that can be. Don't put your clients through that sort of experience, as they may get frustrated and not finish the questionnaire. Also, though not as structured as fixed-alternative and scale items, you want open-ended questions to be directed so that the answers will be useful. You should also always leave an area that requests comments and additional suggestions so that your clients can provide you with information that you may not have considered requesting. Numbers 5, 6, 7b and the "Comments and Suggestions" area are examples of open-ended items in Figure 21.1. Open-ended items can be written as questions or statements.

PHOTO 21-2 *Evaluation allows consultants to determine client satisfaction.*

WRITING QUESTIONNAIRE ITEMS

When writing questionnaire items, there are some common wording problems that you will want to avoid. In this section, five types of poorly written items and their more appropriate counterparts will be presented.

First, avoid double-barreled questions. Babbie (2003) explains that double-barreled questions are those where you ask the respondent to give a single answer to a combination of questions. This problem frequently emerges in scale items. For example, consider the two options below for a scale item where you are assessing the respondent's level of agreement:

Poorly written item: *"My wedding consultant was punctual and organized."*
Better: *"My wedding consultant was punctual."*
"My wedding consultant was organized."

In the poorly written example, two questions are presented in one statement, and it could be the case that the consultant was punctual but not organized, or vice versa. Make sure that each question can stand alone.

Second, avoid writing questions that have confusing language such as double negatives. Consider the scale items below:

Poorly written item: *"I was never not satisfied with the communication skills of my wedding consultant."*
Better: *"I was satisfied with the communication skills of my wedding consultant."*

The poorly written item is incredibly difficult to interpret and sure to lead to confusion.

Third, avoid writing items that are overly vague. Consider the open-ended items below:

Poorly written item: *"Please talk about your vendors."*
Better: *"Please list the three vendors that you enjoyed working with the most."*

The poorly written item creates more questions than answers. The respondent is left to think: "Which vendors?" "What do you want to know about them?" On the other hand, the item that is clearly written will help you hone your list of vendors to recommend to future clients.

Fourth, items should be written as concisely as possible. Babbie (2003) explains that a respondent should be able to read an item quickly, understand the intent, and provide an answer quickly. Consider the following open-ended items:

Poorly written item: *"Wedding planning can be stressful with various influences and thoughts that you are dealing with, not to mention the pressure of family and financial burdens that you have to worry about all the time; nonetheless, your wedding consultant probably helped you deal with this stress so please explain how."*

Better: *"Please list three ways in which your wedding consultant made your wedding day less stressful."*

The poorly written item is so long and complicated that it is almost impossible to discover the point.

Finally, avoid items that are leading or biased. Questions that exclude respondents or encourage respondents to answer in a particular way are problematic for two reasons. First, leading or biased items remove the neutrality of the evaluation process by excluding certain groups or thoughts from consideration. Second, leading or biased items often are embedded with social desirability cues, which means that the respondent will be pushed to answer in a certain way because it appears that there is a "correct" answer that the consultant wants to get. Consider the following scale item:

Poorly written item: *"All intelligent brides will hire a wedding consultant to help make wedding planning less stressful."*

Better: *"My wedding consultant helped make the wedding planning less stressful."*

The poorly written item assumes that only brides hire wedding consultants, which is biased in that it excludes grooms, couples, or parents from being the point of contact. Furthermore, it has the social desirability cue of intelligence; that is, if the respondent wants to be perceived as intelligent s/he will feel forced to agree to the statement.

FORMATTING THE QUESTIONNAIRE

When formatting the questionnaire, keep the usability in mind because you want it to be as easy as possible for respondents to answer all items efficiently. Below are 15 formatting rules that you should take into consideration:

- Start with a clear heading that has your business name and sets forth the fact that this is a client questionnaire.
- The heading should be followed by a brief statement that gives the purpose of the evaluation.
- Below the purpose statement, include an assurance of confidentiality. If there is a particularly fabulous statement from a client that you would like to include on your Web site, you should follow up and ask permission to do so.
- Include a space where you fill in the name of the client, the couple's names, the wedding date, and the name of the consultant. The client may or may not be the same as the couple. In some

cases, the client may be a parent of the bride or groom—for instance, if the couple is out of town and a parent is planning on their behalf. Mail the evaluation to your primary point of contact to avoid confusion.

- Similar item types (fixed-alternative, scale, open-ended) should be clustered together so that the respondent can easily flow from one item to the next.
- As necessary, include instructions to facilitate the completion process. This is usually needed prior to the presentation of scale items. Do not take anything for granted or assume that the respondent will understand what to do.
- The items themselves should be easy to read, so make sure the font is big enough so that the respondent does not have to squint. Avoid unusual font styles that are difficult to read.
- The layout should be organized and straightforward. Items should neatly line up, and all of the open-ended lines should be the same length.
- There should be adequate room for the respondent to write, in particular for open-ended items. If the lines are squished together, it will discourage feedback.
- Do not try to crowd too much on a given page, as this will create confusion.
- If the questionnaire is more than one page, consistently direct the respondent to the next page. For example, "Please continue on the opposite side" can be used when designing a two-sided questionnaire.
- Do not expect your clients to write a dissertation. Usually 10 items, and certainly no more than 20, will be sufficient.
- At the end of the document, you should include a message of thanks and a request for the return of the questionnaire.
- Always include a self-addressed, stamped envelope to facilitate the return process.
- Grammatical, typographical, and printing errors will harm your credibility. You are better off having no evaluation than having a sloppy evaluation.

THE COVER LETTER

Once you have carefully crafted your questionnaire, you will be anxious to send it off to a client. But not so fast. If you just toss it into an envelope without an appropriate cover letter, all of your efforts may have been in vain. When writing a cover letter for a post-wedding evaluation, be certain to include the following seven elements: (1) date sent; (2) greeting; (3) naming of the couple and reminder of the wedding; (4) purpose of the questionnaire; (5) desired return date and indication of an included return envelope; (6) contact information; and (7) final words of thanks. The cover letter should be short and to the point. Invest in letterhead stationery for a professional touch. Figure 21.2 offers an example of a cover letter. Give the couple a few weeks to enjoy their honeymoon and get settled in before mailing out the questionnaire packet.

VENDOR FEEDBACK

While the examples in this chapter have primarily applied to your clients, the same rules apply when creating a vendor questionnaire. Vendor questionnaires should be used with extreme discretion; do not send a questionnaire to the same vendor each time you work with her or him, as the vendor is bound to get annoyed. The best time to request feedback is the first time you work with a vendor. Once vendors get to know you personally over time, you can send an e-mail or make a quick call if you have anything you would like to discuss about a particular wedding. A sample vendor questionnaire can be found in Figure 21.3.

Similar to the client questionnaire, you need to fill in the top part of the form. If you do not remind the vendor of the couple's names, your name, and the wedding date, the vendor will have no idea which is the wedding of interest. Do not get distressed if vendors do not return the form or if their feedback is not stellar. During the busy wedding season, there simply may not be time. Moreover, some vendors do not fully appreciate the services that consultants provide. Don't try to force the issue, and be appreciative of any feedback you do receive. Sample question number 5 is included as a cross-check to make sure you have not requested feedback from this particular vendor in the past. If you have several associates, you will need to be very careful not to bombard your vendors with questionnaires. Compare notes and create a master list of vendors who have given feedback that can be readily accessed. Again, over time you will get to know your vendors well and they will know you, so the need for structured vendor feedback will decrease.

☙ the wedding summary

The hardest part about evaluation is giving it meaning. As Getz has observed, "Evaluation results often get filed and forgotten, especially if they are negative" (2005, p. 381). When you plan your first wedding, it will be incomprehensible that you will ever forget even a single minute detail; however, over time your weddings will start to morph together, and you will not remember the specifics unless you make a point of always completing a wedding summary.

It is only in taking the time to review and summarize the details of each wedding that you can make adjustments and improve upon your skills. There will always be small things that don't go quite right during

Wakeside Weddings

Business Address, Telephone, and E-mail

August 8, 2008

Client Name

Client Address

Dear Karina,

I hope that you and Ethan had a fabulous honeymoon in Hawaii. It was such a pleasure working with you and watching your sunset orange theme come to life at your wedding.

I am writing to ask you to fill out a brief questionnaire. The Wakeside Weddings team is always looking for ways to improve our services, and your feedback is very valuable to us.

Please complete the enclosed form and return it in the postage-paid envelope by September 1. If you have any questions, do not hesitate to call or e-mail me.

Sincerely,

Jamie Carrolton

Associate, Wakeside Weddings

FIGURE 21.2 *Sample cover letter*

Wakeside Weddings
Post-wedding Vendor Questionnaire

By completing this questionnaire, you are helping the consultants at Wakeside Weddings
to consistently improve their services when working with vendors

Your answers will remain confidential

Vendor's Name: _____

The Couple: _____

Wedding Date: _____

Consultant's Name: _____

Please rate the quality of your interactions with the Wakeside Weddings consultant,
where 5 = Strongly Agree and 1 = Strongly Disagree

1. The wedding consultant was…	Strongly Agree	Agree	No Opinion	Disagree	Strongly Disagree
…helpful	5	4	3	2	1
…organized	5	4	3	2	1
…professional	5	4	3	2	1
…knowledgeable	5	4	3	2	1
…easy to contact when needed	5	4	3	2	1

2. Working with a wedding consultant…	Strongly Agree	Agree	No Opinion	Disagree	Strongly Disagree
…saved me time	5	4	3	2	1
…saved me money	5	4	3	2	1
…made my job less stressful	5	4	3	2	1
…made working with the couple easier	5	4	3	2	1

3. What services did the consultant provide that helped you perform your job more effectively?

_____

_____

4. What other services would you like to see our consultants provide that would help your company?

_____

_____

5. Was this the first time that you worked with a consultant from Wakeside Weddings?

[ ] Yes   [ ] No

FIGURE 21.3 *Sample post-wedding questionnaire for vendors*

6a. Based on your experience, would you recommend the consultant to your clients?

[ ] Yes   [ ] No

6b. If no, please explain: _____

_____

Comments and Suggestions:

_____

_____

_____

THANK YOU FOR YOUR FEEDBACK!

Please return this questionnaire in the postage-paid envelope that has been provided.

FIGURE 21.3 *Continued*

wedding implementation. By reflecting on these issues a few days later and talking with other consultants, you can come up with ideas for handling similar situations in the future. Careful documentation and honest self-appraisal will allow you to be your own best critic. The wedding summary includes creative solutions so that you are better prepared for the next wedding.

If you have been organized all along, compiling the final wedding summary should be a fairly efficient process. Each client should have a separate file folder. In your file cabinet, order them alphabetically by last name. Also, create a cross-reference spreadsheet on your computer that includes the client's name as well as the date of the wedding. The wedding summary should include six parts: (1) an executive summary; (2) the write-up of the wedding if announced in a local newspaper (as this generally also includes a picture of the couple, which is a useful reminder); (3) the entire production schedule including the vendor list; (4) the final budget breakdown; (5) the returned client questionnaire and any completed questionnaires from new vendors; and (6) samples of materials from the wedding that can be shown to future clients, such as the program, invitation, escort cards, favors, and swatches of fabric.

The executive summary should be a one- to three-page overview, including the most important and unique aspects of the wedding. If carefully written, the executive summary should immediately spark your memory and bring you back to the wedding, even if it took place 10 years ago. Consider including the following aspects in each executive summary:

- The names of the couple, both before and after the wedding
- Ceremony and reception venues
- Theme
- Final budget
- Vendors who were especially excellent
- Vendors who presented difficulties
- Elements and ideas that were particularly unique
- Moments that did not go well, how they were addressed, and how similar problems can be avoided in the future
- Feedback from the clients that will assist with continuous improvement
- As applicable, feedback from vendors that will assist with continuous improvement

Complete the bulk of the wedding summary as soon as possible after a wedding. Although it may take several weeks to receive final feedback from a client or vendor, do not wait until this information arrives to initiate the summary. First of all, the feedback may never come if a client or vendor is not inclined to return the questionnaire. Second, as days and weeks pass, you will start to forget the specifics of one wedding as you move on to the next.

As a final follow-up, consider sending each of your couples a first anniversary card. This should only be done for the first anniversary and is a nice touch that will keep your business on the couple's radar screen. During a casual conversation with an engaged friend, a former client may mention how thoughtful it was that you remembered their anniversary date, and this just might lead to a new client!

REFERENCES

Babbie, E. (2003). *The Practice of Social Research*, 10th ed. Belmont, CA: Wadsworth Publishing.

Getz, D. (2005). *Event Management and Event Tourism*, 2nd ed. New York: Cognizant Communication Corporation.

Jordan, D. J., DeGraaf, D. G., and DeGraaf, K. H. (2005). *Programming for Parks, Recreation and Leisure Services: A Servant Leadership Approach*. State College, PA: Venture Publishing.

PHOTO 21-3 *(opposite) Vendor questionnaires are useful the first time you work with a vendor.*

Consultant Checklist and Reminders for Post-wedding Evaluation

☐ Prepare an evaluation in order to pinpoint areas of success and those in need of improvement.

☐ Evaluate the product, process, and psychosocial elements.

☐ Keep wedding questionnaires concise and limit the number of open-ended items.

☐ Format questionnaires with usability in mind.

☐ Include a cover letter to introduce the purpose of the questionnaire.

☐ Use vendor questionnaires with extreme discretion.

☐ Complete a summary of every wedding.

☐ Be your own best critic through careful documentation and honest self-appraisal.

☐ Consider sending each of your couples a first anniversary card.

review questions

1. Name three reasons why evaluation is important.

2. Distinguish between formative and summative evaluation and explain why one of these is inappropriate for wedding evaluation.

3. Distinguish between quantitative and qualitative evaluation.

4. Name the three types of questionnaire items and explain how they differ.

5. Give three examples of common wording problems that you want to avoid when writing questionnaire items.

6. Name a minimum of five rules for formatting a questionnaire.

terminology

- Constructive criticism
- Double-barreled items
- Fixed-alternative items
- Formative evaluation
- Leading items
- Process evaluation
- Product evaluation
- Psychosocial evaluation
- Qualitative evaluation
- Quantitative evaluation
- Questionnaire
- Response fatigue

- Scale items
- Social desirability cues
- Summative evaluation
- Open-ended items
- Usability
- Wedding summary

section three

BUILDING YOU

BUSINESS

if you have decided to embark on a career in wedding planning, you need more than just a business card to get started. before you can call yourself a wedding consultant, you must have a thorough understanding of what it takes to own and operate a sole proprietorship, partnership, or corporation. the third and final section of this book will detail the key steps to follow when building your business.

You should begin with the important task of writing a business plan with a clear focus on your target audience, as presented in depth in CHAPTER 22. Once you have a business plan, you need a strategy to carry it out, so CHAPTER 23 explores the keys to successful marketing. When potential clients start contacting you, effective interview techniques, communication skills, and knowledge of contracts become essential and are therefore highlighted in CHAPTER 24. Remember, you do not have a client until you have a signed contract. With a client in hand, proficiency in vendor relations, networking, and negotiating becomes a must, so these areas are the focus of CHAPTER 25.

As your business expands, your office and staffing needs will grow, as examined thoroughly in CHAPTER 26. You will become familiar with the other consultants in your area, and you should understand the influences of competition, obligations, and ethics, all of which are discussed in CHAPTER 27. This section and the book will conclude with CHAPTER 28, which presents information that will help you manage the stress associated with this demanding career. Simultaneously, this chapter offers ways to continually enrich your business and maintain your personal life.

business plan and target audiences

Before opening the doors, a new business owner must have a well-thought-out business plan in order to increase the likelihood of success. Starting a business without a plan is like learning to ski from a triple black diamond run...maybe you can make it down, but it's not going to be pretty.

he Small Business Administration (SBA) is one of your best resources for starting a small business. The SBA (2006) explains the importance of having a business plan:

A business plan precisely defines your business, identifies your goals, and serves as your firm's résumé. The basic components include a current and pro-forma balance sheet, an income state-

PHOTO 22-1 *(opposite) Business plans allow you to pinpoint a target market.*

ment, and a cash flow analysis. It helps you allocate resources properly, handle unforeseen complications, and make good business decisions. Because it provides specific and organized information about your company and how you will repay borrowed money, a good business plan is a crucial part of any loan application. Additionally, it informs sales personnel, suppliers, and others about your operations and goals.

This chapter outlines the basics of your business plan while also pinpointing the importance of having a target market.

✍ writing your business plan

Developing your plan is an important first step in showing the world you are serious about starting a business. After all, if you can't find the time or energy to put together a game plan for your business, how are you ever going to find the time or the energy to run a business? If you want to be taken seriously by lending institutions, vendors, colleagues, and competitors, you need a business plan to achieve your goals and objectives.

Before you begin writing your business plan, the SBA (2006) suggests you consider four core questions:

- What service or product does your business provide, and what needs does it fill?
- Who are the potential customers for your product or service, and why will they purchase it from you?
- How will you reach your potential customers?
- Where will you get the financial resources to start your business?

In short, your business plan will help you describe your business, select a target market, manage day-to-day operations, and handle finances. Although there is no single formula for developing a business plan, some elements are common to most business plans. They are summarized in Table 22.1.

While the information in Table 22.1 may seem overwhelming, the complexity of the business will dictate the complexity of the information required. Starting with Section I, you will want to describe your business by first providing a mission statement, which is a clear and concise (usually one-sentence) statement of being. Begin the sentence with, "The mission of (insert your company name) is ... " Complete the thought by stating your focus and philosophy. A more detailed description of your business can follow, which might include an overview of your vision, products, services, goals, and objectives.

In addition to the business description, the first section of the business plan should include a marketing plan (Chapter 23), a statement detail-

TABLE 22.1 Elements of a Business Plan

Cover Sheet
Statement of Purpose/Executive Summary
Table of Contents

    Section I: The Business
- Description of business
- Marketing
- Competition
- Operating procedures
- Personnel
- Business insurance

    Section II: Financial Data
- Loan applications
- Capital equipment and supply list
- Balance sheet
- Income statement
- Breakeven analysis
- Pro-forma income projections
- Pro-forma cash flow

    Section III: Supporting Documents
- Tax returns
- Personal financial statement
- Copy of lease
- Copy of licenses and other legal documents
- Résumé

Source: Adapted from SBA (2006).

ing your competition (Chapter 27), a clear means of operation (Chapter 26), and a listing of personnel needs (Chapter 26). Many consultants start out working alone, and building a staff comes with business growth. This section ends with an overview of your insurance coverage, as discussed later in this chapter.

Section II of your business plan includes your financial data. Many consultants start out small and work from their homes, keeping them from the immediate need to apply for a small business loan. Once you have built a reputation and a staff, you will need to rent a separate space and will have the business clout to secure a loan. Your list of capital equipment and supply list details the materials you need to run your business. Equipment is permanent or reusable over a significant period of time, such as your vehicle, computer, printer, desk, fax machine, copy machine, bookshelves, file cabinets, stapler, scissors, and tape dispenser. Supplies, on the other hand, are consumed after one use or a short period of time; examples are printer paper and cartridges, pens, tape, staples, and sticky notes. Keep an organized spreadsheet that details the equipment and supplies that you utilize in your daily operations.

A balance sheet is a summary of the dollar value of everything your business owns and owes. This details the overall financial state of the company. Your income statement identifies total income, which is your revenue minus your expenses. A breakeven analysis is your projection of the amount of business you would need to do to simply break even over a defined period of time, that is, where your expenses are equal to your revenue. Pro-forma income projections are "what-if" analyses in which you estimate your expenses, revenue, and income over a defined period of time. Finally, your pro-forma cash flow is a projection of cash receipts and cash payments over a specified time period. Financial projections are critical to your business success because they help you determine your pricing structure.

The third section of your business plan includes the supporting documents that are critical to obtaining loans as your business grows. Information such as your tax returns, personal financial statements, lease (if you are renting a space), licenses, and résumé should be readily accessible.

You don't have to reinvent the wheel when writing your business plan; you simply need to get it down on paper. There are many resources

Photograph by www.RodneyBailey.com

PHOTO 22-2 *Online resources can guide you in writing your business plan.*

and individuals available to assist you in this task including Web sites, books, software, and accountants. Bplans.com is an excellent resource that includes over 50 free business plans for review, including one that pertains to a wedding consultancy business.

☞ beyond the business card

Many aspiring wedding planners believe it takes little more than a business card to get started in the field. However, whether you are starting from home or leasing executive office space, you will need to establish your business as a formal legal entity before attracting your first customer. This may seem like a tedious exercise, but rest assured, prospective clients will check your credentials to ensure you are a legitimate business before hiring you. If you don't have a legitimate business, the client will hire another consultant. Getting married is stressful enough. A couple doesn't want to hire someone to manage the most important day of their lives only to find out the person wasn't properly insured or legally permitted to operate a business.

WHAT'S IN A NAME?

In a word: Everything! Before you fill out the first form to register your business, you must have a business name. When selecting a business name, use your imagination and conduct research. Check out the competition. Your business name should be as unique as you are. The name can be formal, contemporary, casual, funky, or elegant but ultimately should reflect your style, so make the decision carefully.

In creating a business name, do not make it too complicated, cutesy, or confusing. "Happily Ever After" might sound like a wedding planning business to you but it may suggest "travel agency" to someone else. An overly complicated name like Fran's Fabulous and Fancy Wedding Planning and Design is too wordy for a business card and would not lend itself to a concise logo. Be innovative but keep it simple. Potential clients are more apt to remember your business name if it is concise, unique, and interesting. In addition, many wedding planners choose to use their own first and/or last name in their business title; for example, business names such as "Events by Holly" or "Sue Serene Wedding Planning" allow for a personal approach. You might also consider starting your company name with the letter "A." This tactic will ensure that your company is listed at or near the top of listings such as bridal showcase directories or the white pages.

After you have developed three or four possible ideas for your business name, share your thoughts with family and friends. Get their feedback and support. Often, someone else will think of a good reason to use or not use a name. Once you digest their feedback, narrow your choices to two or three.

Once you have narrowed down your selection, check to make sure the ideas for your name are unique and not already in use. Beyond a general Internet search, a few other places to check are the U.S. Patent and Trade Office Web site at uspto.com, the white pages, and Network Solutions, which is the clearinghouse for Web site name registrations. The Association of Bridal Consultants and the Association of Certified Wedding Consultants are additional places to check before choosing a name for your business. Remember, just because the name you select does not have a Web site does not mean that the name has not already been taken. Do your homework and check. If the name you like best is available, register it immediately so that you are not left out in the cold. If it is taken, move on to your second and third options.

"DOING BUSINESS AS" STATEMENT

Once you have a business name, you must register it with your local government. This is called filing your Doing Business As (DBA) statement. To learn more, go to your local city or county government's Web site, where you can find information regarding where to register and how much it will cost. The fee is generally between $30 and $60 and entitles you to use your business name for a set period of time, most often three years. When your DBA expires, you simply renew your statement. Prior to issuing a DBA, the local government will do a search to make sure your name is not currently used by another business. If you haven't done your homework in advance, you might learn that your idea has already been taken.

THE CORPORATE STRUCTURE OF YOUR BUSINESS

Having filed your DBA, you must next determine the structure of your business. The three primary types of business entities are sole proprietor, partnership, and corporation, and many hybrids, such as limited liability companies, exist. Of these, the sole proprietorship, which is one individual operating a business, is the most common for wedding consultants because it is the simplest and least expensive type of business to set up. Be aware, however, that if your business fails, your personal assets may be used to pay off your business debts because the business does not exist separately from the owner and you accept all associated financial risks. If you open a business in your own name as a sole proprietorship, you can use your social security number for filing business taxes.

A partnership, on the other hand, is a relationship existing between two or more persons who join together to carry on a trade or business. If you elect to form a partnership, have an attorney draw up a formal partnership agreement so that each partner is aware of his or her rights and responsibilities. Don't just assume that your best friend will understand his or her responsibilities. This is a business, so get it in writing.

A corporation is a separate legal entity from the business owner. It requires filing of articles of incorporation, electing officers, holding an annual meeting, and paying corporate taxes. It is often easier to obtain financing from banks or other sources as a corporation; thus, if you should decide to franchise your business, it will make sense to form this type of entity.

EMPLOYER ID NUMBERS

If you form a partnership or corporation, you will need an Employer ID Number (EIN), which is a federal tax identification number used to recognize a business entity. The IRS uses this number to identify individuals who are required to file business tax returns. You may apply for an EIN in various ways, including online at the www.irs.gov Web site. To obtain an EIN, you will need to complete Form SS-4 from the IRS. Again, this form can be found on the IRS Web site or at your local IRS office. You may also call 1-800-TAX-FORM to request the form by mail; be certain to follow the line-by-line instructions for your business type (IRS Publication 1635, 2002).

THERE'S NO PLACE LIKE HOME

Many wedding planners operate out of their homes, especially when they are first getting started. If you decide to go this route, be sure to call the Zoning Commission in your local town to check on the zoning ordinances that may govern this type of activity. Some towns prohibit home-based businesses that have clients coming and going. You will want to determine if any special permits are required for your wedding planning business. An alternative to seeing clients in your home would be to meet them at a mutually convenient location like a coffee shop.

LICENSE, PERMITS, AND INSURANCE

Many communities require business owners to have a business license. It is obtained by filling out a form at your local city hall. The license is usually good for one year and the fee is nominal. Your local government's Web site will have further information on obtaining this license.

You will also need to apply for a permit from your local health department if you are planning to provide food or drink for your clients. For example, if you promise your client that you will make 100 miniature wedding cakes as favors, you will need a permit from the health department. If you don't plan on baking or providing catering to your clients, you will not need this permit.

Insurance is not just for homes and cars; it is important for businesses as well, especially small businesses. While you are in the process of establishing your business, an important component of getting started is to make sure you are insured against potential damaging situations. For example, it is frequently your job as the wedding consultant to make sure the wedding gifts get from point A to point B. If a gift goes missing or a money envelope is stolen, you might be held liable; or, if you are working at a venue and accidentally drop a waterford vase, you will want to have insurance to replace the damaged item. Most insurance companies offer a variety of policies that can be designed to suit your wedding planning business. Contact a local insurance agent in your community to discuss what type of insurance is right for you.

If you already have standard homeowner's insurance, you may have a certain amount of general liability coverage. Check the amount that your policy carries. If it is too low, you may need a rider to the main policy. A rider acts as an addendum to your main policy and can cover specific items like office equipment and computers. Another type of rider you should investigate is one for general liability that protects

Photograph by www.RodneyBailey.com

PHOTO 22-3 *Insurance will protect you should an accident happen at a venue.*

you, your employees, and vendors from personal injury claims (Sandlin, 2003). For example, if the florist you hired backs his delivery truck into the couple's limo, you will be covered. Insurance riders can be very economical and give you the peace of mind and confidence to conduct your business with less worry and stress. For a nominal fee, you can acquire the rider you need to protect your assets.

General liability policies are excellent choices for those running a home-based business without significant foot traffic. If you wish to hire a staff that will work out of your home, you will need business owners insurance. This particular type of insurance will cover you against physical injuries to you, your clients, and your employees, damage to your property, and other situations that may arise. This type of coverage is in addition to your homeowner's policy and is more expensive than a rider.

If you decide to establish your business outside of the home, you will need commercial business insurance. Rates for this type of insurance depend on where your business is located, the type of business you own, and state/local regulations. A knowledgeable insurance agent can help you determine if this type of coverage is right for you.

Because we live in a world that is quick to litigate, it is critical that you take care of insuring yourself and your business before the first client walks through the door. This could be the most important decision you make regarding your business.

REFERENCES

IRS Publication 1635. (2002). *Understanding Your EIN, Employer Identification Number.* Washington, DC: U.S. Department of the Treasury.

Sandlin, E. F. (2003). *Start Your Own Wedding Consultant Business, Your Step-by-Step Guide to Success.* Irvine, CA: Entrepreneur Media.

Small Business Administration. (2006). SBA: Your small business resource, available at http://www.sba.gov/starting_business/legal/forms.html

4

review questions

1. What are the four questions that guide a business plan?

2. What is a DBA, and why do you need one?

3. Name and distinguish between the three primary types of business entities?

4. What is an EIN?

5. What is an insurance rider?

terminology

- Balance sheet
- Breakeven analysis
- Capital equipment and supply list
- Corporation
- DBA statement
- EIN
- Income statement
- Insurance rider
- Partnership
- Pro-forma cash flow
- Pro-forma income projections
- Sole proprietor

developing a marketing strategy

Marketing is an umbrella term that pertains to a company's activities that are associated with selling a product or service and developing a competitive advantage. Marketing has traditionally been packaged with the four Ps: product, price, place, and promotion. Product is the tangible and intangible goods and services that you offer. As a consultant, you act as the liaison between the couple and many of the tangible purchases they make; you also add the intangible elements related to design and organization. Price is the exchange value of the product—in other words, your fee structure. Place involves the radius or area that you serve, that is, the distance you are willing to travel as a planner and the primary communities that you serve. Promotion involves the advertising, sponsorship, publicity, sales promotion, and personal sales that you use to grow your business.

PHOTO 23-1 *(opposite) When selecting a target market, make sure there is a substantial customer base.*

t is commonly thought that marketing is all about advertising and making sales. In addition, marketing is about the little things a company does to reach its target audience like driving to a client's house to make a delivery in person instead of dropping it in the mail, having an annual party to thank clients, or sending cards to vendors. If a business matches its products and services to the people who need them, then marketing has been successful. This chapter points out the three key factors that will allow you to develop a marketing strategy for a wedding consultancy business: determining your target audience, marketing tool development, and learning the four secrets of selling to brides.

determining your target audience

After you have established your business as a formal entity, it is time to get the word out that your doors are open for business. The best way to do that is through marketing. But before you spend the first dollar on marketing or advertising, you must determine your target audience, which is the defined group of people you wish to serve. One of the hardest things about establishing a business is finding your style and defining it. Many consultants struggle because they want to be everything to everybody and are afraid to turn away business, but this generalist approach means that they can't focus their energy on a specific, target market. To get focused, consider the following questions:

- Who are your customers going to be?
- Is this a growing market in your area?
- How are you going to reach your customers?
- What pricing strategy will you implement?
- What will be your specialty area of expertise?
- What will differentiate you from your competitors?

When selecting a target market, you have to make sure there is a substantial customer base to justify the choice. For example, if you decide that you want to focus your wedding business on same-sex weddings, you should know the facts: Are same-sex marriages or civil unions legal in your state? How many same-sex marriages or civil unions have there been in your state since it became legal? Are there enough couples to support a wedding consultant who focuses on same-sex weddings? The same series of questions pertains to any niche group, such as the over-40 market, the cross-cultural market, and the second marriage market. Once you have drilled down and answered the questions about your potential clients, you are ready to develop a marketing plan to reach them.

ϲ➢ marketing tool development

For a new business, the two best marketing tools you can create are your business card and your Web site. However, before you develop either of these tools, it is important to consider developing a logo for your business.

What would McDonald's be without the golden arches? Or Nike without the famous swoosh? Or Starbucks without the mermaid? Each of these businesses is known by the company's graphic representation, known as a logo, as much as the business name. When forming your company, you spent a significant amount of time selecting a business name; now it is time to work on a logo that captures your essence graphically. Once you have a logo, you can move forward with developing your associated marketing tools.

For such an important task, seek professional help from a graphic designer or artist. If you have minimal start-up funds, there are Internet-based logo design firms that are reasonably priced. Alternatively, secure the assistance of friends who have artistic talent or consider hiring an art or graphic design student to generate ideas for you. Meet with the designer in person to describe your business, style, the type of client you hope to attract, your mission statement, philosophy, and other relevant details from your business plan.

Give the artist some ideas to get the ball rolling, and then allow the artist free rein to come up with designs for you to review. When the artist presents some options to you, take time to think about them. Ask yourself some questions: Which idea will carry you through many years? Which idea has the most flexibility? Which idea really personifies what you are all about? Remember, this logo will be seen on letterhead, signage, work shirts, brochures, and your Web site. Make sure the logo you select looks like a wedding planning business rather than a florist, caterer, or other wedding-related specialist. Now that you have a logo, you are ready to develop your other key marketing tools.

BUSINESS CARD BASICS

The business card may seem like an antiquated business tool, but it is in fact one of the best marketing tools at your disposal and also one of the least expensive. Plain or fancy, self-made or professionally designed, the business card is indispensable for marketing your business.

Since your business card is a tangible personification of your business, the style of your card should echo the style of your business. For example, if your business plan is to cater to those with small budgets, your business card should reflect that. Conversely, if you hope to capture high-end weddings, your card should be on expensive paper and the lettering should be engraved. If you hope to target recent college graduates, your card should be modern so that it will appeal to a young audience.

Your business card should include the following information: your logo, the business name, your name and title, and your contact information, including mailing address, home telephone number, mobile telephone number, e-mail address, fax number, and Web site address. If you are going after a certain market, reflect that with your business card. For example, if you wish to target Japanese brides, you should consider having your information printed in Japanese on the reverse side of the card. This way, when you meet with a Japanese client, you can present your card in both languages. Small efforts like this will distance you from your competition.

In addition, if your business has a specialty, you might list that on the card. Statements like "Specializing in multi-cultural celebrations" or "Fluent in English, Spanish, and French" would provide valuable information to potential clients.

Have 500 cards printed and always keep a stack with you. Invest in a nice leather or metal cardholder so that when someone asks for your card, they are not tumbling out of your purse or briefcase. You always want to present a new card, not something that has been kicking around at the bottom of your bag. Remember, your card is a representation of your business. If you want to present a neat and organized image, make sure your card speaks to that.

WEB SITE UNDER CONSTRUCTION

While your business card is a mini-billboard for your business, a professional Web site is an electronic billboard capable of reaching millions of potential clients. Ed Chung is the creative director of Ditherdog, a marketing and design firm specializing in Web site development. Ed offers the following reasons why wedding consultants should have a Web presence (Chung, 2006):

- The Web is an inexpensive, proven, mass-market vehicle to communicate corporate objectives and description of products and services.
- Unlike print marketing, a Web site is easy to regularly update and keep fresh.
- A Web site is a great vehicle for creating a stimulating, 24-hour multimedia portfolio (pictures, sound, video) to sell your company.
- Web e-mail forms allow for a passive (hands-off) way to accumulate new leads and garner customer interest.
- You can cross-market with print campaigns (direct mail or advertising) by promoting a unique URL (e.g., www.wildlandweddings. com/holidayspecial), which will better explain services and at the

same time track the effectiveness of a campaign or publication by analyzing user traffic.

- Newsletters created in e-mail or Web form are an inexpensive means of sending promotional updates.

Your e-mail address should be linked to your Web site address. For example, if a wedding Web site is wildlandweddings.com, an associate's e-mail might be leanna@wildlandweddings.com. This is much more memorable, professional, and marketable than something like leanwedplnr1234@email.com.

MARKETING APPEALS

When constructing your Web site or other marketing materials, you should appeal to potential clients through logic, emotion, and credibility. Logical appeals answer all of the nuts and bolts questions that arise: who, what, where, when, why, cost, and contact information. Specifically, there should be a person attached to the company (who), a description of the services you provide (what), your location and/or the areas you serve (where), how long you have been planning weddings (when), and a mission statement (why). When you are brand new to the business, you probably don't want to directly state the when (e.g., "We've been in business for three months!"). Over time, however, this can add significantly to your credibility (e.g., "During the past five years we have planned over 100 weddings") . If you do not want to put your price structure on the Internet, the cost information can be alluded to by detailing the various packages you offer. Clients who want to follow up can then use your contact information to get more specific details.

Emotional appeals draw your clients more closely to your services. Specifically, many consultants include pictures from weddings they have planned as a means to personalize their Web sites. Potential clients can get a better sense of your style and specialty areas through the visual representation of past work. If your business caters to ski resort weddings, make sure that is made obvious with a number of associated photographs. Brides love looking at pictures from other weddings as this creates a sense of anticipation for their own day. When utilizing pictures, make sure that you get copyright permission from the photographer. Many consultants have excellent professional relationships with area photographers who will allow them to post pictures from weddings that showcase their work.

Appeals to credibility can come from quotes taken from letters or feedback from satisfied clients. Furthermore, if you receive any awards or outside recognition related to wedding planning, that information should be prominently displayed on your Web site. Credibility can also be obtained through related courses, seminars, or conferences that you have either attended or participated in as a guest speaker. Any

PHOTO 23-2 *Tantalizing photographs appeal to brides' emotions.*

involvement with event or wedding associations such as the International Special Events Society or the Association of Bridal Consultants should also be evidenced on your Web site to boost your credibility.

Beyond your own Web site, advertising on wedding sites such as The Knot can be an effective form of promotion. You will be charged based on the type of listing, with premium positioning coming with an extra charge. Fees that run $150 or more a month may be cost-prohibitive at first, but if you get one or two clients from this listing, before you know it, you've covered the fee for the entire year.

the four secrets of selling to brides

Marc McIntosh, who is featured in Vendor Spotlight, Case 23.1, is the CEO of Showcase Productions, which produces 10 bridal shows each year. In the course of his career, Marc has interacted with thousands of wedding vendors and over 100,000 brides. When he is not produc-

marc mcIntosh

showcase productions

What is your background? I have spent my entire working career in the wedding business, first working as a DJ and then managing a DJ business. When I decided to go into the business of bridal shows, the biggest show in the area had 75 booths and 1,000 visitors. So I rented the largest venue in town and spent a year putting together a show that was bigger and better. I was initially projecting about 150 exhibitors, and everyone thought I was crazy. Well, 150 booths turned into 250 booths and 4,000 people showed up, and it literally launched me into a new career. Here I am 12 years later still doing it. My wife is a divorce lawyer—we work both ends of the wedding spectrum.

Under what circumstances do men attend bridal shows? Under duress! Actually, guys make up a pretty small percentage of our audience. It is a 95 percent female audience, and that's how it has always been.

But do men get involved in the actual planning? Yes, very much so. Brides and grooms more and more often are paying for the wedding themselves or contributing a large amount of money to it. Because the grooms are paying, they become more involved in the decision making.

Can you share a funny vendor story? I have many fond ones, like the DJ who did some genius gorilla marketing and ordered chicken wings for all of his competitors and had them delivered to the show about 15 minutes before the show started. They thought that he was the greatest guy in town. And you know what the end result was? They're all sitting in their booths eating chicken wings and the doors open and thousands of people fall in. That was a funny one.

Web site: www.bridalshowcase.com

ing shows, Marc spends much of his time helping vendors, including wedding consultants, discover ways to better market their businesses. In 2003, Marc was awarded the Bridal Show Producer's International Cup Award, the highest honor of the association. Below are Marc's four secrets of selling to brides, adapted to apply specifically to wedding consultants.

SECRET #1

Secret #1 is that you have to connect with the bride. Connecting with the bride simply means that you have to create awareness of your business in the mind of the bride. In other words, she has to be able to find you. Traditional media options such as newspapers, radio stations, or the yellow pages can be cost prohibitive. With these forms of advertising you are paying to reach a large percentage of the population; however, you are only trying to reach the 1 or 2 percent who are planning a wedding. Advertising in wedding-specific media can be much more effective. Direct marketing using mail can be cost effective because you are putting your message in the hand of a bride. You can obtain lists of brides as part of an exhibit package at a bridal show, as part of an advertising program with a Web site, or through a list broker.

The next way to connect to the bride is referrals. You ask the bride for referrals not only after the wedding, but also during the planning stages. Almost every bride knows someone else who is planning a wedding, and referrals are a huge way of getting business. Another source of referrals is accomplished through networking with other people in the business of weddings. When you are new, make appointments with all the major wedding vendors in your area so they get to know you. Join the major associations and begin to socialize with other people in the wedding business. If you establish friendships with other consultants, they will refer business to you if they are booked at a certain time or they meet someone who fits your specific niche.

While you absolutely need a Web site, it only works if it contains a message that is compelling and if the bride is able to find it. One of the biggest criteria that search engines use when ranking sites is how many other sites are linked to it, so cross-linking with other wedding-related Web sites will have a positive impact. You should be careful, however, that you do not give away your trade secrets on your site. The bride is paying for your knowledge, contacts, and experience, and you do not want to give her too much information for free. You are selling a very personalized service and you will be most effective when you have the opportunity to meet with the bride in person. Your site should only give enough information to entice the bride to call you for the complete details.

A final way to connect with the bride is through bridal shows. Bridal shows typically include fashion shows, demonstrations, and a variety of wedding-related businesses arranged in a trade show format. Shows give the vendor the opportunity to reach many prospective customers in just a few hours and allow the bride to visit one location to see all of the options available for her wedding.

Once you've decided to be in the wedding business, you can never ever stop marketing your company. Unlike companies that rely on repeat business, you will be dealing almost exclusively with first-time customers. Newly engaged brides continually enter the marketplace as prospective customers but then exit the marketplace when they get married. Your investment in marketing your business is every bit as important as your investment in the tools of your trade.

SECRET #2

Secret #2 is that you have to reach the bride at the right time. Your marketing will only be effective if your timing is right. Junk mail is only junk mail and spam is only spam if it contains a message that is not relevant to the person who reads it. The biggest challenge for wedding consultants, bar none, is the challenge of convincing a bride that she needs you while she still needs you.

If you are selling full-service planning, your goal is to reach the bride shortly after she has become engaged. Providing day-of coordinating services allows you to capture the brides who did not hire a long-term planner and allows you to gain valuable experience. The most effective time to market day-of services is three to four months prior to the wedding.

SECRET #3

Secret #3 is that you have to gain credibility with the bride. The more times you can get your message to the bride, the more chances you have to gain her trust. Perhaps the bride meets you through a friend or at a bridal show. She might then see your ad in a bridal magazine, receive an e-mail from you that directs her to your Web site, and then she gets referred to you from another company.

When establishing credibility, make sure you focus not only on the features of your business, but also on the benefits that will be very important to the bride. Features are things such as 10 years of experience, highly trained staff, and personalized attention. Features are important, but only when they are combined with corresponding benefits. For example, if the feature is "unmatched customer service," the benefit is "so that you will be able to relax and enjoy your wedding day."

More than anything, the bride is buying you. The bride only does business with you after she first buys you. If she likes you, chances are she will like doing business with you. If she's comfortable with you as a person, she will be comfortable doing business with you. Become someone who she is certain will not take advantage of her. Become someone she trusts.

PHOTO 23-3   *The focus of the wedding sales process is on the bride.*

SECRET #4

Secret #4 is that you have to give the bride what she wants. The bride has lots of details to take care of and not a lot of time to take care of them. She has problems. She has needs. Do not get wrapped up in the glories of your product or service. You need to concentrate on how you solve the bride's problems and how you fulfill the bride's needs.

The wedding sales process is about her; it's not about you. The bride really does not care about your company. She cares about her wedding. You have to make it as easy as possible for the bride to do business with you. Be accessible, answer your phone professionally, and return calls promptly. Maintain a business etiquette that will impress her and she will not only do business with you but will also refer you to her friends.

REFERENCE

Chung, E. (2006, January). Salient reasons to have a web presence for a wedding planning business (personal communication), Ditherdog, available at http://www.ditherdog.com

review questions

1. What are the four Ps of marketing?

2. Name a minimum of three questions to consider when determining your target market?

3. What information should be included on your business card?

4. What are four benefits of Web sites?

5. Name and explain the three types of appeals that should be represented in your marketing materials?

6. What are the four secrets of selling to brides?

terminology

- Appeals to credibility
- Emotional appeals
- Logical appeals
- Logo
- Marketing
- Place
- Price
- Product
- Promotion
- Target audience
- Web site

the client interview, *communication, and contracts*

One of the most difficult aspects of starting a wedding planning business is attracting your first client. Getting that initial bride to sign a contract can seem like a Herculean task, but with good planning, marketing, and creative thinking it will happen. This chapter discusses the elements of securing a client, including the initial screening, client interview details, follow-up communication, contracts, and compensation.

PHOTO 24-1 *(opposite) The client interview will illuminate the couple's dreams for their wedding day.*

☞ initial screening

Through your marketing efforts, you will eventually receive a telephone call or e-mail requesting a meeting with a potential client. By and large, the primary point of contact will be the bride. Before you grab your briefcase and rush out the door, it is wise to have a brief conversation over the telephone. During the conversation, you can screen the potential client by asking her a few preliminary questions such as: When is your wedding date? What is your wedding budget? Where will your wedding and reception take place? These questions will allow you first to quickly check your calendar to make sure that you do not have another wedding scheduled for that day; second, determine if the bride has an unrealistic budget, allowing you to judge whether this wedding will be worth your time; and third, find out if the wedding and reception are taking place in an area where your profits won't be eaten up at the gas pump. If the venues are significantly far away, make sure you build the additional travel time and transportation costs into your fee.

After the initial screening over the telephone, arrange to meet with your prospective client face to face. This meeting can take place at any number of locations such as your home office, the bride's reception venue, or the bride's home. Try to make the appointment as convenient as possible. If you elect to meet with your prospective client at a public place, make sure the environment is conducive for a long conversation. You do not want to compete with the sounds of baristas making lattés in the background or, worse, be asked to leave.

During the screening, set some ground rules regarding whom the bride can bring to the client interview. The groom is a good addition to the meeting, but the mother, father, and nursing sister with a new baby are too much. A bridal entourage participating in the meeting will hamper the process. Remember: this is your opportunity to hear what a potential client wants, and it is your chance to sell yourself and your planning business. If there are competing messages and agendas at the meeting, you will not get the information you need.

☞ client interview details

Think of the client interview as a "first date" or a "get to know you" meeting. If you have decided to specialize in outdoor country weddings, a bride who has visualized her wedding in a chic hotel ballroom will not be a good fit for your business. If this information comes out during the course of your interview, it will save everyone time and money if you gently steer the bride toward another planner. The client interview is a golden opportunity to find out what the bride wants and expects for her wedding day. Chances are she has been dreaming of

TABLE 24.1   Client Interview Questions

- How did you and your fiancé meet?
- Where are you going on your honeymoon?
- What are your hobbies and interests?
- What type of music do you like?
- What colors are appealing to you?
- Where are your favorite places to travel?
- Where did you grow up?
- What is your cultural background, and would you like to incorporate special traditions or customs into the wedding day?
- What tasks have you completed for the wedding?
- How many guests are you expecting?
- What are your "must haves" for your wedding day?
- How would you describe your style?
- Where do you like to shop?
- What is your budget?
- What are your expectations of your wedding planner?
- What are your greatest fears for your wedding day?
- Do you have any special needs or requests?
- Is there anything that I have not asked that I should?

this special day all her life, and now it is your responsibility to translate those dreams into reality.

When you meet with your prospective client, remember to dress appropriately. You should look neat and professional while conveying a sense of good organization. No bride is going to hire a rag-tag planner who forgot business cards or shows up late to the initial meeting. When you sit down, allow the bride to do 75 percent of the talking. Listen carefully to your client, maintain eye contact, and ask questions that encourage her to offer details. In order to start the conversation flowing, Table 24.1 includes a list of open-ended questions you can ask. The objective during this conversation is to find out as much as possible about your potential client and her wishes for her wedding day.

Once she has sketched out the details you can pick up the conversation by telling her about your background and experience, especially as it relates to her wedding. If you don't have much experience, tell her about events you have assisted with, the classes you have taken, or the ideas you have for her wedding day. This is your chance to make the sale and convince her that she needs to hire you to plan her wedding.

follow-up communication

Immediately after the meeting, send additional communication that reinforces what you learned at the meeting and that highlights why the bride should hire you. Often, a bride will interview three to five planners before selecting the one she likes best. Your follow-up communication may be just what it takes to set you apart from the other planners. You can send a simple thank-you note or you may write a more thorough recap of the meeting with a wedding planning contract attached. Whichever path you select, your communication must be flawless. If sending a thank-you note, it is wise to invest in some elegant personal stationery or letterhead. Any communication that leaves your office is a reflection of you. Take time to review for typos, spelling mistakes, misused words, and factual errors. A sample thank-you note is found in Figure 24.1.

✑ Contracts

Sometimes, either during or after the initial meeting, a potential client will express readiness to commit to hiring you as a wedding planner. This excellent news should be followed up immediately with a contract. A wedding contract is a written set of obligations that clearly spells out the responsibilities of the consultant and the client.

Whether you send the contract via e-mail or surface mail, it is important that you already have a standard version on hand that can be quickly customized and sent out without delay. If you wait a week or two to mail the contract, your potential client may have already secured another planner.

Send your contract out with a cover letter thanking the bride for selecting you to plan her wedding and reassuring her that you are excited about working with her on this event. While there is no standard contract for all planners to use, the following key elements should be included in all contracts:

- Today's date
- Wedding date and time
- Rehearsal date and time
- Name of the bride and groom
- Contact information for both including address, all phone numbers, and e-mail address
- Conditions, including roles and restrictions
- Your compensation including total fees, initial deposit, and payment schedule
- Terms, including liability and other legal issues
- A listing of your duties
- A Force Majeure clause, which protects you from natural disasters or other "Acts of God"
- Signatures of all parties and the associated dates

Important! You do not have a client unless you have a signed contract. Until you have the executed contract in your hands, you should not

Carla's Creative Events

Business Address, Telephone, and E-mail

November 12, 2007

Dear Toni,

I'm so glad we met yesterday at the Ritz Carlton to discuss your December 6, 2008 wedding. I enjoyed hearing your ideas for your special day, and I especially liked your color scheme of platinum, gold, and black. How elegant!

As I mentioned during our meeting, I have worked with the Ritz Carlton staff on many occasions and feel that my knowledge of the venue and my considerable background in the floral industry are key elements that set me apart from other planners in the area.

I enjoyed meeting with you and look forward to the possibility of working with you in the days ahead.

Sincerely,

Carla Davis, Owner

Carla's Creative Events

FIGURE 24.1 *Sample follow-up letter*

begin working for that bride. Without a contract, a bride is only a potential client. No contract, no client!

A sample contract is included in Figure 24.2 and can be used as a guide. In preparing your own contract, it is recommended that you show your contract to a lawyer, mentor, or small-business advisor.

433

Today's Date:

Wedding Date/Time:

Rehearsal Date/Time:

Names of Bride and Groom:

Name of Client:

Address:

Phone Number:

Mobile Number:

E-mail address:

Conditions:

The role of the wedding consultant is initially that of an advisor. The client will make actual

selection of service providers, and the consultant will implement those selections.

The client makes payments directly to the service providers and not to the consultant.

The consultant does not accept any commissions from the recommended vendors.

The consultant must be notified of any necessary changes made between the client and the

selected service providers.

Fees:

The agreed upon fee for this wedding is $_____

Payment Schedule:

A nonrefundable deposit in the amount of $_____ is due with the signed contract to

hold the wedding day. The remaining balance should be paid in accordance with the following

schedule:

Partial payment of $_____due on _____ (Date)

Final payment of $_____due on _____ (Date)

FIGURE 24.2 *Sample wedding consultant contract*

Terms:

Service providers accepted by the client shall be liable for their own business practices.

XXX wedding consultant does not assume responsibility for the negligent acts nor omission of such professionals.

The client agrees to hold harmless the consultant for any error, nonperformance, or change made by any vendor.

This contract shall be construed according to the laws of the XXX (state/district).

The parties agree that exclusive jurisdiction and venue for all claims of breach of this agreement shall be in XXX.

Liability is limited to the fee paid. The client understands that XXX wedding consultant will not enter into this agreement without this clause.

Force Majeure clause: The client agrees to hold harmless XXX consultant for an Act of God, weather conditions that may affect the event, acts of war, etc.

Duties:

XXX wedding consultant agrees to provide the following services to client XXX:

(Note: these duties will vary from contract to contract, below are sample duties)

- Provide a list of three vendors for the bride to select in each of the following categories: reception venue, rental items, caterer, pastry chef, floral décor, musicians, invitations, and transportation.
- Manage day of duties as agreed upon by the bride and XXX consultant.
- Oversee the delivery of the gifts to the bridal suite.
- Return cake topper to the mother of the bride.

FIGURE 24.2 *Continued*

The client by signing this contract agrees to the terms and conditions of this contract.

Client's signature	Date
Consultant's signature	Date

Adapted from Horne-Nestor (2005).

FIGURE 24.2 *Continued*

Laws vary by state and country, and what may work for a planner in Austin, Texas, may not work for a planner in Kamakura, Japan.

The best contract is the one that is signed, filed, and does not have to be pulled out again, because when it is, that means there are problems. Should the need arise, the contract is there to protect you. When you deviate from the contract provisions, you are taking a risk, as illustrated in Consultant in Action, Case 24.1.

compensation

When you were writing your business plan, you probably thought about setting the fees for your business. Start off by determining what other consultants in your area are charging. Keep in mind that planners in Honolulu, Hawaii, typically can charge more than planners in Fargo, North Dakota. After you have a good idea of what the market will bear in your area, it is time for you to set your fees. If you are a new planner with little or no experience, you cannot expect to charge as much as a seasoned wedding consultant. You must start out small and gradually increase your fees as your reputation grows.

There are various ways to charge for your planning services, including a flat fee, an hourly rate, a package deal, a percentage of the wedding budget, or a day-of fee. Each of these options has pros and cons, so you must decide which type of fee structure will work best for you. Regardless of the approach you take, do not expect to be able to fully support yourself full-time from the onset. Most consultants start out part-time and gradually build their businesses.

A flat fee works well when you have a client who wants you to manage the wedding from start to finish. With a flat fee you do not have to keep track of billable hours, and you know exactly how much you will earn based on the set price.

the $30,000 question

You landed your biggest client yet. The bride is Gretchen McConnell, the daughter of two prominent attorneys. Gretchen's parents, Shane and Juliet, have set a budget of $150,000. After the contract is signed and sealed, Shane informs you that he wants you to handle the funds as he is concerned that his daughter will get carried away. While you usually do not make payments on behalf of your clients and this is stated in the contract, you do not want to jeopardize this relationship and decide to make an exception. Every few months Shane cuts you a check for $30,000, and you make payments from a special account that you set up just for this wedding. This proceeds with no problems and six weeks before the wedding, Shane sends you the last check just in time, since you need to make several final payments to vendors. Two weeks later you get a notice from the bank and are receiving irate calls from vendors; four checks you have written bounced due to insufficient funds, and the fees are piling up. You contact the bank, and realize that Shane's last check for $30,000 bounced.

What do you do?

An hourly rate works well when your client only wants a few things from a planner; for example, you may be asked to provide a list of venues that already have a piano or recommend three florists who carry both live and silk flowers. Sometimes a client will hire a consultant on an hourly fee basis and end up needing the planner for many more tasks than initially thought. When you meet with your client, try to determine what the exact needs are and suggest the compensation package accordingly.

Many wedding planners come up with clever names for various types of package deals for their services using names like gold, silver, and bronze, or diamond, emerald, and sapphire. No matter what titles you apply, include a defined list of services for each option, where the fee increases along with the number of duties. Common services associated with various wedding packages were introduced in Chapter 1.

Some planners charge a percentage fee of the overall wedding budget, generally in the vicinity of 10 percent. This is a simple and effective way to charge for your services. However, if you do not have a fair amount of experience, this method should be avoided. As a new

Photograph by www.RodneyBailey.com

PHOTO 24-2 *Day-of wedding planning is a good way for a consultant to get started.*

planner, you will probably start out with weddings with modest budgets, and if you charge a percent of a modest budget, your compensation is likely to be very small.

Lastly, many consultants, especially those who are new to wedding planning, will take on day-of weddings. What this means is that you will agree to do a small amount of work prior to the wedding day (usually just confirming vendors), and then you will be on hand the day of the wedding to carry out all the plans the bride has made. For this type of service, you will charge a day-of fee.

Some seasoned planners specialize in day-of service, while many new planners find this type of work a good way to break into the field. If you are hired for day-of duties only, this does not remove you from the responsibility of producing a trouble-free wedding. "I didn't hire the DJ" is no excuse when a consultant is faced with a microphone-hogging bore dressed in a tux and belting out commands. You still must intervene when necessary to pull off a lovely wedding even if you didn't plan it. Be careful to invest the time up front getting to know as much as possible about the venues, vendors, and VIPs for each day-of wedding. Whether you are hired to plan the entire wedding or just manage the day-of duties, it is your responsibility to meet your client's expectations. After all, a wedding full of impressed guests can lead to more work for you down the road.

REFERENCE

Horne-Nestor, B. (2005). Wedding and event contracts (personal communication). I-do Weddings & Events, available at http://www.i-do-weddings.com

review questions

1. Why is it difficult to get your first client?

2. What screening questions should you ask a potential client over the telephone?

3. Name and explain three different types of compensation methods?

4. Name three crucial elements that should be found in every wedding contract.

terminology

- Client interview
- Client screening
- Compensation
- Contract
- Day-of fee
- Flat fee
- Follow-up communication
- Force Majeure clause
- Hourly rate
- Package deal
- Percentage fee

PHOTO 25-1 *Catering managers are a good source of referrals.*

vendor relations, networking, and negotiation

While waiting for your first client to walk through the door, one of the least expensive and most effective marketing strategies you can employ is to systematically get out there and meet your fellow wedding vendors. Meeting vendors is a valuable exercise that will pay dividends to your business for years to come. As you will learn, wedding professionals form a close-knit community. All of the stationers know the calligraphers, and all the caterers know the rental companies. Ideally, all of these vendors know you. This chapter highlights the importance of establishing vendor relationships, networking, and negotiation.

⚡ establishing vendor relationships

Introducing yourself to other wedding vendors is critical because they will become an endless source of referrals for you. For example, Ashley Davis has just become engaged. She and her mother rush out to find the perfect wedding gown. They make an appointment and begin their search at an exclusive boutique. During the process of trying on gowns, Ashley becomes overwhelmed and says, "If picking out a wedding gown is this tough, I don't know how I will handle the rest!" The boutique assistant might casually ask Ashley if she has thought about hiring a wedding planner to help ensure a beautiful and stress-free wedding day. Ashley's mother might say that they hadn't thought about this option because Ashley has only been engaged for a week. Her interest piqued, however, Ashley's mother might ask the assistant if she has any recommendations for a wedding planner. It is at this point that cultivating a sterling reputation with other vendors will pay off, as the boutique assistant might mention your name.

Wedding vendors get to know each other by working for the same clients and at the same events, during which they develop a sense of camaraderie. They quickly discover who is reliable and who is not. They grow to trust each other, and they develop an esprit de corps, meaning a sense of enthusiasm and morale-building for the entire team that puts on a wedding.

Often, couples begin the wedding planning process by securing one or two elements for their wedding. Somewhere along the way, they might decide to hire a planner to help them with the numerous decisions that have to be made. So, if the local country club event manager thinks highly of you and your work, he or she might refer you to a new client. Or, if you have successfully guided many brides down the aisle of a specific church, the altar guild of that church is usually more than willing to recommend your services.

You never know where your next referral might come from, which is why it is so important to get out there and meet everyone in the business. Think beyond the usual vendors by touching base with local makeup artists, travel agents, or ballroom dance instructors. In addition, make sure you introduce yourself to all the local wedding consultants in your market. Other planners are not your competition; instead, they can be a tremendous source of leads.

Four hypothetical planners—Sue, Dave, Heather, and Gary—will be used to illustrate the benefits of working with other consultants in your area. Imagine that Sue is a long-established planner in your market. When Sue gets a call from a bride who has a small budget and she does not want to take the job, she might gladly give the bride your name and number. That way she has helped the bride and you at the same time. Another planner, Dave, might get a call for day-of help, and, if he does not offer this service, he might pass along your name and number if he knows that you offer day-of assistance. If another consultant, Heather, is already committed on a certain date, she might refer the bride to you if your calendar is free. Last but not least, if a bride is looking for a certain style or specialty such as knowledge of Asian wedding customs, another planner, Gary, might give the bride your contact information if he knows that this is your area of expertise. Cultivating friendships with other wedding planners is an excellent way to grow your business.

MAKING A LIST

As you begin identifying and meeting other wedding vendors in your area, you should develop a list of specific individuals you would like to meet. You can develop this list from a variety of sources, such as:

- The Yellow Pages
- Vendors close to your home base
- Local vendors listed on The Knot
- A "best" list, often compiled in regional magazines

PHOTO 25-2 *Meeting vendors is a good use of your time when you are starting your business.*

- By category; for example, you may want to meet all florists
- Vendors who specialize in what you specialize in (e.g., Mexican weddings)
- A listing of vendor names in a bridal show program or local wedding publication

After you have compiled a list of names, set a goal to meet a certain number of vendors each week. Depending on your time commitments, you might meet two or even five new vendors each week. By systematically meeting all the players in your area, you will set yourself up to be a player, too.

After you have your list, call each vendor to arrange a brief (e.g., 15-minute) appointment to introduce yourself. By taking the time to make the call, you are showing respect for the vendor's time and you are conveying a professional image. You don't want to just drop in on a vendor unannounced. Make the appointments for early in the week because most vendors get busier as the week unfolds. Also, keep in mind that the busiest wedding months are May, June, September, and October. With that in mind, try to schedule your appointments during the quieter months of January, February, and August.

After you have secured the appointment, you should sketch out what you are going to say in advance. Learn about vendors by familiarizing yourself with their Web sites. Reading about their products and services will help you during these meetings. If you are going to meet with a local florist, you might make a note of any recent awards or recognition the owners have received. In addition to doing your research, you might practice what you want to convey about your business. If you have completed your business plan, as discussed in Chapter 22, you will be prepared to answer any questions about your business with confidence.

The last point you will want to consider is what you can do for the vendor. Vendors are going to remember you if you have a unique specialty, shared interest, or helpful skill, or if you can cross-market their goods and services with a posted link to their business on your Web site. Anytime you go out of your way for another vendor, you increase the chance of that vendor going out of his or her way for you.

SHARP AND CENTERED

When you meet with vendors, you should dress as you would for a client meeting. You should look neat and professional, not rumpled and wrinkled. Remember that you are representing your business and that first impressions are lasting. Don't forget to bring extra business cards to each meeting in case a vendor asks to keep a few on hand to share with clients.

One last piece of advice: give the vendor your full attention. Center all of your energy on the vendor during the meeting. Turn off your cell phone, BlackBerry, and/or pager. Keep in mind that vendors may not extend the same courtesy to you, so do not get flustered if the meeting gets broken up by telephone calls, staff questions, or clients who require the vendor's attention. For that moment, you are on their time, and patience is a key personality trait for any wedding consultant. Also, a certain vendor may not be willing to take the time to meet with you or may not be helpful or welcoming during the interaction. Do not take this personally, because the vendor likely treats everyone in the same manner. By and large you will find that wedding vendors are friendly, generous with their time, and eager to meet with consultants.

ᎠᏃ networking

Networking "denotes the relationship of entrepreneurs and their small businesses with the outside world" (Donckels and Lambrecht, 1997, p. 13). Laird (2006) explains that, over time, exceptional business leaders are those that not only have significant individual talent but also are able to successfully leverage their social assets in order to advance. Other terms that have been used to clarify the meaning of networking are social capital and community capacity (Pawar, 2006). The bottom line is that networking involves the ability to effectively relate to others in order to help position oneself and one's product or service. Hyväri (2006) assessed leadership behavior in 14 managerial practices in project-oriented companies and found that planning/organizing, networking, and informing were the three most significant assets to effective management. Cultivating these three skills will allow you to work successfully with both your clients and your vendors.

The best way to start your networking program is by joining the organizations where people involved in the business of weddings gather. One of the most popular networking groups for wedding planners is ISES, the International Special Events Society. ISES has chapters in most major markets and offers a wide variety of services such as educational and professional development, professional resources, subscription to *Special Events* magazine, discounted business services, and listings for all members on their Web site. If you are still a student, the time to join ISES is now because annual student membership dues are only $35, whereas professional dues are $450. The professional membership fee, however, is a tax-deductible business expense, so joining is a win-win situation once you have started your business.

ISES holds monthly meetings at different venues, and vendors associated with the society supply the linens, floral, catering, entertainment, invitations, and other event elements as a way to showcase their businesses. Attending these gatherings is an excellent way to meet wedding vendors and consultants. Keep in mind that networking takes time and you will get out of it what you put into it. Many people join associations and get frustrated or give up after one or two meetings because they feel they aren't meeting anyone or feel left out because it seems that everyone already has a set social group. Keep in mind, however, that many of those relationships took years to cultivate, and you will break in over time.

Other groups to consider are the Association of Bridal Consultants, the Association of Certified Professional Wedding Consultants, and the International Festival and Events Association. These groups, like ISES, encourage ongoing training, education, and professional development and host meetings and conferences that allow you to associate with people who have similar goals and interests. You should also familiarize yourself with business-related groups in your area such as your local Chamber of Commerce. The Chamber will have monthly meetings where leaders introduce new members and initiate conversations about issues facing the business community as a whole.

Other networking groups that will offer you the opportunity to meet a range of interesting people who may need a wedding consultant include the Young Democrats/Republicans, the Junior League, Toastmasters, the "Friends of" or event planning arm of any major museum or art gallery, the American Cancer Society, Habitat for Humanity, or the alumni association of your college or university. These are all excellent resources for community networking.

KICKBACKS VERSUS GIVING BACK

Some vendors and consultants believe that an effective networking tool is to promote kickbacks, which involves receiving a percentage of the price your clients pay to given vendors. Here is how this works. A hypothetical transportation specialist, Joe Limo, might tell you that for every client you send his way, he will give you 10 percent of the client bill as a kickback. In other words, you are getting paid to recommend this vendor. Taking it a step further, some consultants even work in their own kickbacks, in particular when the client cannot be present for the vendor meetings and negotiations. For instance, the caterer might present a food and beverage proposal to the consultant for $90 a head, and then the consultant brings the proposal to the client, explaining that the cost is $100 a head. The extra $10 per person goes into the consultant's pocket as a self-imposed kickback, often given the notation of "administrative fee."

While the practice of kickbacks is not illegal, the ethics of it are shaky, and many consultants and vendors are offended by the proposition of kickbacks. If you have a clear policy against kickbacks, it is best to

PHOTO 25-3 *(opposite) Monthly meetings offer vendors an opportunity to showcase their products and services.*

put this in your contract, as seen in the contract example found in Chapter 24, as this will build trust. Those consultants who are perfectly comfortable with this practice and use a kickback strategy on a regular basis should still let their clients know about this practice. If you choose to employ a kickback strategy behind your clients' backs and they find out, they may feel angry and betrayed.

Instead of kickbacks, we suggest the process of giving back, which can be even more lucrative in the long run. This process works in a couple of ways. If vendors offer you kickbacks, tell them that you would rather pass that savings along to your clients. When your clients discover that you were able to secure a discount on a good or service on their behalf, they will be even more likely to talk up your excellent skills as a planner to their friends. Giving back also applies to the groups and associations to which you belong, as well as your local community. For example, after Hurricane Katrina, many vendors offered free goods and services to New Orleans' residents whose homes and wedding plans had been ravaged by the storm. These generous donations allowed many weddings to take place that would have otherwise been indefinitely postponed.

✎ negotiation

Another valuable skill that you will need is the ability to negotiate. Whether you are working with a bride who wants a discount on your fees or a vendor who wants to charge your client a premium for delivering ice cream in August, you will be faced with many situations that call for thinking on your feet.

Much of your time will be spent honing your skills in the art of negotiating. For example, suppose your clients have ordered apple green linens for their wedding. The rental company arrives with green linens, but they are a shade off from what your clients wanted. It is your job to negotiate with the rental vendor in order to secure the exact linens for your clients in time for the wedding.

As an additional example, assume you are meeting with your clients and the manager of their chosen wedding reception venue. During the course of your discussions, you learn that your clients want the venue's "cherry drop ice" for their signature drinkable dessert. The catering director for the venue might say that this specialty drink is not available during the month of your clients' wedding, because fresh cherries are prohibitively expensive at that time. It will now be up to you to negotiate with the venue to make sure your clients get what they want for their wedding day. While most negotiation occurs with little conflict, sometimes you will find yourself in the midst of emotionally laden situations, as highlighted in Consultant in Action, Case 25.1.

mother-daughter mania

You have made an appointment with your client and the stationery specialist, and the bride's mother insists on coming along despite the bride's objections. As the vendor pulls out different albums, you watch the communication quickly deteriorate between the mother, who wants traditional invitations, and the bride, who wants something more contemporary. As they continue to bicker, you realize that this is one manifestation of a much bigger problem—the two have completely different visions for the wedding. It becomes obvious that they are not getting along well and that the mother is agitating the daughter. The vendor is clearly uncomfortable with the situation. Suddenly, the daughter jumps up and runs out the door. You think for a moment and then follow the bride, hoping that you can get her to come back and reconcile with her mother. After talking with the bride for a few minutes, she says, "It is better if I just cool down and my mother cools down." So, you walk back into the stationer's office to calm down the mother and speak with the vendor. As you approach, the mother jumps up and yells, "You took her side! I am paying for this wedding and I can't believe you took her side!"

What do you do?

Case submitted by Lynne Sandler

HOW DO YOU NEGOTIATE?

Michael Kaplan from *Money Magazine* (2005) tells us that there are seven rules for getting what you want on your own terms, each of which is applied below to the business of wedding consulting.

1. *Don't look at a deal as an either/or proposition.*
    Good negotiating is all about compromise. Giving a little, getting a little. In order to get the cherry drop ice mentioned earlier, your client might have to forego one of the hors d'oeuvres to offset the cost of getting a multitude of out-of-season cherries.

2. *Know what you can part with—then part with it hard.*
    Prioritize what you really want as a result of the negotiation. Don't lay your cards on the table but know in your own mind what it will take for you to feel good about the outcome of the deal. If you know that your client is not truly worried about the exact color of the linens, and the vendor offers a discount to spare an extra trip to the warehouse, letting go is an easy decision.

3. *Figure out the other side's timetable. Then use it.*
    Is the dress shop ready to get in next season's gowns but hasn't yet discounted the one your bride loves? Suggest a reasonable discount and negotiate the price. The dresses will soon be outdated. Use this knowledge to your advantage.

4. *Show people that you understand their position.*
    Here's where the skill of good empathy will come in handy. You must convince the upset mother from the Consultant in Action case that you empathize with her feelings. You do not have to agree with her, but allow her to express her thoughts and feelings. Ask open-ended questions to solicit more information and validate her feelings. The stationery vendor will be sure to note how you calmly balanced the emotions of both the bride and her mother.

5. *Stifle your emotions.*
    Stay on the issue and leave personalities out of the discussion. Remember: you don't want to burn any bridges with vendors or clients. You do not have to like a given vendor or even a given client in order to have a successful working relationship.

6. *Don't believe everything, but don't call anyone a liar.*
    Negotiations are a strategy. Both sides know that each is trying to gain the upper hand. If, for example, a local florist says she can't do better on her price for centerpieces, you might accept that statement, but then let her know that your client will need to step back and reevaluate the options for selecting a floral designer.

7. *Devise a backup plan.*
    Before entering into the negotiations, think through your options. If your clients want a specific ballroom for their reception that

you learn is not available, present some other options that they might not have considered. Have at least three other venue ideas in mind, or encourage your clients to consider changing the wedding date if it is early in the planning process and their hearts are set on the venue.

So whether you are just beginning to develop skills that will establish positive vendor relationships or want to hone what you have already learned, networking and negotiation are two valuable talents to cultivate. Like any complex interpersonal skill, proficiency in networking and negotiation will develop over time.

REFERENCES

Donckels, R., and Lambrecht, J. (1997). The network position of small businesses: An explanatory model. *Journal of Small Business Management* 32: 13–25.

Hyväri, I. (2006). Project management effectiveness in project-oriented business organizations. *International Journal of Project Management* 24: 216–225.

Kaplan, M. (2005, May 3). How to negotiate anything. *Money Magazine*, available at http://www.cnnmoney.com.printthis.clickability.com/pt/cpt?action=cpt&title

Laird, P. W. (2006). *Pull: Networking and Success since Benjamin Franklin.* Cambridge, MA: Harvard University Press.

Pawar, M. (2006). "Social" "capital"? *The Social Science Journal.* 43: 211–226.

review questions

1. Why is it important to establish vendor relationships while waiting for your first client?

2. Why is it important to have good working relationships with other wedding consultants?

3. Define networking and name a minimum of two networking organizations for wedding consultants.

4. Explain what a kickback is and why this strategy potentially has ethical implications.

5. Name and explain three of the seven rules for successful negotiating.

terminology

- Community capacity

- Esprit de corps

- Kickbacks

- Negotiating

- Networking

- Referral

- Social capital

office **26**
management

If you are just starting out as a wedding consultant, it is crucial that you lay a solid foundation for your business by making good business decisions right from the start. Whether you work from home or lease office space, there are many facets to good office management, including organizing your work environment, selecting hardware and software, gathering other business equipment essentials, and building a staff. These office management essentials, are the building blocks of a successful wedding consultancy business.

PHOTO 26-1 *(opposite) An organized setting allows consultants to track the details of each wedding.*

✎ organizing your work environment

If you plan to work from home, get started by taking a survey of your current furniture to see what might work in your home office. The most important item is a desk with good workspace, plenty of room for a computer, and an area to review spreadsheets, guest lists, and sample books. Don't forget about space for a printer, scanner, fax machine, and other equipment that will need to be located nearby.

Keeping track of all the details that go into a wedding will be one of your most difficult tasks as a wedding planner. How you choose to manage the wealth of information is up to you, but some options include spreadsheets, three-ring notebooks, 3 x 5 cards, a day timer, or a file folder system. Bookshelves, file cabinets, and storage bins help tremendously by utilizing vertical space and hiding clutter.

You will get a lot of mileage from investing in a comfortable chair that offers good support and fits your body. There are many ergonomic styles to choose from, so take a trip to your local office superstore and test out a few different models. Also, measure the height of your desk to make sure the chair you select will fit comfortably underneath your desk with you sitting in it. You don't want to hit your knees every time you sit down to work.

As a consultant, you know the value of good lighting for weddings, and it is no different for your office. Check the lighting in your office area. If overhead lighting is not adequate, purchase a desk or floor lamp that will let you work efficiently at all hours. If you don't have everything to outfit your home office, buying office equipment doesn't have to be expensive. Beyond frequenting office superstores, you can scour garage sales and thrift shops for affordable furniture and equipment.

In addition to deciding what your office will look like, consider setting some ground rules for yourself. For example, decide on a work schedule that fits with your body's time clock and allows you to work a reasonable number of hours each day. Are you a morning person? If so, then it makes sense for you to begin your workday at 5:00 A.M. If you operate better later in the day, then consider starting later in the afternoon. Remember, you are your own boss, and it is up to you to set your own hours for maximum productivity and profit.

Other ground rules to consider for your home-based business might include limiting your time spent surfing the Internet and making personal phone calls, requiring yourself to take a break every hour or two, eating lunch at the same time each day, not eating in your office, and other no-nonsense policies. Every office has rules, and your home office should be no exception.

A word of caution: working from home can be very lonely, especially when you are just starting to build your business. To avoid going stir crazy, make a point to meet with new vendors, as discussed in Chapter 25, while you are building your client base. If you are home alone without the opportunity to interact with the rest of the world, you risk boredom, isolation, and depression. If you balance your outside meetings with your quiet work time at home, you will feel more productive and energized.

If you decide that working from home is not for you, leasing office space is always a viable option. From browsing real estate ads to using national Web sites such as www.offices2share.com, you can find a wealth of information on leasing office space month-to-month or just for special client meetings. Many of these executive suites are located in business parks, include furnishings, are Internet ready, and have optional add-ons such as mail pick-up, receptionist services, and access to conference space. Whether you want day-to-day office space or just space once in a while, leasing well-equipped space is easier than you think.

selecting hardware and software

Because you will spend a fair amount of time on the road, seriously consider buying a laptop computer rather than a desktop system. Besides having your files with you, a laptop will enable you to give a visual presentation at the drop of a hat, such as showing photographs of recent weddings to a prospective client. Regardless of which system you select, make sure the computer has plenty of storage space, sufficient memory for running several programs at once, and a moderately fast processor. For graphics work, which includes anything involving photographic images, illustrations, or animation, you will need to maximize processor speed, hard drive storage space, and memory (Obringer, 2006).

In addition to a computer, some other hardware purchases to consider (adapted from Obringer, 2006) can be found in Table 26.1.

Now that you have purchased your hardware, there are several software applications that will be necessary. Minimally, you will need software to complete the following functions: e-mail, word processing, spreadsheets, presentations, virus protection, computer maintenance, Portable Document Format (PDF) reading, a graphics and image editing tool, and Internet browsers. Some of this software is available free online, whereas business software is often bundled in packages such as Microsoft Office (Obringer, 2006). Because so much of what you will do requires access to the Internet, you need to select a high-speed Internet provider, and you absolutely must invest in virus and spam protection, as dial-up Internet and constant pop-ups can literally paralyze your computer.

TABLE 26.1 Hardware Purchase Options

- A color laser printer, as many of your documents may include color illustrations, photographs, or charts.
- A fax machine to send contracts to clients and vendors. There is also the option of subscribing to an online faxing service such as E-Fax that allows unlimited monthly faxing for a nominal fee.
- A scanner to digitize documents or photographs. You can use a scanner along with e-mail or fax software in place of a regular fax machine.
- A CD burner if you need to provide clients with large files electronically or if you want to back up your files on CD.
- A digital camera to document work and ideas to be used for presentations, reports, and your Web site, or simply to jog your memory about a wedding detail.
- For those short on space, a multipurpose scanner, fax machine, copier, and printer might be worth the investment.
- The best cell phone and cell phone service you can afford. A cell phone that is also a PDA (Personal Digital Assistant) and/or a digital camera is a great multifunctional addition to your office equipment.
- If your cell phone does not have one, you may also need a separate PDA (e.g., BlackBerry, Palm Pilot, Handspring) for ready access to contact information, e-mail or the Internet.
- For home office use, a telephone with a speaker function and Caller ID is useful. A second telephone line for your business phone, fax, and Internet access is also a plus.

Source: Adapted from Obringer (2006).

other business equipment essentials

In addition to hardware and software, it is essential for a wedding planner to own a reliable vehicle. The last thing you want is to break down en route to a job. If you can't afford a premium automobile because you are just starting out, buy or lease the most reliable one possible. On a cold, rainy evening at midnight, you will be thankful your car starts and carries you safely home after an all-day wedding. Both the exterior and interior of the vehicle should be kept clean, as the appearance of your car is a reflection of your business.

A smart business wardrobe is also essential equipment for a wedding consultant. This wardrobe should include suits for client meetings, professional casual wear for setup, as well as elegant but functional formal attire for the actual wedding day. Your clothing should be as nice as you can afford, even if you can only purchase one good suit. Each time you wear your suit, make sure it is clean and pressed. You want to project the image of a calm, cool, professional wedding planner rather than someone who slept in his or her clothes. You should never look out of place or draw unnecessary attention to yourself during a wedding. Take the time to think about your working wardrobe in advance and add the appropriate pieces as necessary. You will not have time to shop for something suitable the day before a wedding. Make sure you are ready to go before you land your first client.

Without a doubt, the most important piece of clothing you will need is a good pair of shoes. It is essential to your comfort and safety that you own a pair of good-looking, sensible, nonslip shoes. As a wedding planner, you can expect to be on your feet for long stretches of time. Don't find yourself in a situation like the one presented in Consultant in Action, Case 26.1.

Another important point to consider when selecting your shoes is that a wedding planner must often walk through the kitchen in order to communicate with the catering staff. Kitchens are notorious for having wet, slippery floors. If your shoes have slick soles, you could take a fall and perhaps injure yourself. If the thought of wearing practical shoes makes you cringe, bear in mind that many wedding planners will wear dress shoes at the beginning of a wedding and then quietly slip into their sensible shoes after the wedding starts. Whatever you decide, opt for safety over fashion.

building a staff

Even if you are just starting out and money is tight, it is important to consider having a small staff, which might simply include bringing in a volunteer assistant for day-of implementation support. An assistant can manage the ceremony activities, freeing you to oversee the details at the reception. If the wedding you are planning is large, you may even need two assistants to make sure everything runs smoothly. Assistants can complete tasks such as directing vendors for setup, gathering the bridal party for photographs, or running out to complete last-minute errands. With guidance, they can do almost anything to help you manage a wedding.

Finding a qualified assistant is a challenge. Although many people will be interested in learning the ropes as your assistant, not all of them will possess the skills necessary to succeed. Interview a few candidates to see who has the most experience and/or enthusiasm for the position. Students from a local college or university are often willing to volunteer for day-of implementation to gain experience. If they are studying a related area, such as events management or business, they may be able to work with you over an extended period of time for course credit, in association with a practicum or internship experience. Check with the internship coordinator of the associated program to determine the restrictions and requirements of working with students for credit. Typically, students complete 150 hours for a practicum and

footwear fiasco

You have hired an assistant to help you with an outdoor wedding that will have 200 guests. The evening ceremony and reception are being held at a plantation with a long, winding gravel drive. One of the primary jobs you have for the assistant is to walk along the gravel drive just before dusk to fill, set up, and light over 100 luminaries (paper bags filled with sand and holding a votive candle), which will require at least 10 trips up and down the drive to get everything in place. As you set up for the ceremony, you watch for her arrival, as you know this task will take at least an hour, time that you do not have to spare. Your assistant arrives right on time, 1½ hours before the wedding. As she walks over to greet you, you realize that she dressed as a wedding guest rather than an assistant. She is wearing a tight silk dress and a lovely pair of 3-inch spiked heels.

What do you do?

PHOTO 26-2 *Having a staff allows you to be in one place while your assistant is in another.*

400 hours for an internship over a period of 10 to 15 weeks; you will therefore want to make sure that you have enough work to justify a student's for-credit experience.

One point you will want to stress to your candidates is that most weddings take place on Saturdays, so they will need to be available on Fridays for the rehearsal, the wedding day itself, and possibly Sunday. If weekend work is not possible for your candidate, you need to keep searching. In addition to weekend availability, a good assistant should possess the 15 skills listed in Table 26.2.

PAY AND NONCOMPETE CLAUSES

Although some assistants will work for the experience alone, you should be prepared to pay your assistants for their time and effort. An experienced assistant can earn as much as $25 per hour and up, especially in a large city. If you do not want to pay on an hourly basis, you should negotiate a flat fee for the entire wedding, such as $100, depending on the duties that the assistant is required to perform. Consult with your tax advisor regarding how to appropriately docu-

PHOTO 26-3 *Brides appreciate it when consultants have assistants to help with wedding day details.*

TABLE 26.2 Skills to Look for When Interviewing Assistants

• Able to follow instructions	• Composure under stress	• Politeness
• Attention to details	• Does not gossip	• Professional demeanor
• Bright personality	• Good multitasker	• Organized
• Can stand on feet for many hours	• High energy level	• Self-confidence
• Common sense	• Looks comfortable even when it is hot or cold	• Quick and creative problem solver

ment payment for short-term assistance. Many wedding consultants hire the same assistants over and over. This is the perfect scenario because, over time, the assistant will develop a feel for what the planner expects and needs, even before the planner has to ask for it. Sometimes, two or three wedding planners will share the same assistant.

When working with the same assistant over time, bringing on an intern, or, most importantly, when hiring your first associate, it is in your best interest to have a noncompete clause as part of the arrangement. Most wedding consultants are hesitant to host interns because they fear that an intern might work with them for 15 weeks and then turn around and open a business using all of the information and secrets they have just learned. It takes successful wedding consultants years to establish a system that works, and they are justifiably protective of their materials and methods.

A noncompete clause is a condition of employment statement found in an employment agreement that indicates a time frame during which the employee, upon leaving the company, cannot work for the company's competition. The purpose is to prevent former employees from taking trade secrets to start a similar type of business or to work with a competitor. For example, the clause might state that an employee is not permitted to start a wedding consulting business or work for a competing consulting firm within 18 months of leaving the position. Noncompete clause determination and enforcement are governed by state law, so you are advised to consult with an attorney when drawing up this document. A refusal to sign is a justifiable means for nonhiring. If the clause is violated, both the former employee and the employee's new company can be sued.

A noncompete clause may also include a radius clause, which indicates a region of exclusivity to which the agreement applies. To extend the preceding example, the clause might say that an employee is not permitted to start a wedding consulting business or work for a competing consulting firm within 18 months of leaving the position if the new company is located within a 200-mile radius. This clause allows a former employee to start a business immediately if and only if the new business if located outside the specified radius.

REFERENCE

Obringer, L. A. (2006). How setting up a home office works. How Stuff Works, Inc., available from http://money.howstuffworks.com/home-office.htm

review questions

1. What are three things you can do to organize your work space?

2. Give four examples of hardware you might purchase for your business.

3. Name five attributes you would look for in hiring an assistant.

4. Define and give an example of a noncompete clause.

5. Define and give an example of a radius clause.

terminology

- Executive suites

- Hardware

- Internship

- Noncompete clause

- Practicum

- Radius clause

- Software

PHOTO 27-1 *Brides continue to far outnumber planners*

competition, obligations, and ethics
27

Competition has been shown to be useful up to a certain point and no further, but cooperation, which is the thing we must strive for today, begins where competition leaves off.

—Franklin D. Roosevelt

With nearly 2.2 million couples marrying each year in the United States (McMurray, 2006) and millions more around the globe, there is tremendous opportunity to start and grow a wedding consultancy business. As discussed in Chapter 6, Hollywood movies and reality television have thrust the wedding planning profession into the spotlight. Hiring a wedding planner is no longer a luxury reserved for the rich and famous. Couples with all types of budgets are hiring consultants to manage various aspects of their wedding day.

spiring wedding consultants have also benefited from the increasingly positive portrayal of wedding planning in the media. Thanks to this unprecedented publicity, more women and men than ever before are entering the field of wedding planning and enrolling in event management and wedding planning classes. This chapter sets forth the increasing demand for wedding consultants, which creates a level of competition, and then discusses the obligations and ethical practices that are key factors for successful wedding consultants.

❧ demand and competition

Richard Markel, president of the Association for Wedding Professionals International, attributes the tremendous growth of wedding consultancy to a strong economy (Pasquale, 2006). He explains that the growing economy has given people a little more money to spend on their weddings. However, it is not just the demand for consultants that is growing, but also the supply. With the pool of certified consultants getting bigger, competition is keen. Markel contends that consultants are more assertively marketing and hashing it out for brides' attention and business. In the process, they are spreading the word about the pluses of having a consultant on board for the wedding planning process (Pasquale, 2006).

Thankfully, even with the up-tick of those entering the wedding planning field, there is enough business to go around. Brides continue to far outnumber planners. The Association of Bridal Consultants (2006) is a professional organization with over 4,000 members from 26 countries; this same organization estimates that in the United States alone, there are approximately 10,000 consultants. This means that for every U.S. planner, there are approximately 220 potential couples—certainly more work than most wedding planners could handle in one year. However, not all couples hire consultants, and the current estimate is that 19 percent of couples are doing so (McMurray, 2005), which equates to 418,000 couples per year. Even at that rate, there would be nearly 42 weddings per planner per year. Because so much work is available, there exists a strong sense of cooperation rather than competition among wedding consultants.

Despite a spirit of cooperation, consultants in a given market must still compete for the best weddings. A bride generally interviews three to five planners before deciding on the right consultant for her wedding day. This process of elimination causes some new consultants to get discouraged. They may quickly become jaded, seeing the business as cut-throat or down and dirty.

PHOTO 27-2 *(opposite) Some consultants specialize in Jewish weddings*

Also, significant competition exists between consultants who specialize in the same type of weddings. For example, if a bride is looking for a planner who specializes in Jewish weddings, then she will interview all the planners in the area who have that focus. The bride you meet today may very well be interviewing your competition tomorrow. When a high-profile or high-budget wedding is at stake, planners will put forth their best efforts in order to land the prominent client.

This sense of competition can actually benefit the wedding profession as a whole by encouraging consultants to constantly raise the bar in terms of standards and practices. Competition keeps planners sharp and up to date, urges them to be constantly on the lookout for new trends and ideas, and inspires them to create something unique for each client. Competition also leads to continuing education through classes, workshops, and seminars. Wedding consulting is a business, and, like any business, those involved in it must consistently study their market and hone their skills to stay on top.

Competition can take an ugly turn, and it would be false to say that it never results in questionable actions. Throughout this text, we have

Photograph by www.RodneyBailey.com

PHOTO 27-3 *Competition keeps planners sharp and up to date with the latest trends*

emphasized the necessity of ethical, trustworthy, and respectful inter-actions with clients, vendors, and other consultants. While antagonis-tic and dishonest practices may help a consultant in the short run, once the word gets out, vendors and clients will shy away from working with such a planner.

⬧ obligations

As a wedding planning professional, you will have many important obligations, including those to clients, vendors, the wedding profession as a whole, your own business, and, of course, to yourself and those in your social network. The challenge is to manage all of these responsi-bilities that compete for your time with grace and finesse. As a consult-ant, your primary business obligation is to your client, typically the bride. If the bride's parents have hired you, then your obligation is to them as well. As a rule of thumb, if the bride is happy, then everyone around her will be happy. It is your job to make the bride happy, even if that means negotiating with your vendors to ensure the bride's satis-faction. For example, suppose a bride has selected an historic Federal-style hotel for her late November wedding reception. The hotel has a lovely staircase leading to the front door. It has long been the bride's dream to be photographed outdoors on the staircase on her wedding day. The wedding day arrives, and the photographer tells you that he would prefer not to take the outdoor photographs because it is too cold. This is where your obligation to your client comes into play. You must diplomatically tell the photographer that the bride still wishes to be photographed outside despite the cold because being photo-graphed on the staircase has long been the bride's dream and this photo is therefore nonnegotiable. You then tell the photographer that you will have hot coffee sent out to keep everyone warm.

Wedding planners also have obligations to their vendors. So, in our example, the planner should try to accommodate both the bride's wishes and the photographer's desires. Sometimes this is a balancing act and, if the planner must choose, the bride's needs almost always come first. However, be careful. If you anger your vendors and treat them poorly, soon they will refuse to work with you. Treat your vendors with respect and courtesy, and they will recommend you time and time again.

As discussed in Chapter 11, you have an obligation to feed your vendors. No one works well on an empty stomach. When determining the final headcount for the caterer, remind your clients to include the total number of vendor meals. It is your responsibility to make sure that your clients understand the importance of feeding the vendors, includ-ing yourself and any assistants you have. It is also your duty to tell the vendors when their meals are ready and where they can take a break to eat. A well-fed staff is a highly productive staff.

Planners should also make sure that vendors are given water and other cold or hot beverages while setting up. If a company is installing tenting on a 95-degree day in August, the staff members are sure to appreciate you and recommend you to others if you show up with a cooler full of ice-cold beverages. The same holds true in the winter. Moving in catering equipment or installing floral arrangements outdoors can be a difficult job in cold, raw weather. Make sure you have hot coffee and tea on hand. This courtesy will go a long way toward getting the job done on time.

In addition to obligations to the client and vendors, wedding consultants have an obligation to the wedding profession. Since wedding planning is a relatively new career path, it is important for consultants to give back to the profession in order for all facets to move ahead. As discussed in Chapter 25, giving back might include joining associations, speaking at conferences, teaching a seminar, or letting a student shadow you for a day.

Most important are your obligations to your business, yourself, and those closest to you. When you are in business for yourself, it is entirely up to you to ensure that your company succeeds. Part of that success will be driven from the decisions you make on a daily basis. One of your most important business policies is to always collect your final payment at least two weeks prior to the wedding day. There are countless hair-raising stories of planners not collecting their final payment until the last minute or even after the wedding, which can lead to situations like the one described in Consultant in Action, Case 27.1.

Once a wedding has ended and your services have been provided, it is often impossible to collect the money without the assistance of a legal professional. Rather than learning a lesson the hard way, always collect the final payment well in advance of a wedding to give the check enough time to clear the bank. If there is a problem such as insufficient funds, you will still have the leverage of not managing the wedding day. The vast majority of couples do not set out to intentionally defraud their wedding consultants. However, as the wedding approaches, couples face many financial pressures and may look for ways out of making final payments. Ultimately, it is up to you to ensure that you are paid for your wedding consulting services.

You also have obligations to yourself in terms of balancing your career and your personal life. Chapter 28 details numerous ways to manage the stress that is associated with wedding consulting as a career. Top planners emphasize that you have to remember that the more clients spend for your services, the more they expect from you. This adage includes the fact that your personal crises are not your clients' crises, and it is the case that your clients will expect to come first. Consultant in Action, Case 27.2, highlights one such scenario.

payment postponement

You have been working on a 250-guest, lavish outdoor garden wedding
to take place in Santa Monica, California, for your clients, Mark and
Monica. As stipulated in the contract signed prior to engaging your
services, they paid you the initial $3,000 deposit and made an on-time
second payment of $3,000 six months prior to the wedding date. Two
weeks before the wedding, you remind Mark and Monica that their final
payment of $3,000 is due. One week prior to the wedding, the check
still has not arrived. Five days prior to the wedding, you tell the couple
that you will not be on hand to manage their wedding day unless they
pay you before the rehearsal on Friday. Monica knows that they are
not remotely prepared to coordinate the extensive wedding activities
themselves and encourages Mark to write the check. On Thursday
evening, you finally receive a check for the final payment of $3,000. You
are so busy with the rehearsal on Friday and the wedding on Saturday
that you don't deposit the check into your account until Monday
morning, at which point you learn that Mark has issued a stop payment
order on the check.

What do you do?

chad's crisis

Your consultancy business is located in St. Louis, Missouri, and you eagerly agreed to manage a destination wedding in Belize, which is just south of Mexico. Your spouse and 4-year-old child, Chad, understand that you will be gone for five days, but your spouse reassures you that they can manage for a few days without you and all will be fine. On the second day in Belize, which is the day before the wedding, you receive an urgent call from your spouse, who tells you that Chad fell off the swing set at preschool and broke his arm and they are currently at the hospital. You are able to speak to a nurse who reassures you that Chad is fine, but that he keeps asking for you.

What do you do?

✤ ethics

In the wake of such high-profile business scandals as Enron, World-Com, and Martha Stewart Living Omnimedia, it becomes easy to believe that the business world rewards bad behavior. However, the fact remains that there is a documented connection between strong morals and business success (Lennick and Kiel, 2005), which is why it is imperative that you become a business owner with clear ethical principles right from the start. From your first day in business you must lead by example and show others that you are honest, fair, responsible, compassionate, and just.

For example, assume you have back-to-back appointments with two different brides who are considering your services. The first bride, Maria, asks what the fee would be for your comprehensive planning services and you tell her $3,000. Later in the day, the second bride, Jean, asks you the same question. You notice that Jean is wearing an expensive designer outfit and showing off her 5-carat diamond engagement ring. For her, you quote your comprehensive planning fee as $5,000. Both weddings will require the same amount of work on your part, yet you have quoted two different fees based on what you believe each bride can afford. Imagine the consequences if these women are friends and compare notes of their meetings with you. Your inconsistent pricing structure will be exposed, your credibility will become suspect, and neither bride will hire you to plan her wedding.

When discussing your fees with potential clients, remember that you must be consistent in your pricing structures regardless of what you think the bride can afford. If you want a flexible price structure, set forth your fees as a firm percentage of the overall budget, which allows for a consistent application and addresses the fact that a $100,000 wedding is likely to be more labor intensive than a $20,000 wedding. But do not just randomly throw out fees based on appearances, because you will come across as disorganized, in particular if you are unable to remember the amount that was quoted at a later date. Your fee structure should have no ambiguity whatsoever. Entertainment specialist David Fletcher, introduced to you in Chapter 16, offers the following gem of wisdom regarding honesty in the wedding profession, "I'm a truthful person, not because I'm a good person, but because it is easier to remember." The bottom line is that it is much tougher to keep a series of lies straight than it is to be honest in your practices.

A second ethical issue pertains to kickbacks, which were introduced in Chapter 25. Take for example the scenario of the wedding planner, Chris, who always takes clients to meet with the same florist, regardless of a couple's floral vision. Whether the couple wants romantic, contemporary, Asian-influenced, English garden, or herb-inspired

PHOTO 27-4 *Through established vendor contacts, you can save your clients money*

wedding flowers, Chris takes them to "Lily's Florist" because Chris and Lily are friends and Lily will give Chris a percentage of the total order placed by the couple. This practice does a disservice to both the client and the wedding planning profession. A more ethical approach involves listening to your clients' requirements, directing them to a few carefully chosen vendors, and ultimately letting them make the final decisions. If, after doing repeat business with a vendor, the vendor decides to give you a discount, it is only fair to pass along that savings to your clients. After all, the couple has hired you with the hope that through your contacts and expertise you will be able to save them money. This is the perfect opportunity to show your clients just how smart of an investment it was to hire you as a consultant.

Some consultants go so far with kickbacks that they ask vendors what sort of deals they will cut. For example, a consultant may approach a caterer and say, "I will refer you to my bride. How much will you pay me to do that?" The practice of kickbacks has caused a great divide in the wedding profession between those who do and those who do not engage in the practice. Most consultants and vendors avoid kickbacks for three reasons. First, the consultant's vendor recommendations are based on who will kick back the most, which has nothing to do with what will ultimately be best for the bride and groom. Second, vendors will jack up the price to cover the amount of the kickback, causing an artificial inflation of the prices of goods and services. Third, regardless of the money, kickbacks encourage consultants and vendors to cultivate dishonest relationships with their clients.

Ethics also pertain to private information that your clients share with you. As you begin working with a couple on their upcoming wedding, you will become privy to all kinds of secrets about the bride, the groom, and the families. It is your responsibility to treat this information with the utmost discretion. What is told to you in confidence must remain between you and your client. Imagine the consequences if comments such as "I'm not crazy about my new father-in-law," "Please keep Aunt Cheryl away from the booze," or "I'll just die if my boss speaks to the other guests during the wedding" were made public. As the wedding pressure begins to build, the bride, the groom, and other family members will let off steam by telling you how they feel. A good wedding consultant will listen intently and empathically, and then keep their clients' secrets forever.

Sometimes during a reception, guests may come over to you and strike up a conversation, usually beginning with an innocent compliment about the wedding. After you acknowledge their comments, they might slyly ask you how much your clients have spent on a certain item. A conversation might go like this:

Guest: What a great idea for dessert. I don't think I've ever seen such an elaborate chocolate fountain before. And the flowers are magnificent. My, the Jones family has certainly outdone themselves with the reception tonight. How much do you think an event like this would cost?

Wedding Consultant: I couldn't agree with you more. The décor and special touches are fabulous. In fact, this is one of the most spectacular weddings I've ever managed. As for the cost, that's between me and my client.

The ability to keep your clients' secrets is a quality every planner should possess in abundance. If you have this skill, it will serve you well.

Finally, it is the responsible consultant who thinks of those in the community and makes a point to give back when feasible. For example, any floral arrangements that your clients do not want and that are not carried off by the guests might be delivered to a nearby hospital to cheer those most in need. Small gestures will make the world a better place and will make you a better wedding consultant.

REFERENCES

Association of Bridal Consultants. (2006). Available at
http://www.bridalassn.com/index.tmpl

Lennick, D., and Kiel, F. (2005). *Moral Intelligence: Enhancing Business Performance and Leadership Success*. Philadelphia: Wharton School Publishing.

McMurray, S. (2005). The Wedding Report: 2006 Statistics and Market Estimates, available at http://theweddingreport.com

Pasquale, P. (2006). Why you might need a consultant. *Modern Bride*, available at http://modernbride.com/printer/index.ssf?/budget/wb_helpmbc

480

review questions

1. Why do you think it is difficult to pinpoint the exact number of wedding consulting businesses?

2. What are the benefits and drawbacks of competition?

3. Discuss the multiple obligations of a wedding consultant.

4. Why should you always collect your final payment at least two weeks prior to the wedding?

5. List three things that you can do to help maintain the highest ethical standards as a wedding consultant.

terminology

• Competition

• Discretion

• Ethics

• Morals

• Obligation

stress management and career enrichment

Though not as nerve-wracking a profession as being a 911 operator or an air traffic controller, wedding planning is not for the faint of heart. It is a stressful job with demanding clients and little margin for error. In order to succeed, a top-notch wedding planner must be part diplomat, part counselor, part cheerleader, part negotiator, and part sponge. Sponge? That's right. As a consultant, you have to be part sponge because you are hired in large part to absorb the wedding stress and pressure from the couple. It is the planner's job to stress over the details so that the couple can enjoy their wedding day. If the cake has not arrived, the officiant has caught a cold, or the maid of honor is missing in action, it is the wedding planner who worries while the bride and groom are blissfully unaware of these potential disasters. First, this chapter presents stress management tips that will help keep you calm and energized. Second, career enrichment techniques are highlighted to keep you feeling fresh and moving forward.

PHOTO 28-1 *(opposite) A consultant absorbs the couple's stress*

☙ stress management tips

Because wedding consultants often find themselves in pressure-packed situations, they must learn to be effective stress managers. Imagine the stress level that would occur if during an upscale wedding reception, two tables of guests complain that the band is too loud and demand to be moved immediately. An easily flustered consultant might fly off the handle and tell the guests to sit down and deal with it. This flippant response will only anger the guests and encourage them to take matters into their own hands. The last thing you want is to have anarchy among wedding guests. A composed planner will jump into action to resolve the problem with the least amount of disruption possible to both the guests and the couple. Issues arise at weddings, and, if you remain calm and can think on your feet, you will be able to handle anything that might be thrown your way.

While it is the planner's job to deflect wedding tension from the bride and groom, who will take on the job of helping to manage the consultant's daily pressures? As an independent wedding planner, it is up to you to recognize the stressful nature of the job and to take the appropriate steps to reduce the stress level in your life.

 One of the best methods for reducing anxiety is to know the details of each wedding inside and out. The more familiar you are with the details, the less nervous you will be. For example, have you confirmed with all the vendors? Do you have copies of the contracts? Have you finished the seating assignments? Have you thought about event security? Do you have a Plan B in case of inclement weather? Have you checked in with the couple to see if there are any last-minute changes? If you plan your work and work your plan by organizing and confirming each element in advance of the wedding, you will lower your stress level and feel confident that everything is under control. A structured approach will allow you to focus on execution rather than being overwhelmed by an issue that was neglected. This is not to say that unexpected emergencies will never crop up. However, knowing that you have covered all the essentials will give you the flexibility to pass responsibility on to an assistant if you need to troubleshoot.

Another great way to reduce stress is to recommend vendors you trust based on successful past experiences. These go-to vendors should have a stellar reputation for superior service, professionalism, and punctuality. Each vendor recommendation is a reflection of you and your business. You will be calm when you are absolutely certain that a recommended vendor is an excellent fit for the couple and will come through on the wedding day. Will the florist drive through a snowstorm to deliver flowers to the wedding? Will your caterer find authentic sake cups for your Japanese clients? Will your tent company search high and low to find the exact shade of blue that you require for your tent liner? After you have planned many weddings, you will

PHOTO 28-2 *A structured approach will allow you to focus on execution*

know which vendors are dependable and trustworthy. Surrounding yourself with a team of dedicated, reliable, and knowledgeable professionals will greatly reduce your stress and make your job easier.

Even with months of dedicated planning and the profession's top vendors working by your side, there is no escaping day-of wedding stress. Regardless of how long you have been in business or how many weddings you have planned, most wedding consultants admit to feeling some degree of stress on the day of each client's wedding. This is only natural. You just have to know in your heart that you have done everything possible to prepare for the wedding and that it will run smoothly. Simultaneously, make a point of learning and applying stress management skills. Perkins (2003) offers a series of effective stress busters, adapted to apply specifically to wedding consultants, as summarized in Table 28.1.

Stressful situations come in all shapes and sizes, and how you handle them will often determine how much of a production they become. Avoid making a mountain out of a molehill. For example, assume you are checking on the preparations for a 6:30 P.M. reception. You enter

TABLE 28.1   Stress Busters for Wedding Consultants

1. *Learn to say no.* Building a business from the ground up is a daunting challenge. While you are establishing your business, don't be afraid to say no to such requests as babysitting your niece and nephew, researching your family tree, or rewriting the bylaws for your local volunteer organization. Give yourself permission to say no to any request that will not further your new business, especially during your busiest times.

2. *Don't overdo it.* If you know you need at least eight hours of sleep in order to function at top speed, don't push it by pulling a series of all-nighters before your first wedding. No one will thank you for it. What counts is your ability to think on your feet and manage the wedding. If you are running at half-speed, your clients will suffer.

3. *Take breaks.* If you are working from home, don't chain yourself to the phone or computer for 10 hours straight. Take a break. Listen to music. Go to the gym. You will return to your work with a fresh perspective.

4. *Pace yourself.* Break tasks down into manageable steps. Give yourself adequate time to meet your deadlines. If you are facing a large task such as assigning the seating for 200 people, break the job down into three or four smaller steps. That way you won't feel so overwhelmed.

5. *Plan ahead to rest.* Schedule resting periods after events that you know will drain you. The last thing you want to do is schedule a meeting with a potential client for the morning after a large wedding. Give yourself time to catch your breath and get reinvigorated.

6. *Take a relaxing bath without interruptions.* Don't answer the phone. Fill up the tub, light a candle, and relax while reading a magazine or the latest book by your favorite author.

7. *Listen to music.* Music is a great way to bust through the stress and tedium of day-to-day details. Listening to your favorite musical artist can help to relax you and put you in a good mood.

8. *Get out.* To break up your day, schedule a site visit to meet with a vendor who is located at or near a beach, lake, zoo, or park. After the meeting is over, stroll around and take a quiet moment or two for yourself.

9. *Participate in activities that are meaningful to you.* Many new wedding consultants complain that they don't have a life, since they are always working on the weekends. Find a club or activity that has gatherings during the week or plan an evening to get together with friends for dinner and a movie. Don't let your business take this away from you. You will want to keep as much joy and fun in your life as possible.

10. *Eat a healthful, balanced diet.* Consultants running on sugar and caffeine will be edgy and lack the staying power needed for day-of implementation.

11. *Develop insight.* Deep breathing, yoga, meditation, and prayer are all ways to touch base with what is meaningful to you. Engage in the activities that are most soothing to you.

12. *Exercise.* The release provided by regular exercise operates to burn calories and stress. It will also keep you trim and healthy.

13. *Vent.* If you are angry or excited about something, talk it over with a close friend, family member, or another consultant. Just by talking it over, you will begin to feel better.

14. *Take a nap.* If time permits, take a 20-minute power nap. It will revive you and help to calm your nerves for the tasks ahead.

15. *Keep your sense of humor.* Make sure you take the time to laugh, as humor is great for the spirit. Every wedding has its ridiculous moments. If you can see the humor in the lunacy, you are well on your way to successfully managing the situation.

Source: Adapted from Perkins (2003).

Photograph by www.RodneyBailey.com

PHOTO 28-3 *Stress busters will help keep you calm and motivated*

the ballroom of a downtown hotel only to find a DJ's equipment set up where the couple's dinner buffet table is intended to be. By being prepared and catching the mistake early, you can remedy the situation quickly and use your sense of humor. Instead of making a negative statement such as, "Move this equipment now or I'll scream!" you can joke with the DJ that he is supposed to enhance the meal, not be the meal.

By working in a few stress busters each day, you will greatly reduce your desire to snap at clients and chew out vendors. Remember, brides and grooms will take their cue from you. If you are stressed, they will be stressed. Conversely, if you exude a sense of quiet calm, the couple will pick up on this vibe and be able to relax.

If you ask 10 wedding consultants what they do to relax, you will get 10 different answers. There is no one-size fits all relaxation strategy. One consultant, a dedicated exerciser, gets up at 5:30 A.M. and goes for a power walk regardless of the weather. Another takes time out of her busy schedule each week to have a pedicure. She gets a kick out of having her toes painted in funky colors and styles and uses this as a conversation starter during her events. A third loves to refinish furniture purchased from thrift stores and garage sales. Whatever hobby or interest you enjoy, continue to pursue it. You will be a much happier person.

career enrichment

In addition to monitoring your stress level, it is also important for wedding planners to seek out opportunities to enrich their careers. Instead of waiting until you are bored with managing the same type of wedding over and over, sign up for a floral design class to learn about different styles of floral arranging. Maybe branch out by learning calligraphy. Perhaps take a seminar taught by a leading catering expert. By attending workshops and classes, consultants from all over the world learn about new ideas and products and begin incorporating them into the weddings they plan.

The last thing that you want to hear a guest say at one of your weddings is, "This must be an event planned by (*insert your company name*), they always use the tuxedo strawberries arranged around the cake." You don't want your clients to think that their wedding will look exactly like the last five weddings that you planned. Clients want something new and different. It is this ability to present the unexpected that will keep a planner in demand.

Travel is another excellent way to enrich your wedding planning career. With the explosion of multicultural brides and grooms, it is particularly helpful to your clients if you have traveled and experienced different cultures. If you have toured Asia extensively, you will be better informed to plan the wedding of a Japanese bride and a Vietnamese groom. You can always read about Asian customs and solicit advice, but nothing takes the place of travel in opening your eyes and giving you cultural insight.

CAREER SHIFT

After you have built a successful career as an independent wedding consultant, you might find yourself growing tired of the business. You may wistfully dream of the day when you won't have to leave your house at the crack of dawn on a lovely Saturday morning in June to head off to work. The important thing to remember about a career as an independent wedding planner is that you can accept as many or as few jobs as your time and budget will allow. If you want to take the month of August off, then do it. Your schedule is entirely up to you.

Planning flawless weddings week after week can become tiring. Seasoned planners frequently move their businesses in a different direction, with perhaps less stress and more manageable hours. This is called a *career shift*. As you break into wedding planning, you might think that there is nothing you would rather do than plan weddings for the rest of your life. The good news is that you can, or, alternatively, you can take your business down a different path.

Many consultants will keep their hand in planning while exploring other opportunities, usually still related to the business of weddings. For example, Laura Weatherly, a top Washington, DC consultant, is now writing mystery novels in addition to planning weddings. Her debut novel *Better off Wed* and the follow-up *For Better or Hearse* are exciting whodunits in which the super sleuth is a wedding planner and the victims are a nasty mother-of-the bride and a haughty hotel chef. Wendy Joblon, a sought-after planner in the southeastern Massachusetts area, recently opened her own invitation and stationery boutique, much to the delight of her clients. Joyce Scardina Becker, a very popular northern California wedding planner, teaches a wedding consultant certificate program at California State University—Hayward. Celebrity wedding consultants are no different. For example, Colin Cowie has written wedding and entertainment books and has a home décor line with JCPenney, Sharon Sacks has a line of clothing, makeup,

Photograph by www.RodneyBailey.com

PHOTO 28-4 *Seasoned planners will frequently take their businesses down a new path*

and leather goods, and Preston Bailey has authored several books and partnered with Sandals Resorts to create his signature WeddingMoons (Muhlke, 2005).

Whether you plan two weddings a year or have a team that plans two hundred, a career as an independent wedding consultant is rewarding, challenging, and meaningful. You will have the privilege of working with clients as they prepare for one of the most important events of their lives. Because of your hard work, their wedding day memories will be of their commitment and carefree enjoyment rather than the nuts and bolts of planning.

Whether you long for a career in wedding planning or you simply long for your own perfect wedding day, it is our sincere hope that *Wedding Planning and Management: Consultancy for Diverse Clients* has inspired you to think about the cultural significance of weddings and the intricacies of the wedding profession. These are exciting times for wedding consultants, with trends such as the growth of destination weddings, the changing family, an increase of multicultural traditions, and the legalization of same-sex unions broadening the scope and visibility of this career. Now, perhaps more than ever, the wedding profession needs consultants who understand and respect today's diverse clients and can translate their needs into extraordinary weddings.

REFERENCES

Muhlke, C. (2005, January 16). The wedding banners. *New York Times*, Section 6, p. 57.

Perkins, C. (2003). Holistic stress management. Available from http://www.mental-health-matters.com/articles/print.php?artID=820

review questions

1. Why is the job of wedding consultant so stressful?

2. Name two things you can do as the planner to help each wedding go smoothly.

3. What are four simple things you can do to reduce your personal stress?

4. What are three steps you can take to enrich your career?

5. If you ever grow tired of wedding planning, what are some new directions you can explore for your business that relate to the profession?

terminology

*   Career enrichment

*   Career shift

*   Day-of stress

*   Stress busters

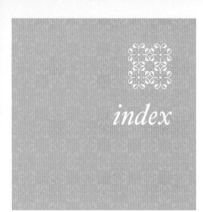

index

493

494

496

498